MW01258125

ALSO BY JEFFREY SELINGO

*College (Un)bound: The Future of Higher Education and
What It Means for Students*

*There Is Life After College: What Parents and Students Should Know
About Navigating School to Prepare for the Jobs of Tomorrow*

Who Gets In and Why: A Year Inside College Admissions

DREAM SCHOOL

Finding the College
That's Right for You

JEFFREY SELINGO

NEW YORK   AMSTERDAM/ANTWERP   LONDON
TORONTO   SYDNEY/MELBOURNE   NEW DELHI

Scribner
An Imprint of Simon & Schuster, LLC
1230 Avenue of the Americas
New York, NY 10020

First Scribner hardcover edition September 2025

SCRIBNER and design are trademarks of Simon & Schuster, LLC

For information about special discounts for bulk purchases, please contact Simon & Schuster Special Sales at 1-866-506-1949 or business@simonandschuster.com.

The Simon & Schuster Speakers Bureau can bring authors to your live event. For more information, or to book an event, contact the Simon & Schuster Speakers Bureau at 1-866-248-3049 or visit our website at www.simonspeakers.com.

Interior design by Erika R. Genova

Manufactured in the United States of America

1   3   5   7   9   10   8   6   4   2

Library of Congress Cataloging-in-Publication Data has been applied for.

ISBN 978-1-6680-5620-2
ISBN 978-1-6680-5622-6 (ebook)

To my children, Hadley and Rory—
never stop dreaming as you explore the wonders
of the world around you

CONTENTS

Author's Note   *xi*

Introduction   *1*

PART I: Why Your Assumptions About Elite Colleges Are All Wrong   **15**
Chapter 1: Great Expectations
  Why You Need a Backup Plan   *17*

Chapter 2: Swimming in Calmer Waters
  The Elite College Degree Matters Less Than You Think   *47*

PART II: Mapping the New Admissions Landscape   **69**
Chapter 3: The Rise of the Out-of-State Recruit
  What's Driving Teenagers to Cross Borders   *71*

Chapter 4: Value Over Prestige
  Skipping the Next Tier of Schools to Get a Deal   *91*

Chapter 5: The Age of Agency
  Why This Is Your Time to Explore   *115*

PART III: What to Look for in Your Dream School   **127**
Chapter 6: On the Hunt for a Good School
  How the Information Marketplace Fed Our Obsession with Admissions   *129*

CONTENTS

Chapter 7: Mentors Matter
Finding Colleges That Put Teaching First 153

Chapter 8: Finding Your People
How Belonging Shapes Your Undergraduate Experience 175

Chapter 9: The Doom Loop of College Finances
*How to Make Sure a College Will Continue to Have
the Dollars to Invest in You* 197

Chapter 10: Better Than Average
Making Sure the Degree Pays Off 219

Conclusion: *Dreams* 241

Appendix: *The "New" Dream Schools—A Selected List* 247
   Hidden Values 251
   Breakout Regionals 265
   Large Leaders 273

Acknowledgments 293

Notes 297

Index 317

AUTHOR'S NOTE

In reporting on high school and college students over the years—and with two teenagers of my own at home—I've come to appreciate that time in life when we make more mistakes than we care to remember. I'm always glad that I didn't grow up in an era of smartphones where every moment of my life could be traced and recorded and then shared with the world.

With that in mind, names of students and their parents throughout this book have been changed. All other details of their lives are true, except for those that would reveal identities. For example, you'll notice that, in a few cases, I didn't mention the name of a college a young adult attended because doing so could identify them given the small size of the school. In such circumstances, I tried to give readers a sense of the *type* of college. Every person in this book identified with a full name explicitly chose to be.

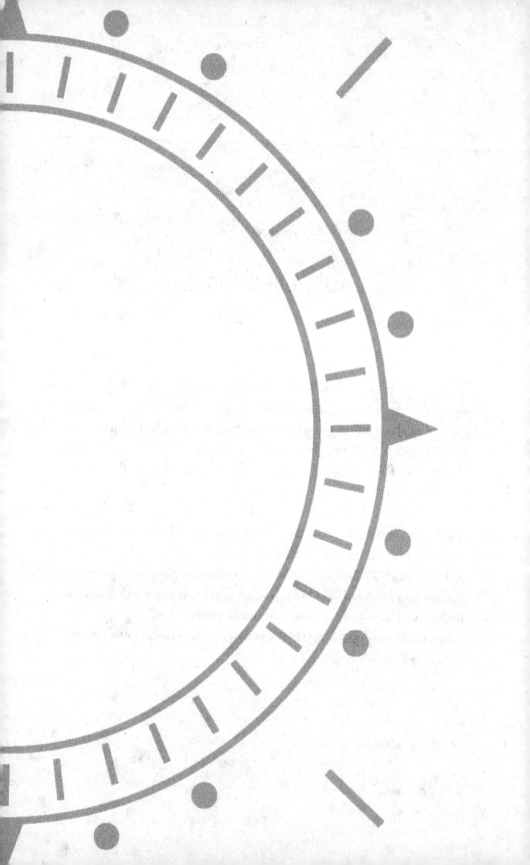

INTRODUCTION

When I first met William, a high-achieving teenager from the Midwest, he rattled off stats most high schoolers would dream of: a 4.0 grade-point average, a perfect 36 on the ACT, a three-time debater at nationals, a lab researcher at a Big 10 university. The college counselor at his high school encouraged him to place a bet on the most selective school he could get into. He deliberated between three top 20 universities—Northwestern, Stanford, and Columbia—and just before early decision applications were due in November of his senior year he put all his chips on Columbia. Applying early decision meant that, if he were accepted, he was committing to going no matter what. "I knew I wanted prestige," he said. "I knew I wanted to go to school in a big city."

A month later, while he was working the register at his retail job, the acceptance email arrived from Columbia. It felt akin to holding a "winning lottery ticket," he said. It's an analogy I've heard often over the years about admission to highly selective colleges, and it's an apt one. The year William was admitted to Columbia, it rejected the vast majority of applicants: some 58,000 out of 60,000.

But soon after William arrived in New York in August 2022 for his first year of college, the high of his win started to wear off. During the college search, he'd been enamored of the brand name. Now elements of the Columbia undergraduate experience he hadn't really paid attention to began to surface.

A class he wanted in the psychology department had a waiting list so long that he likely wouldn't get in until he was a junior or senior, if at all. A professor he'd hoped to do research with on addiction didn't allow undergraduates to work in his lab. Instead of building a collective community of first-year students, Columbia's core curriculum, William told me, amounted to "collective suffering." The pace in the humanities was so fast that he never had a chance to thoroughly think about the books he was reading.

More than anything, the "true colors of the student body started to come out," he said. "I realized that a lot of people were there exclusively for their studies, to land an internship, to work in a lab. That was the number one priority [rather than] making friends, maintaining friendships, and being a kid, or really having a college experience." When exams came, the libraries were packed. "No one was off enjoying the lack of classes at the end of the semester," he told me.

By winter break, he was already thinking of transferring to the University of Minnesota. His mom worried he was taking the easy way out. "This was a hard ticket to win, and so once you leave, you can't get it back," she said. In a conversation before he returned to New York for the spring semester at Columbia, his mother reminded him, "You'll need to figure out what story you're going to tell because people will want to know." Few students leave Columbia on their own, she told him. Indeed, the year before, all but fifteen freshmen returned for their sophomore year.

William ultimately gave up his "winning ticket." When I caught up with him in the spring of 2024, he was thriving as a sophomore at the University of Minnesota. He told me he finds his courses just as challenging as at Columbia, even if the size of classes is larger and he doesn't know his professors as well as a result.

On the flip side, he's able to work in a research lab, and his family's yearly tuition bill has been cut in half. But the biggest difference, he finds, is his classmates. They are as bright and curious as those at Columbia, but their "primary focus is building meaningful connections," William told me. "There's not this feeling that if at any given moment you're not doing something quote-unquote productive then you're either lazy or just not progressing in life."

My conversations with William stayed with me as I met other teenagers and their families who craved the ticket to the elite education he'd won. Although one-third of college freshmen transfer each year, William made an uncommon choice: He traded an Ivy League school ranked thirteenth in the nation by *U.S. News & World Report* for a big public university ranked some forty spots lower.

William got a taste of his dream school and then realized it wasn't worth it.

My last book, *Who Gets In and Why: A Year Inside College Admissions*, was a peek into how colleges make *their* decisions. This book is a companion, focusing on how you should make *your* decisions about college. For my last book, I spent a bunch of time inside admissions offices, talking with administrators and others to pull back the veil on what seems like a secret system, especially at selective colleges. This book, though, doesn't put the colleges at the center. Instead, it's about how you should make your decision among a much broader set of schools.

We approach the college search as if there is a dream school, a single choice, a perfect match for us. There isn't. There are more than 3,900 colleges and universities in the U.S. If you exclude two-year colleges and those institutions focusing on a single purpose such as the arts, music, or theology, we're still talking about 1,700 schools. If you take out small colleges—those more like the size of a typical high school, with fewer than 1,000 students—we're left with a universe of around 1,200 campuses.

With so many options, research suggests that uncertainty clouds the judgment of both colleges and applicants, making it impossible to find that perfect fit we hear about during the college search. A group of economists who researched the idea that students and colleges are trying to match with each other concluded that teenagers are "ignorant of the types of colleges" that would be a good fit for them. Meanwhile, researchers found "colleges evaluate students, trying to gauge the future stars, and often don't succeed." Countless factors affect how students and colleges sort through the process, and no teenager or admissions dean can adequately explain their decisions without them seeming any less arbitrary than their choice of cereal in the supermarket.

So why did I call this book *Dream School* if I'm suggesting there's no such thing? Because the dream isn't about a single name or a universally understood brand like the Ivy League. It's about finding a place where you can thrive, learn, and become the person you're meant to be. It's about considering a range of colleges that fit both your personality and how you like to learn. Do you want a small school in a college town, an urban university with ample city life, or a big public flagship where football on Saturday and Greek life are the main attractions? What about academics? Do you want a pressure cooker like William experienced at Columbia, where every day felt like a competition, or more of a balanced vibe like he found at Minnesota?

This book is for anyone worn out by the endless messages we hear about the value of an "elite college." My hope is that in the chapters that follow, you will find comfort and satisfaction in stepping away from that mindset (and stress) as you discover what really makes a "good" school for you. I'm not saying you shouldn't have aspirational picks on your college list, but too often I've seen eighteen years of academic or athletic striving turn into another endless sprint, first in the pursuit of the college brand, and then in landing the coveted job offer.

Here's the thing: Most of us don't know what a dream school would be (or even why it's a "good" school in the first place). We tend to let others define that dream. Perhaps it's our TikTok feed, with stray clips and hidden algorithms pulling us toward certain campuses and experiences (check out #RushTok, if you haven't already, to see what I'm talking about). Or it could be the names scrolling across the ticker on ESPN, making us think there are only a few dozen universities out there. Or maybe its family ties and stories from relatives about their alma mater at Thanksgiving dinner. In my interviews with parents for this book, I discovered that nostalgia plays a huge role in encouraging our kids to replicate our own college experiences—often on the same campuses.

Unfortunately, what defines a dream school for many families is simply the signal it sends to others. College rankings claim to identify the "best schools," but in reality they're mostly creating a shorthand for managing brands. ("T20" or "T25" is an abbreviation you'll see often in Reddit threads and Facebook groups to describe top schools.)

Go ahead, admit it: One reason you want your kid to go to Yale or MIT is so you can tell others that you're sending your kid to Yale or MIT. Much of the hype over college is about kids trying to make their parents happy or parents trying to impress their friends. That's the wrong way to select a school.

My hope after you read this book is that you'll brag instead about how your kid got accepted into an honors college at a big public university, an acceptance that came with a huge scholarship and a study-abroad grant. And down the road maybe you'll even be able to boast about your son or daughter earning an industry-certified credential in Adobe, while still in college, that will be a gold star on their résumé and end up getting them their first job.

When a student thinks there is only one dream school, one perfect fit, that single choice comes to dominate their college search. Yes, they'll still apply to five, ten, twelve schools. But more often than not, they're simply variations on that top choice or schools added for good measure, not true backup plans. There really isn't a Plan B. So, when Plan A doesn't work out as expected because the student doesn't get in, can't afford it, or it's a bad fit like it was for William, most families are left without a viable alternative.

I didn't write this book to make you give up on Dartmouth or

Amherst or Michigan and "settle" for something that feels like "second best." Rather, I want families to consider other colleges beyond the small group that sucks up all the attention. Our fascination with elite higher ed is understandable, even if it's indefensible.

We're a nation of strivers. Given the opportunity to own an elite brand—Cartier, Ferrari, Hermès, for example—most of us would jump at the chance. However, the landscape of elite higher education has shifted in ways that look wholly unfamiliar to Gen X parents who went to college in the late 1980s and 1990s—and now have kids who are applying. Not only is it nearly impossible to get in, as I'll outline in Chapter 1, but that entry ticket might not matter in life as much as we think, as I'll tell you in Chapter 2.

Still, for those obsessed with getting into a top school, this book will provide an Option B, in case things don't work out as planned and, for the rest of us, show how to widen the aperture of the college search from the very beginning. It will become your playbook for finding *your* dream school.

By pulling together data in novel ways and combining it with insights from three decades of covering higher education as a journalist and author, I've developed a practical framework for finding a good college. It starts by discovering what you value and what you need out of college when you graduate, no matter your major. And then I help you reverse engineer that by finding the campuses during your college search where you'll discover your people as an undergraduate, connect with faculty and advisors, get the job outcomes you want, and do it all at a place with the financial resources to invest in a student experience where you won't sit on the sidelines for four years.

I'll name names throughout—and list seventy-five colleges in the appendix that are what I call the "New" Dream Schools—but this is not another rankings guide or a *Colleges That Change Lives* book. And don't skip right to the list in the back. The list is more of a rough guide because I don't know what's important to *you* or the unique qualities *you* might bring to a school. There is no Easy Button to push or algorithm that yields an answer. That's why the book itself gives you the know-how and leads you to the tools to help you find *your* dream school.

We've been led to believe that elite colleges are something special. Perhaps it's because we *think* prestige is what the majority prioritizes in education. But when you dig into surveys of parents, you see that we all overestimate the importance of gaining admission to colleges with "the best possible reputations." At the same time, we underestimate what the public thinks education should be about: helping students develop "the skills and values needed to build decent lives in the communities where they live."

For this book, I conducted two surveys of more than 3,000 parents in all about how they defined a dream school, the pressures they felt within their family and their community to pick the right school, and what they were willing to compromise on if their child received a scholarship from a college deeper in the rankings. In the surveys—conducted with the assistance of a former pollster at UCLA, who for eight years conducted large nationwide studies of college students, as well as a researcher at Harvard's Graduate School of Education—two findings in particular struck me as significant in how parents are rethinking the pursuit of prestige in higher ed:

- **First, college is mostly about the job afterward.** When asked to name the most important attributes in a "good" college, the top two responses related to getting a job. No. 1 was the availability of experiential learning, such as internships and research projects. No. 2 was the job placement of graduates. The prestige of a college ranked fourth, just below the strength of a specific major or program. This explains why so often in my conversations with prospective families they'll lead with the reputation of a school within the university (the Kelley School or the Maxwell School, for example) before ever mentioning the name of the university itself (Indiana or Syracuse).

- **Second, prestige isn't worth *any* price.** For the parents at every income level in the survey, hands-on learning and job placement trump prestige. Even at the highest income level in the survey ($250,000+), more than a third of parents said they'd compromise "a lot" on prestige if a school cost them half as much as their child's dream college because they received a generous amount of merit aid. It used to be that upper middle-class and affluent parents were willing to pay anything for a degree from a top college. They still are, but the list of schools they consider worth the cost is getting smaller, as I'll outline in Chapter 4. (Just to note: This isn't a book about paying for college. For that, I recommend Ron Lieber's *The Price You Pay for College*.)

Nevertheless, social pressures around going to college—and going to the right college—are real. We tend to think that the sticker on the rear window of our car says something about our parenting, and so the college search becomes this pressure-filled pursuit at all costs. Only 16 percent of parents in my survey said it was important to *them* that their children attend a prestigious college; 27 percent said it was important to *their children*. Then they were asked how they thought others in *their community* would choose. And that's where it got really interesting: 61 percent thought prestige was important to *other* parents.

Whether they think attending a prestigious college is important for their own kids or not, they often feel an achievement pressure that rises in middle- and upper middle-class neighborhoods where families try to cling to their place in the economic pecking order through the college their kids attend. These same places also tend to drive the national narrative about college. If we think everyone in our kid's high school wants to go to Cornell, Berkeley, Williams, or Georgetown, we think we need to as well—even if these highly selective colleges, which accept fewer than 20 percent of applicants, represent a tiny fraction (100,000 students) of the more than 15 million undergraduates in higher education.

INTRODUCTION

Do some parents, even in affluent communities, ignore this "Ivy League or bust" feeling? Of course. But they often feel they're in the minority, and social pressure makes it harder to voice that view. When your neighbor is loudly proclaiming that they're doing everything to make sure their child has every opportunity, you might feel like a mediocre, uncaring parent when you say those highly selective places don't matter. But my survey shows that parents are increasingly willing to compromise on brand name—for the right reasons. If a campus really wants their kid, helps them fit in, is focused on fostering purpose, and launches them into a life of meaning . . . and, oh, helps them find a good job—if it can deliver all that—the sticker on the car window matters a lot less.

This book got its start soon after my last one was released. It was still in the early months of the Covid pandemic, and as I talked with high school students, their parents, and counselors over Zoom, I noticed questions and comments about whether elite colleges were worth north of $300,000 for four years.

One meeting, with parents in Southern California in the fall of 2020, surprised me because they lived in the type of communities where it's expected kids are going to UCLA or MIT. That night, they didn't question the idea of going to college, but they did ask how to find a good experience at a lower cost. "I work in big tech, and we're hiring new grads from Cal State, University of Denver, Arizona State, Santa Clara, etc.," one person in the chat wrote. "So not sure why I'm worried about paying for an Ivy." Other parents started to join in the chat—rejecting elite preferences but struggling to assert alternatives to the status quo.

As schools reopened the following year, I went to speak to students and parents in communities like Pittsburgh, Columbus, Detroit, Houston, Chicago, and Seattle. One winter night in February 2022, I visited Highland High School in Medina, Ohio, a prototypical middle-class American suburb near Cleveland. After my talk, a mom came up to me. All the talk, she told me, is about "top-tier schools." Even when parents aren't talking about Penn and Michigan, they're talking about Kenyon and Ohio State, she said. This mom rightly pointed out that most middle-class and upper middle-class families at this high school won't qualify for much need-based aid, so they look for schools where they can get a decent discount on tuition (what's called merit aid). She thanked me for my "Buyers and Sellers" list, which I outlined in my last book and is a guide to schools that are more generous with merit aid. "But how do I figure out what's a good school on that list?" she asked me. Her question has remained scribbled on the back cover of my notebook ever since.

Parents, in the notes they sent me throughout 2024—a tumultuous year of protests on elite college campuses—asked me for help seeing beyond their own preferences, their own bias. They told me, in these moments of vulnerability, that what they thought others valued in college was not best for everyone, including their own kids. What I sensed I was observing was growing resistance against elite schools.

This book is mainly for parents. That's the "you" and "we" I use throughout because I'm a parent, too, and whether we like to admit it or not, we're usually the ones to blame for focusing too much on brand names in higher ed. But we're also the ones with more experience in making life's major decisions who need to lay guide rails for our kids and be there to nudge them or provide sage advice when needed.

This book is for your kids, too, and their counselors—they are the "you," the "we," and the "us" in the pages ahead because the only way teenagers will find the right fit in a college is if we approach this together as a team with candid and meaningful conversations about what matters in the undergraduate years and why. Only by telling our stories—which usually transcend the name of the college on our diploma and instead are rooted in the experiences we had during those years—will young people appreciate the often-repeated truth: *How* they go to college ultimately matters more than *where* they go.

As you dive into this book, you might get overwhelmed at times by the lists of to-dos I'm suggesting you undertake to really evaluate what is perhaps the biggest purchase you'll make in life. I do realize that you can't do it all. A lot of people spend no more time on a campus during the college search than to take a tour, grab a snack, and stop for a bathroom break, before heading off to another campus to do the same. If you're lucky, you might find a connection to a college you're interested in through friends or on Facebook and Reddit groups where you can learn more even if you can't visit the career services office to learn where students interned last year, or sit in on a class, or corner a professor to see if they're keeping their posted office hours. If you only take a few of the steps I'm suggesting, that's okay. Just like going to the gym once a week is better than not going at all, doing even a fraction of what I lay out in this book can help you find your dream school.

This book starts off by describing how much admissions has continued to change since I wrote my last book and examines what an elite college degree buys you (or doesn't) in the job market. The truly elite group of colleges that we believe matters when it comes to getting a job anywhere we want is much smaller than many of us picture. We might think of the University of Chicago or Colby as elite and pull out all the stops to get in, when what is elite in reality is mostly a handful of places, like Harvard, Princeton, and Stanford.

Once we come around to the idea that we should look for something different from college, we still have a challenge in front of us: figuring out what makes a good one for you. That's what the rest of the book tackles. I'm not giving you a new set of rankings, nor a recipe with every ingredient, but instead a guide you can use to find your dream school whether that's Duke or Denison or Delaware or Drake.

In this book you'll see schools and students all over the admissions map. Expanding your lens usually depends on where you start. If you're focused on a top 25 college in the *U.S. News & World Report* rankings, then my hope is that this book gets you to look beyond—at least, at the top 75. If you're considering a broader range of schools already, then this book will help you make hidden-gem distinctions among the campuses on your list. As I tell this story, you'll read about students with straight A's and 1500s on the SAT who had Ivy League dreams, as well as B-average students with 1100s and 1200s on the SAT who were late bloomers in college.

I was one of those students who ended up blooming later in college. So often in my reporting on higher ed, I think about my own college search back in the 1990s. I tossed aside any college viewbook that didn't list journalism as a major because I thought to be a journalist you had to major in journalism. My father was a high school music teacher whose salary didn't top $50,000 the year I went off to college; my mother didn't go to college and was a teacher's aide earning barely more than minimum wage. The fact that they sent three kids to college still astounds me. I applied to four schools—none at the top of the *U.S. News* rankings. I picked Ithaca College because it was close to home (120 miles) and had a well-regarded communications school. With four other professional schools as well and 6,000 undergraduates, Ithaca felt to me like a smaller version of a much bigger university, one with a liberal arts foundation, something years later I realized I needed. Most of all, Ithaca offered me a generous financial-aid package.

Hard work and a lot of luck means I now live in the suburbs of Washington, D.C., one of America's epicenters of privilege, where the talk of ultra-selective colleges is common at swim meets and at school gatherings for my teenage kids. I live among what *New Yorker* writer Jay Caspian Kang calls the "panicking class," people who fear their kids won't be able to replicate their lifestyle in affluent American suburbs like Scarsdale (New York), Winnetka (Illinois), Buckhead (Atlanta, Georgia), Highland Park (Texas), or Atherton (California). But I also know from covering higher education that my kids and most in the upper reaches of the middle class will generally inherit their parents' social class advantages anyway. In other words, they'll be fine.

When people find out what I do, they want to know how to win the game of college. This book will offer insights on that front, but more important, I want to encourage all of us to redefine what winning means. I have a stack of best-selling parenting and education books on my shelf that advocate dialing down the pressure on our kids. Still, we struggle. It's time to take a new approach. Let's replace anxiety with excitement and make the college search a happy milestone. This book is your road map to finding a college that fits your child, encourages their growth, and sets them up for a thriving life. The quest for a good college should be inspiring, not exhausting.

PART I

WHY YOUR ASSUMPTIONS ABOUT ELITE COLLEGES ARE ALL WRONG

CHAPTER 1

GREAT EXPECTATIONS

Why You Need a Backup Plan

If you're the parent of a college-bound kid, you might recall that when you submitted your own applications, most (if not all) had one deadline, in early January. You either received an answer quickly, if a school had "rolling admissions," or got that thick (or thin) envelope in March along with everyone else in your class. Then you had another month to make your final decision.

How colleges recruit and evaluate applicants has been evolving since the turn of this century. But the intensity and complexity of today's admissions process—the craziness we now experience—came about gradually, then suddenly. You'll see that shift reflected in the Instagram posts of incoming freshmen and in the lists of college placements that many American high schools release each spring. Compare the most recent lists to ones from 2015 or even 2018, and you'll notice that some high schools used to send batches of their graduates to top-ranked colleges but don't as much anymore. Or talk to any parent who had multiple kids go through the college search before and then after 2020—the pandemic year that shook up the age-old, placid picture of admissions like an Etch A Sketch.

Kim, a mother of three in a suburb of Washington, D.C., has been on both sides of that 2020 divide. We met while I was working on my last book. Her son Sawyer, who graduated from high school in 2016, ended up at Carnegie Mellon University after what Kim described as a "pretty easy sprint." In many ways, his process mirrored her own some thirty years earlier, when she went to Duke University. Kim is a runner, so she likes to use running analogies to describe the college search for her three kids. For her second, Taylor, in 2019, it seemed more like a 5K that ended at Providence College. For her third, Mia, after the pandemic, it was a marathon.

Everyone is running that marathon now, and it starts long before the first campus visit or the first time your child takes the SAT. As Kim and I were catching up at a Chipotle, we waited for Mia to stop by for a bite to eat between basketball practice and a shift working the checkout at a local supermarket. Kim laid out Mia's schedule for the rest of the week: four hours volunteering at an after-school program, more basketball practices plus a game, and musical practice three nights. That didn't include several hours of homework each night.

All around us families were doing the same thing—grabbing dinner on their way to yet another sports practice, "enrichment" activity, or test-prep class. To replicate their lives in college and since, every parent there was doing all they could to give their kids an edge. That afternoon, similar scenes played out at Chipotles in American metros everywhere.

As I talked with Kim and met other families in reporting this book, they commented on how stressful the search experience was and, in vulnerable moments, how unhappy they were running this marathon. They often vented to friends and family. "I am really surprised by how awful this process is," a Denver mother had written to her cousin in the middle of her daughter's senior year. "And at the end of it you are not a movie star, a billionaire, a star athlete, or the President of the

United States—you are only a college freshman." Yet the parent who showed me that email and the parents of countless other college aspirants felt channeled into this course set by someone else without the power to deviate from it.

"I sort of transplanted to Mia the excitement I felt for my own experience searching for a college," Kim told me, "without really acknowledging how different the world is."

The world I saw *inside* college admissions offices during the 2018–19 cycle hasn't changed substantially from how I depicted it in *Who Gets In and Why*. Yes, admissions officers can no longer consider race and ethnicity as a factor in their decisions, after the U.S. Supreme Court struck down affirmative action in 2023 (a ruling that mostly impacts highly selective colleges where seats are scarce). Sure, more of the back-and-forth work between admissions officers is done remotely now, by Zoom. And, certainly, the math at the most selective places gets harsher each year as more applications arrive for the same number of spots in the freshman class.

But the biggest change in admissions actually stems from the *outside* world's reaction to three adjustments in the application process during and after the pandemic. That huge behavioral response—by students, parents, and counselors—has altered the course of the whole race.

First, hundreds of schools, including the entire Ivy League, dropped their requirement for the SAT or ACT at the beginning of the pandemic because it was difficult for students to find test sites. The admissions cycle that followed for high school seniors graduating in 2021 got messy: Applications skyrocketed 24 percent at the most selective colleges in that one year, to over 2 million. If Harvard or Stanford or NYU didn't want a test score, the thinking went, then why not apply to those places?

Second, to deal with that deluge of applications, colleges spread out their arrival. Some schools also wanted students to commit sooner, too, and added early decision (ED), where students apply by November 1 and guarantee they'll enroll if accepted in December. Even more schools added early action (EA), which also secures applications early on but does not involve a binding commitment. Encouraging students to apply early worked as intended. By the fall of 2024, the combined number of applications filed for both ED and EA through the Common App—the single application platform used by more than a thousand colleges—jumped by one million, up to 2.6 million, inching ever closer to the total number sent in January for regular decision.

But then colleges had another problem on their hands: determining which early action applicants were serious about enrolling if accepted. As students sprayed more applications into the system overall, less-selective schools worried they might be used as backups. So the third adjustment institutions made was to embrace a practice called "yield management." They deferred early-round applicants to regular decision to see if they behaved like real prospects. Either that, or admissions offices denied applicants outright if the school suspected it was a safety pick.

Assembling a freshman class at any college is like making a complex stew. The adjustments that colleges made in the early 2020s—going test-optional, establishing multiple deadlines, and practicing yield management—messed with a tried-and-true admissions recipe, especially at selective colleges. As a result, it has become much harder to get in, yet kids and their parents still have the same expectations as applicants in 2017 or 2019.

While writing this book, I received a steady stream of texts from friends experiencing this new reality firsthand as they went through the application process with their own teenagers. "This is now getting ridiculous," one wrote when their kid with a near-perfect SAT score was wait-listed at Georgetown, following a similar fate at the University of Michigan and an outright rejection at the University of Pennsylvania. Another texted me after their first meeting with their high school junior's counselor: "I'm going to have to reset in my mind where T. should apply and where she can realistically get in." The parent admitted a little later: "She'll be okay. It's just frustrating to see where this is going." And then, more hand-wringing, in a refrain

I heard repeatedly in my reporting: "It doesn't mesh with the vision that I had!"

Before we go on, let's clarify what we mean when we talk about selectivity. Most colleges are selective in some way; some portion of the students who apply get rejected. For the purposes of this book, however, when I use the term "selective" I'm talking mainly about schools that accept fewer than 30 percent of applicants. While these numbers are always shifting, there are fewer than a hundred colleges and universities in this category most years. Within that group is a small subset of what I'll refer to as "super" or "ultra" selective colleges—about twenty-five schools that take fewer than 10 percent of applicants. All these terms are based largely on one thing: how many applicants a school rejects. Remember, that is a head count measure only; it says nothing about the quality of teaching or the student experience.

As I wrote in the Introduction, this book isn't about how to get into one of those super-selective colleges. Perhaps that's your current goal and that's fine. This book focuses on finding the right fit, whatever your high school transcript looks like and wherever you end up. That said, for better or worse, top-ranked colleges shape the larger admissions game for all of us: Their priorities—whether they want more economic diversity in their student body or families that can pay full freight or more female engineering majors from the Great Plains—chart the course for every runner in this marathon, no matter where they finish.

Lower-ranked colleges often adopt the practices of ultra-selective institutions, since higher-ed leaders perceive this as a way to gain legitimacy. Also, with so many prospective students flooding the system and so few top-tier spots available, applicant pools are increasingly overlapping, making colleges more competitive with each other up and down the rankings. Students can apply to multiple schools, but they go to one. So colleges are always looking for an advantage over rivals.

Getting a wider view of admissions—and how the different actors, from applicants to high schools to colleges, both interact and affect one another—helps you see where you're likely to end up and why. In this story of college admissions, let's examine how each of these groups is playing its part and how each complicates it in its own way.

The Applicants: Swinging from Overconfidence to Self-Doubt

While we talk a lot about "college" in the United States, we struggle to agree on what exactly the word means. That's why most students start their search with a broad and sometimes eclectic list of options—as if they threw darts at a board filled with names of schools. Even Mia, who had the benefit of watching her two older siblings go through their own searches, included a wide range of possibilities in the list she compiled at the beginning of her junior year in high school. "I had Penn and Chicago on it, but I also had Fordham, Michigan State, Temple, and Drexel," Mia told me soon after she arrived to have dinner with her mom. "I didn't really care much about brands." She paused, her voice catching. "At that time."

As Mia shoveled down a taco bowl, she pulled a Chromebook out of her oversize backpack. She opened the laptop, turned it toward me, and clicked on a bookmarked tab for Niche.com, a website she used to manage her college search. Niche includes millions of reviews of colleges from students and alumni, which are used in its own "Best Colleges" rankings. Roughly half the U.S. college-bound students create accounts on Niche by the time they're seniors in high school. This digital gold mine shows the twists and turns of their college search journey. That's why I asked the company to help me figure out how students' dream school lists shift as reality sets in.

What we found is that the college list doesn't solidify until right before the senior year of high school. The company produced a graph for me showing how far the caliber of colleges on students' lists deviates from the average for all places they showed interest in during the first three years of high school. For example, accounts on Niche that are created freshman year have the widest spread of colleges in terms of rankings. As each month of high school passes, the array gradually narrows, as you'd expect.

But then something noteworthy happens in July before senior year: Rather than continue on a fairly straight line, that rankings spread falls precipitously in the months before October, right about the time early applications are due. What that means is that seniors are not only reducing the number of schools they're considering (as expected), but they're also focusing on a narrower range of schools clustered closely in the rankings.

What drives this trend?

Research suggests that as juniors approach this important stretch in the marathon to college they suffer from overconfidence bias. Two things in particular seem to give students—and probably more so their parents—an inflated sense of their academic abilities. The first is their junior-year report card. It's not that students suddenly see their GPAs improve in eleventh grade; rather, they start to view their transcript in a new light, as a critical piece of information in the college application. But it's not the differentiator they assume. According to the U.S. Department of Education, grades have been rising for at least two decades—a trend that only accelerated during the pandemic.

Mia pulled up her grades for me. She had a 4.0 GPA. She began to scroll down to the earlier years in high school, and I didn't see anything below an A, in any class. I counted up the AP classes, ten in all. Mia's grades might seem remarkable to most of today's parents. However, in the context of modern high schools, her transcript is fairly common. When every student receives high marks, it becomes more difficult to separate the top performers from the average performers in a class. Then as students apply for college it becomes increasingly difficult for them and the people close to them, even their counselors, to identify the very best of the best.

I asked Mia if her grades had persuaded her that she was destined for Penn or Chicago, her top two choices. "My grades and test scores were better than Sawyer's," she said with a wry smile, alluding to her brother's acceptance into Carnegie Mellon several years earlier. "So, yeah, I thought I had a good chance."

The second thing that fuels overconfidence as students head into their senior year are their standardized test scores. Before widespread adoption of test-optional policies in 2020, SAT and ACT scores held enormous signaling power for students in the admissions process. Students used a college's middle 50 percent score range to guide their choices and gauge their shot at getting in. Now those ranges don't give applicants a clear idea of where they stand. In a world where only top performers submit scores and then drive up the average for the next crop of applicants, the most-common question I get is "What is a good score anymore?"

Lacking that clarity, students often compare their numbers with those of friends and family who made it into highly selective schools. But the metrics have changed. Mia's 1400 on the SAT put her in the top 7 percent of test takers nationally. Even with a score "higher than my mom's in 1990 that got her into Duke," Mia debated with her parents and high school counselor throughout the fall whether to submit a score or not, and then where to submit one. "Mia's counselor kept telling us to manage her list downward," Kim said. "To me, that sounded like she should settle for second best." In the end, Mia sent scores with all but three of her sixteen applications.

In January, the first round of early action decisions started to arrive for Mia. They weren't decisions, but rather "deferrals." That meant she was still in the running for the regular-decision period, but it certainly wasn't a good sign. "That's when I started to second-guess whether I should have sent scores," Mia said, her face turning sullen. The deferral at Clemson University perhaps stung the most. Mia's SAT score alone should have been a strong enough signal to get her in. Yet, the inconsistency of some students submitting scores and others choosing not to has even seasoned admissions experts struggling to make clear distinctions.

When Stu Schmill, the dean of admissions at MIT, is asked by friends whose children are applying to other colleges whether they should submit scores, he mostly gives them a verbal shrug. "I never have a good answer," he told me. "Like, I have no idea."

Early action today is the regular decision of a generation ago. Students like early action because they get a speedier response. FOMO (the fear of missing out) is real in high school hallways when so many others seem to get an acceptance in January or February of their senior year instead of March. It's also why students look for rolling-admission schools, where they will receive a decision soon after they apply. "Everyone in my school applies to Pitt because they have rolling admissions," Mia said. "At least you can tell friends you've been accepted *somewhere*."

By the time winter rolled around, Mia's overconfidence during the fall application season turned to doubt as decisions started to arrive. Joining Clemson on her early action deferral list were Wisconsin, Northeastern, Ohio State, and the University of Southern California. Early action was supposed to be about getting an early answer, but Mia and tens of thousands of other students weren't getting *any* answer.

In the year Mia applied, both Clemson and USC offered early action for the first time—and both schools were inundated with applications. Clemson received 26,000 applications for early action and then an additional 32,000 regular-decision applications for a freshman class that ended up with 4,500 students. Clemson deferred around 15,000 (and rejected only 300) in its early pool. USC collected 40,000 early applications and then received 40,000 more during the regular-decision cycle for a first-year class of just 3,400. Some 94 percent of its early applicants waited another two-plus months for a decision.

As I heard about these huge deferral numbers, I started calling admissions deans for an op-ed I'd end up writing for *The New York Times*. The deans didn't want to talk about early action or share any numbers. To many, it wasn't a big deal: The admissions process wasn't over, and they were simply telling students to wait. But the reason students applied early, I told them, was precisely to get an answer early. A deferral wasn't an answer.

"Why would we put out a denial when the pool itself isn't settled?"

Kedra Ishop, the vice president for enrollment management at USC, asked when we talked. "Then we're not giving students the full consideration we promise." But they don't get much additional consideration anyway. Most schools don't fully review the deferred applications again during regular decision, when they're already facing another thick pile of files. Are we supposed to believe that, out of the 37,000 or so students USC deferred, there weren't, say, 10,000 that the admissions office knew in December would never be admitted?

At first, Mia took the deferrals in stride; after all, they were a kinder blow than outright rejections. "But then others in her class were accepted," Kim wrote in an email to me in late February. "This resulted in Mia becoming sure she would not get accepted anywhere. In my efforts to cheer her up, I revisited Naviance [a college search tool used by some high schools], where I too concluded she may not get into college!"

By mid-April, when I knew most of the college decisions had likely arrived, I texted Mia. I didn't hear back after a few days, so I sent a note to Kim. "She's been on an emotional rollercoaster the past few weeks," Kim texted back, "between moments of crying/panic" and "days where she pulled it together for school/work."

What Kim described is normal teenage behavior during a time-consuming and unpredictable process. Stress is a perfectly fitting response when students are applying to college, as Lisa Damour pointed out in *The Emotional Lives of Teenagers*. Damour is a clinical psychologist specializing in the development of teenagers, the author of several best-selling books, and a friend. As parents, Damour wrote, "we cannot prevent emotional pain in our teenagers. Rather we should help them manage discomfort when it comes."

Even though Kim didn't know it at the time, she took a page out of Damour's playbook in helping Mia manage her emotions throughout the process. She made sure her daughter got enough sleep; provided distractions (they always took small side trips, for instance, when visiting campuses, like Fallingwater near the University of Pittsburgh or an Eater-rated coffee shop in Davidson, NC, where no college talk was allowed); indulged in small pleasures with her (they took a day off school to go to Mia's favorite crab place near Baltimore—again, with no college talk); and, perhaps most important, helped her adopt a new vantage point.

That last piece is critical in the college search. I call it a "course correction." We go through the application process with biases *for* and *against* certain schools, and I see so many families double down as they move through the junior and senior years of high school. It's hard to knock a favorite college off the list or bring one up that was dismissed early on. But a course correction is often needed as we learn more about colleges—and ourselves. Although more difficult to pull off when delayed, a course correction can even come near the end of the admissions process when weighing offers. We still have time to look at schools in a different light than we did when first submitting applications.

Mia was rejected at twelve of the eighteen colleges she applied to. She had her heart set on Chicago and Penn; she eventually received acceptances to Clemson, the University of Richmond, the University of Pittsburgh, Fordham, Franklin & Marshall, and the University of Delaware. For Mia, the course correction came on Delaware, a school she'd applied to only because, as she told me, "It didn't require any supplements on the Common App."

Ways to Correct Course

How did Mia adjust her perspective? She did so in several ways that you might find useful in your own course correction or even in the early days of your college search:

- **Visit campus for the first time (or again) but be sure to visit.** Mia visited the University of Delaware campus on an admitted student day in April. Meeting students she might actually have as classmates changed her viewpoint on the school. Touring campuses is difficult and expensive during senior year, and so students often wait until they're accepted and making a final decision. While we tend to think the tours happen at the beginning of the college search, about a quarter of them occur at the end—in the month of April. During those visits, about half of families are setting foot on campus for the first time. Bottom line: Don't rule schools out before you visit, and never enroll in one sight unseen.

- **Figure out a budget and have the money talk.** Mia and her parents compared financial-aid offers and discussed how much money she had available to pay for college and, later, medical school (she wanted to be a doctor). While this "money talk" happened too late in the search for her to truly course correct, Delaware's large aid offer, including money for a study-abroad or research experience, worked in her favor. Dashing a kid's college dreams because of the price tag is tough, but determining—as a family—how much you can afford on an *annual* basis for *four* years makes for a smoother process. College pricing works like almost nothing else we buy. Essentially what it will cost you is hidden until after you're accepted. But you can get a sense of what you might pay by using something called the net price calculator, which the federal government requires colleges to display on their websites. You can also find a college's Common Data Set (CDS) on its website to see how generous the school is with merit-aid discounts (I'll explain this in Chapter 9).

- **Give yourself time to process each course correction you make, especially with respect to what you can afford to pay.** Having that money talk early allows time to adjust everyone's expectations. Kim and her husband earned around $130,000 combined. One of their kids had already graduated college and another one would soon. "There was no way we could pay $80,000 a year, or even $50,000 for that matter, for Mia," Kim told me. She and her husband settled on an annual budget of around $30,000. But they hadn't talked to Mia about that number "because we never came to terms with the guilt," Kim said. "She had worked so hard—the hardest of all of our kids—but had the most difficult college search." After Mia completed her freshman year at Delaware, I asked Kim if she had made peace with how Mia finished the admissions race. Mostly, she told me, but then quoted a Taylor Swift song: "The saddest fear comes creeping in." You'll always think *what if*, as Kim did, but as I tell my own kids, you can't live parallel lives. Live in the moment wherever you are in school.

- **Understand what you value and look for it.** In the weeks before she had to decide, Mia finally dug into the curricula of the majors she was considering, an aspect of the college search she'd completely overlooked. When I reconnected with Mia at Delaware, she said she wished she'd done that sooner instead of worrying about some vague idea of fit. On her campus visits, she should have looked for the tangible opportunities that she'd eventually embrace as an undergraduate—being a peer mentor and a writing fellow, for example, and working on research with a professor. That realization highlights one of Mia's missed opportunities before she even started her search: understanding why she was going to college and what she truly wanted. In other words, what did she value? Know your motivations before embarking on the college search: What do you like most about high school? What do you expect from college? What are your unique strengths?

- **Take your own "College 101" course.** Mia had never asked her older siblings about their college searches, what they'd have done differently, or what surprised them when they arrived at college. While she'd toured colleges with them as a younger sibling, later on as a high school junior she couldn't describe what kinds of campuses suited her the best. Don't assume—even if this is your second or third go-around—that your kid understands anything about college. When I'm in the car with my own kids and the subject of college comes up, we'll talk for a few minutes about questions they might not think to ask: What does it mean to major in something? How do you use office hours with professors? What's a liberal arts college? What is the schedule like in a typical week?

Finally, here's an exercise I recommend whenever I'm speaking at high schools: Visit campuses within a few hours of home—whether you want to apply there or not—during freshman or sophomore year of high school. Before the stress of the application process begins, go to a liberal arts college in a rural town, an urban university, a public flagship university with big-time sports and Greek life. Don't put any names of colleges on your list yet. Just figure out what you like (and don't like) and how you might feel if you end up at a college *like* the one where you're walking around without the pressure of a "visit." My research shows that informational drive-bys often lead to the first course correction—helping us shed preconceptions about brand names and prestige and broadening our understanding of what makes a good college.

The High Schools: Feeding Too Many Reaches

Rob Franek peered out at the parents and students who'd gathered on a midwinter night in the auditorium at D'Evelyn Junior/Senior High School in Denver. As the editor in chief of The Princeton Review, which publishes college guidebooks in addition to offering test-prep courses, he headlined more than a hundred similar events at U.S. high schools in 2023. At nearly all he started out the same way he did this night in Denver.

"Take out a piece of paper or your phone and write down three schools you'd want to go to if cost were not a factor," Franek told the audience.

He set the timer on his phone for twenty-seven seconds. He then asked people to cross off the names of schools on their lists as he named them. He started a roll call of colleges at the top of various rankings, a mix of Ivy Leagues, a few public flagships, and some small liberal arts colleges. He named thirty colleges. Then he paused.

"How many of you still have three schools left on your list?" he asked. No one raised their hand. "Who has two?" A few hands shot up. "Who has one?" A couple more hands raised. "Who has zero?" Nearly every hand in the auditorium went up.

This was the third time in six years that Franek had spoken at D'Evelyn as part of its annual college night. I asked Molly Harrington, D'Evelyn's director of college counseling, if Franek's opening spiel had an impact. Did students look further afield for colleges beyond the top of the rankings as a result? "Nothing changes," Harrington said with a resigned sigh. Indeed, if anything, it's had the opposite effect. Since 2014, the number of applications from D'Evelyn's senior class to the top 50 colleges has tripled. "There's always going to be parents who really want these highly selectives," Harrington said, "even when it's not reasonable for their kid."

While D'Evelyn is a public school, it's what Colorado calls an "option school," meaning students enter a lottery to enroll. Situated on former ranch land, fifteen miles southwest of downtown Denver, D'Evelyn, with about 600 students in the high school, is consistently ranked No. 1 in the state and among the top 100 schools in the nation. Harrington feels a constant push-and-pull as a counselor there: Families chose to enter the school lottery for D'Evelyn's unique liberal arts curriculum, but they also care about its ranking and reputation. "There's a little bit of 'D'Evelyn is a great school, so why aren't we getting more kids into these highly selectives?'" she told me. "That's where the pressure comes."

Harrington walked me through a PowerPoint presentation about D'Evelyn's college-placement trends over the last decade. I noted with some irony the reason Harrington had compiled the slides: It was a presentation for the school's "accountability committee." One slide showed a decrease in D'Evelyn graduates who stay in Colorado for college. About half stick around now, compared with 65 percent a decade ago. A key reason is that students are applying to more selective schools elsewhere. But another is that the University of Colorado and Colorado State, like publics everywhere, are recruiting more out-of-state students. As a result, Colorado's public universities are more selective for everyone (a topic I tackle in Chapter 3).

As Harrington ran through the slides, two caught my attention. One listed the schools among the top 50 colleges that D'Evelyn students *applied to* most often in the previous decade: Michigan, Stanford, Vanderbilt, USC, and Purdue. The other showed schools among the top 50 colleges that *accepted* D'Evelyn seniors most often: Lehigh, UC Davis, Case Western Reserve, Virginia Tech, and the University of Wisconsin. The lists didn't match up at all. Why the disconnect? "No matter what I say," Harrington said, "parents feel their kid is different, like this is going to be the time *that* student gets into Stanford."

I call this phenomenon "list creep," and it's happening not only at D'Evelyn but everywhere these days. Overconfidence caused by inflated grades and by test-optional admissions means what used to be reach schools are increasingly seen as target schools by students and their parents. Let me explain: When students apply to college, they put their choices into three buckets—reach, target, or safety. (Most counselors dislike that last term because too much is unknown these days for a school to be a true safety; they prefer "foundation school.") A well-balanced list has schools evenly spread among the three buckets. But too often, students have more reaches than target or safety schools.

When Niche provided me with national data on teenagers managing their college search on the platform, several patterns emerged. The company analyzed the range of schools on students' lists, looking especially at how the most recent year compared to 2020. Students in most GPA levels are now considering a wider variety of schools than they did a few years ago. And students with the highest GPAs (3.9+) showed the most diverse range. On the surface, that suggests these students are following the central premise of this book—they're widening the aperture.

However, look more closely and we see a different story. While they're adding more schools to their lists, the new additions among A-average students at top high schools still skew toward big-name colleges (University of Wisconsin, for instance, with an 18 percent acceptance rate for out-of-staters). Compare that to teenagers at less-rigorous schools who add colleges easier to get into (University of San Diego, for example, which accepts about half of its applicants). So, many of these teenagers are essentially choosing campuses that fit mostly into a single bucket—reach schools. Only when they veer close to graduation do top students seem open to adding a broader range of schools. The impetus? Receiving news of rejections and referrals. It often takes the perception that time is running out for these students to face reality and begin looking at a wider array.

When I applied to college in late 1990, I recall petering out after completing four applications on my family's Smith Corona electric typewriter. In 2024, nearly one in five applicants applied to ten or more colleges. That's about double the proportion of students who applied to the same number of colleges a decade earlier.

The rise in students applying to more colleges has driven record-breaking increases in overall application volume cycle after cycle, as shown in *Figure 1.1*. For the first-year college class that enrolled in the fall of 2023, 13.1 million applications were filed overall on any platform, a jump from 11.5 million in 2019, and way up from 4.4 million in 2001. To put those numbers in context, the number of high school graduates in the U.S. has remained relatively constant over that time, rising by just 800,000 since 2001.

Figure 1.1

Application Inflation

The surge in applications since the turn of this century has largely been the result of students applying to more schools, as first-year enrollment hasn't kept pace.

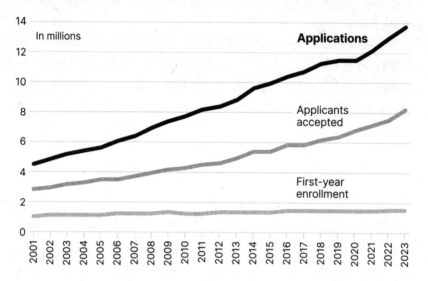

Source: U.S. Department of Education, National Center for Education Statistics, Integrated Postsecondary Education Data System (IPEDS)

It's not that more students are applying to college; it's that the same number of students are sending more applications. And many who are filing a high volume of applications tend to come from the same types of high schools nationwide: private and large public schools in middle- and upper middle-class zip codes.

One of those schools is Minnetonka High School in the western suburbs of Minneapolis. The number of applications filed by each senior class of 900 students since 2019 has doubled to nearly 7,000. What makes that number even more remarkable is this data point from Norma Gutierrez, a counselor at Minnetonka: About half the class goes to community college or trade school or is a "one and done" applicant (i.e., they file at only one place, usually a Minnesota public college).

Among the other half of the senior class, "everyone's list just gets longer," Gutierrez said. "Kids aren't applying to noncompetitive schools; they're all applying to more competitive schools." Echoing what other counselors told me, Gutierrez said, "Sometimes the students are kind of shocked when I say, 'These are reaches.'" What's frustrating to counselors is that the conversations they have with seniors about the rising competition at highly selective schools aren't filtering down to subsequent classes. "It's rinse and repeat" with the senior class that follows, Gutierrez said. Seniors look at the college placements of the previous year's graduating class, get nervous they won't get into their dream school, and then apply to even more colleges—but ones that are copies of one another.

You can see this happening by looking at the scattergrams for any competitive high school. This popular feature of counseling software, such as Naviance or Scoir, shows students their chances of gaining acceptance to specific colleges through a graph of anonymous applicants with similar grades and test scores from their high school. When you study these scattergrams, two trends come into focus.

One is what we've just been talking about. While more students are applying to the same top-ranked schools, the number accepted at each college is holding steady (or in many cases dropping). I looked at Dougherty Valley High School, forty miles east of San Francisco, as a fairly representative sample of kids in an upper middle-class suburban school. In 2018, 251 seniors applied to the University of Southern California; 36 were accepted. Five years later, in 2023, 350 applied but only 22 were accepted. I saw a similar pattern at Reservoir High School in Maryland, south of Baltimore. Some 170 students applied to the University of North Carolina at Chapel Hill in 2018, and 24 were accepted. In 2023, nearly double the number of seniors applied, but only 10 more students more were accepted than in 2018.

This creates a compounding effect that's hard to see from the vantage point of a single high school. Students know that four years earlier, a classmate's older sister—with the same grades and test scores and extracurriculars—got in seemingly everywhere. What's invisible from your own Naviance scatterplot is that thousands of high schools are flooding the system with more applications.

The second trend in the scattergrams is that students are making next-tier colleges more competitive as they apply to more schools. Jeff Makris has become keenly aware of this in his role as director of college counseling at Stuyvesant High School in New York, one of the top public schools in the country. As we talked, he rattled off a bunch of colleges his students apply to after the Ivy League and elite liberal arts colleges—Northeastern, Case Western, Boston University, and Binghamton University among them. In 2016, 298 students applied to Northeastern, and 91 were admitted; by 2022, applications had jumped to 422, but only 49 were admitted. In 2022, 129 Stuyvesant students applied to Case Western, about the same number as in 2017, but admits were cut almost in half, to 36. In 2016, the acceptance rate for Stuyvesant students who applied to Boston University was 43 percent; by 2022, it was 14 percent.

Normally, Makris said, about 50 to 75 graduates enroll at Binghamton University, one of the state's top public universities but a safety school among many Stuyvesant students. In 2022, 124 students went there. I'm sharing these specific numbers to illustrate a crucial point: The college admissions landscape has shifted dramatically. What once seemed unusual—strong students not getting into their target schools—is now commonplace.

As applications arrive in bulk from certain high schools to the most selective colleges, we can see in the admissions results that these colleges don't want to accept too many students from the same place. They don't have a quota for students from a single high school, but most value geographic diversity.

Admissions officers at selective colleges also use a tool from the

College Board called Landscape. It provides key data points about an applicant's school and neighborhood, including average SAT scores, percentage of students eligible for free or reduced-price lunch, crime statistics, and median family income, providing more context than the high school profile that counselors send along. Plus, as these colleges enroll more kids from a given high school, they collect more data on how its students go on to perform as undergraduates. Using that information, admissions officers sort out what GPAs and specific courses really mean from that high school, and those insights come into play in the selection process for applicants who follow. Often, the admissions bar then rises for kids from ultra-competitive schools. Does that mean you should switch to a less competitive high school? Not at all. Colleges still value feeder schools that send them hordes of applicants. What's more, you'll get a good education at a top high school that will prove useful no matter where you go to college.

Another challenge with application inflation, especially for colleges a little further down in the rankings, is yield management. Yield rates—the percentages of accepted applicants who actually enroll—are a truer gauge of popularity than acceptance rates when students have multiple options. And those have plummeted at all but the super-selective schools, as depicted in *Figure 1.2*. Take, for instance, colleges such as Villanova, Kenyon, and Florida State that accept between 20 and 40 percent of applicants. Two decades ago, their yield rates were about the same as the most highly selective colleges. Both groups on average had about four in ten students they accepted agree to enroll. Now, though, this less-selective group has seen their yield plummet, to below 30 percent, while the ultra-selectives have yields now above 50 percent. For colleges and universities, yield is an institutional status symbol and a signal of financial strength.

Figure 1.2

The Haves and Have-Nots In Admissions

Yield rates—a truer gauge of popularity than acceptance rates when students have multiple options—have plummeted at all but the most selective schools.

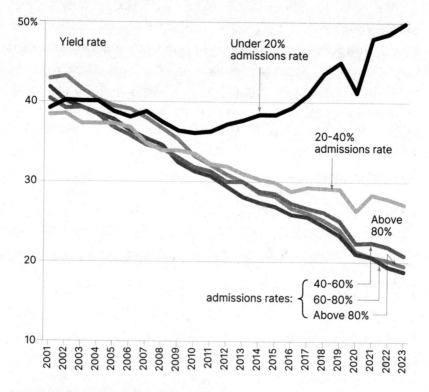

Note: Admissions rates based on 2021 first-year class.

Source: U.S. Department of Education, National Center for Education Statistics, Integrated Postsecondary Education Data System (IPEDS)

When schools believe they are being used as a backup, they use deferrals, wait lists, and even outright rejections to protect their yield rates. Remember when Mia was deferred from early action at Clemson? That was likely yield management on its part. Why? Normally, only 15 percent of out-of-state students accepted by Clemson end up enrolling, compared with half of applicants from South Carolina. By deferring Mia, admissions officers could wait and see how much interest she would show in the months between early and regular admissions by visiting campus or attending virtual admissions events—and then, if she seemed serious, offer her a spot.

All of this is to say, as you widen the lens on your college search, you should recalibrate it as well. Putting more of the same type of top-ranked colleges on your list doesn't increase your chances of getting in; it increases your chances for disappointment. Again, I'm not trying to discourage you from aiming high. But if you fail to balance the top-ranked options on your list with good schools deeper in the rankings, you won't have enough opportunities for the course correction you'll likely need to make later on.

The Colleges: Looking for More Than Perfect Scores

Colleges invest heavily in first impressions. The admissions "welcome center"—with an auditorium to meet prospective students, a comfy gathering place for tours to start, and iconic spaces for Instagrammable moments—is now an enrollment must-have, even at super-selective campuses like MIT (the most extreme example is at the University of Alabama, which you'll see in Chapter 3).

On an early fall day in 2023, I was waiting in MIT's new welcome center, just above the Kendall/MIT stop on the T, as Boston's subway is known. I was there to see Stu Schmill, MIT's dean of admissions since 2008. I first met Schmill a year earlier while writing a feature article for *New York* magazine on MIT's return to requiring the SAT after a two-year pause during the pandemic. When I wrote that piece, I expected others to quickly follow. But at that point, they hadn't. I wanted to ask Schmill why.

As I waited, a student tour finished up. One teenager was hanging back with his parents, and when everyone else left, they approached the undergraduate tour guide. "I was wondering if I could leave my research portfolio," I overhead the prospective student say. His father interjected: "He's worked on three major research projects in high school." I couldn't overhear the entire conversation, though the crux of the exchange was that the student believed his research portfolio set him apart, but the tour guide, without sounding discouraging, was trying to indicate that kind of portfolio is not unusual anymore for the typical MIT applicant. I could tell the undergraduate tour guide at MIT was already setting admissions expectations—on the tour.

A few minutes later, sitting in Schmill's office two floors up, I recounted what I'd witnessed in the lobby. Schmill graduated from MIT in 1986. When he arrived as an undergraduate, he told me, the acceptance rate was 33 percent. "I don't even know if that would be considered selective today," he said with a playful smirk. I asked him if he'd be admitted if he applied now. "Probably not," he said, but quickly noted, "I would have been a different applicant."

Like most teenagers back then, Schmill wasn't aiming to get into a college like MIT from almost the moment he was born. His activities, he said, "weren't picked with anything in mind other than 'Hey, what would you like to do?'" He then added in a nostalgic tone: "Which I wish we could get back to." Schmill told me he took accelerated math courses in high school, not because "I was trying to accelerate, but I was just kind of good in math." He didn't visit MIT before enrolling. He was a walk-on to the MIT crew team but had never rowed in high school.

I could tell from our conversations that Schmill is uncomfortable with many of the tactics employed by his counterparts in elite higher education to boost selectivity rates. MIT isn't on the Common App. It doesn't send mail needlessly to students it has no intention of accepting simply to increase the denominator in calculating its acceptance rate. And at the beginning of the pandemic, Schmill was reluctant to drop the requirements for SAT scores because he knew schools that had gone test-optional were receiving a bump in applications, and a deluge was sure to follow. And at MIT it did: The first year of the pandemic, applications to MIT jumped 66 percent, more than at almost every other selective college. "We certainly did not increase our staff by 66 percent," Schmill told me. "Our staff got very burned out." MIT had every intention of restoring its test requirements after one year but, as the pandemic lingered, the school extended the policy for a second year.

Schmill wanted to return to the tests for another reason as well: He believed they provided a signal of student preparedness for MIT, particularly the math score. He repeatedly pointed out to me that MIT's undergraduate curriculum—and its focus on mathematics—is unique even among top-ranked colleges. Earlier in Schmill's tenure, the school admitted students with a wider range of SAT scores who ended up dropping out.

By the time the pandemic hit, however, MIT was essentially taking only perfect scorers. In 2020, the top 25 percent of the class scored a perfect 800 in math and the bottom 25 percent scored a 780 or below, with none scoring under 700. (To put these numbers in perspective: If a student missed *two* math questions out of the fifty-eight on most versions of the SAT, they'd score 770, lower than 75 percent of that 2020 first-year class at MIT.)

After two pandemic-disrupted application cycles, MIT announced in 2022 that it would require test scores again. At first, it was alone among elite schools, but a year later several Ivy League institutions, including Dartmouth, Yale, and Harvard, announced they were returning to the tests, as did the University of Texas at Austin. Despite those moves, test-optional policies seem to be here to stay for most colleges. Admissions offices don't want to give up the flexibility they provide in crafting their classes.

At Case Western, for instance, test-optional has meant that students who want to major in management aren't discouraged from applying by average tests scores that in the past were inflated by students interested in engineering. As a result, applications from would-be management majors are up at Case. Even the makers of the SAT and ACT have acknowledged the tests aren't returning to their pre-2020 days. The all-digital SAT, introduced in the spring of 2024, is an hour shorter than the old three-hour paper version. College Board executives told me they hope students will *want* to take the shorter test to decide if their score is worth submitting, instead of feeling they *must* take the longer one. The experience has been redesigned for higher-ed consumers in a test-optional era.

Though test-optional became the norm during the pandemic, our relationship with testing remains complicated. If you're a parent of a good test taker, you probably want to return to the days when basically every college required an SAT or ACT score.

Nearly eight in ten parents who responded to my survey already think you need to submit a test score to get into a prestigious college anyway, even if it's test-optional. Requiring test scores is particularly appealing if your kid goes to a high school where grade inflation is prevalent, making it tough to distinguish top students. Here's the problem with that viewpoint: A high score no longer means as much as it once did, with so many more applications now flowing to elite institutions. Double 750s is no longer the master key to getting in.

Although application inflation runs rampant throughout higher education, it's even more pronounced at the super-selective colleges your kid might desire (or, be honest, you might desire). Schools that today accept fewer than 20 percent of students collected 1.9 million applications in 2023. They received just 600,000 in 2001. It's as if every applicant back then applied again in 2023, and then found three of their classmates *also* applying to the same top schools. Meanwhile, the number of seats at these colleges hasn't budged much since the late 1970s.

When Duke's dean of admissions, Christoph Guttentag, started his job in 1992, the university received a quarter of the applications it does now. Nearly 48,000 regular-decision applications arrived in 2024, up 37 percent since 2019. Every cycle, admissions officers at Duke and other elite colleges need to move faster and be tougher in their assessment of applicants. Fewer than half of Duke's applicants go through the full evaluation process. The ultimate destiny of many applicants is determined in initial readings by a single admissions officer that can take less than fifteen minutes. In that early pass, "I have to say no to about two-thirds to three-fourths," Guttentag said. He reads roughly a dozen applications each morning.

These days, Guttentag told me, far fewer applicants "knock your socks off." A decade ago, admissions officers at Duke regularly talked about a "wall of 5s"—applicants with stacks of that top AP score. "You'd just see this long list of eight or ten or twelve 5s," Guttentag recalled. "That's the sort of thing that would by itself have moved the needle and now doesn't" because those stats are a lot more common for applicants to Duke.

The numbers he rattled off shocked me, but I was even more surprised by his nonchalant attitude about them, given how few teenagers score a 5 or even have access to a slew of AP courses. Only 14 percent of the 4.39 million AP tests administered in 2023 were scored a 5, according to the College Board; only half of American public high schools even offer more than five AP courses.

What gets students into Duke now? They need not only the "best possible grade in every subject across the board in as difficult a curriculum as the school offers," Guttentag said, but also evidence "that they've gone beyond the strong students at the school in pursuing their academic interests." The difference between 55,000 and 25,000 applications is that "you see more ways for students to excel academically than through the traditional AP, SAT, IB [International Baccalaureate curriculum offered by some high schools] measures."

When does this fascination with super-selective colleges—and getting into one—end, if it ever does? When will we come to understand how random it is, that getting in is truly like winning the lottery? When will we concede that colleges control the rules of the game and have no incentive to care about us until we stop engaging with them? You may be wondering whether the college admissions pendulum is about to swing back the other way. Given that fewer children were born in the Great Recession and the decade that followed, colleges face a demographic cliff through the 2030s. With some colleges struggling to stay afloat, could getting in become easier for your younger children than your current high schoolers? Unfortunately, when it comes to the top universities, that demographic cliff is unlikely to throw the gates wide open. Plenty of colleges are going to struggle (and we'll talk in Chapter 9 about how to keep an eye on their finances), but the top brands aren't going to feel that pinch.

From the floor where Stu Schmill's office is, on a clear day you can see the MIT campus and beyond. It's a view that reminded me of college brochures that fuel the dreams—and anxieties—of countless students. Schmill's own family story, though, provides perspective we all need as we embark on this journey.

His older daughter, Samantha, raised in the hotbed of the Boston suburban achievement culture, had her heart set on an Ivy League school. The daughter of the MIT dean of admissions, she'd done everything "right." But she got never got into those top places. She ended up at Franklin & Marshall College. (Nothing to sneeze at, of course, but Lancaster isn't Cambridge or Palo Alto.)

Schmill's younger daughter, Becca, took a different approach from the start. She'd had enough of that pressure-cooker world of high school and wanted something different. "I was comfortable with that because I knew that she could be successful wherever she went and might be more successful at a place a rung or two down the ladder," Schmill told me. "You can go to any college and find your people, find serious students."

She chose the University of Richmond. But Becca and her family never got to see how that choice played out. In September of her first year, she died from fentanyl poisoning with drugs bought on Facebook, a tragedy that's reshaped everything for the Schmill family.[*]

So when Stu Schmill hears from parents of rejected applicants that their life is ruined because they won't be able to attend MIT, he

---

[*] The Schmill family has been outspoken about the dangers of social media. Becca died after taking fentanyl-laced drugs bought on Facebook. She was raped by a boy she met online and cyberbullied on Snapchat. The family established the Becca Schmill Foundation in her memory (https://beccaschmillfdn.org).

understands they're upset, but he also thinks to himself: "You're not counting your blessings here, and you're probably not helping your child, either."

As I left Schmill's office, the weight of his family's sorrow put the college admissions frenzy into perspective. What is this relentless pursuit of prestige doing to us? And how can we focus more on the journey and less on a specific destination? Yes, the path ahead may be more challenging than you anticipated, but it's also rich with opportunities you might not have considered.

CHAPTER 2

SWIMMING IN CALMER WATERS

The Elite College Degree Matters Less Than You Think

A month after the newest class at Harvard Law School arrived in Cambridge, study groups began to form among the first-year students. To Beth, the process looked like a mating ritual. Some of her fellow classmates angled to work with those they considered the smartest kids in the class. A few steered clear of those groups on purpose because they didn't want to partner with their toughest competitors for internships and other opportunities down the road. Many students felt a tinge of impostor syndrome if they weren't asked to join a particular group. And several, like Beth, didn't get invited simply because they lacked an elite academic pedigree.

"It was silly," she said. "It was all based on perceptions." With a lighthearted smile, she told me the fuss over the study groups was yet another reminder of why she'd avoided going to a pressure-cooker elite college. Her father hadn't gone to college at all, but he encouraged his kids to get a degree so they'd have options in life. At Beth's high school, students were measured by the number of AP courses they took and got paid by their parents for good grades. She wanted a less competitive college. "I made the mental choice of being a big fish in a small pond because I thought that I could always go somewhere fancier for grad school," she said. Beth applied to two liberal arts schools and chose one that didn't even crack the top 100 in the *U.S. News* rankings.

When Beth left for college, she wasn't sure what she wanted to study. Accounting seemed like the safe major. But she also had dreams of becoming an FBI agent. During her first semester, she took a seminar taught by a lawyer using the Socratic method. His style of rapid-fire interrogation, popular at law schools, was new to her. But right away she was hooked. Growing up, she didn't know any lawyers, but frequent interactions with the professor helped Beth better understand the career track.

At her small, laid-back college, Beth wasn't intimidated by her classmates—or, as she got to know the faculty through office hours and between classes, her professors. So she dove in without hesitation and quickly distinguished herself as a sharp, dedicated, and academically motivated kid. In turn, the faculty looked out for her throughout her undergraduate years. Several profs wrote her glowing recommendations for law school.

"I saw my professors as people who believed it was part of their job to assist in my personal, academic, and career development," Beth said. "They wanted to teach. They knew me. They were family." They also mentored her and made introductions. When the activist Amanda Knox came to speak on campus about her wrongful conviction for murder, Beth got an invitation to a small dinner beforehand. Even the college's president knew her by name.

Feeling supported and confident, Beth fully immersed herself in her experiences and relationships as a student. The college encouraged undergraduate research, and so one summer she delved into the papers of former U.S. Supreme Court Justice Harry Blackmun—a project she credited later in law school for teaching her how to read bench memos.

Listening to Beth, her words quickening with excitement as she talked about her college experience, I was reminded of other students I'd met who ended up at little-known schools that embraced them during the admissions process and then as budding undergraduates. Though these colleges lacked the vast resources of an Ivy or other top-ranked university, they nevertheless offered plenty of opportunities that students didn't need to stand in line for and that weren't reserved for a precious few.

———————

The week I met Beth, after she'd graduated from Harvard Law, the school released a list of where its newest class had gone as undergrads. That list included Arizona State, Canisius University, DePaul, Drake, Montclair State, The College of New Jersey, and other schools further back in the prestige pack. It was impossible to know whether these colleges had been first choices or backup plans. Either way, the students who picked them ended up at Harvard by taking a page from Beth's playbook: Thrive at a college not on anyone's list of standouts, and then go to a graduate school with a fancy name to pave the way to an elite job.

That strategy carries a risk, of course. You might not get into your dream grad school. But there are no guarantees the other way, either—and, according to one popular theory, you might put yourself at *greater* risk by enrolling in an elite undergraduate program. That theory, the big fish–little pond effect that Beth alluded to, was introduced in 1984 by two psychologists, Herbert Marsh and John W. Parker.

As Marsh later told Malcolm Gladwell for his book, *David and Goliath*, most parents and students make their college choices for the wrong reasons. Just because a school is selective or highly ranked doesn't mean it's a good choice for *you*—even if you can get in. In reality, the outcomes for students who go to such schools are mixed. Sure, very few students drop out of places like MIT and Duke, for example. But every year when smart, accomplished kids from around the world gather as freshmen in Cambridge and Durham, it's not clear who among these top performers in high school will reach the same heights in college. In some ways, they're all little fish who swim in "one of the deepest and most competitive ponds in the county," as Gladwell wrote.

Gladwell cited data from UCLA researchers who concluded in a seminal paper that the biggest factor associated with dropping out of a STEM (science, technology, engineering, and math) program was the academic ability of one's classmates. You might assume—as I did before reading Gladwell's book—that being around smarter kids is better because they encourage you to work harder. But the opposite sometimes happens, at least in STEM fields. Many students give up altogether on the major. That result seemed so counterintuitive that I went looking for the original paper, where I found this crucial line: "For every 10-point increase in the average SAT score of an entering cohort of freshmen at a given institution, the likelihood of retention [in the major] decreased by two percentage points."

I mentioned this statistic during a 2022 talk to parents and the local community at Energy Institute High School, a STEM-focused public magnet in Houston. Afterward, a mother named Michelle came up to tell me about her son, who went to Stanford to major in electrical engineering. Early on, he got tripped up by college calculus, which most of his classmates seemed to understand. The professor and the teaching assistant weren't much help, she added. Their message, according to her son, was that if he couldn't find help on his own, maybe he wasn't cut out for that major at Stanford. He switched majors and, eventually, schools.

Had Michelle heard the stat about STEM dropouts during her son's college search, she said, she probably wouldn't have believed it'd apply to him. She's not alone. Most of us think that if our kids performed well in high school, they'll be fine in college. I asked Michelle about the school search that led her son to Stanford. His second choice, Texas A&M University, was closer to home. All other things being equal, according to the UCLA research cited above, Michelle's son had a 68 percent *higher* chance of dropping out of engineering at Stanford than at Texas A&M. What swayed his school choice in the end? The rankings. Stanford was No. 3 in *U.S. News*, while Texas A&M was No. 47.

Despite its physical size, Texas A&M was the smaller academic pond. It was more accessible to a range of kids. Michelle didn't realize it at the time, but a place like that could have given her son the support and confidence he needed to succeed in his major. Beth, the Harvard Law School graduate, understood that intuitively before making her undergrad selection.

Little ponds "might be scorned by some on the outside," Gladwell wrote, but they are "welcoming places for those on the inside." As Marsh and Parker established with their theory—and as other researchers have since found as they applied it to various educational environments—many big fish from high school actually struggle at highly selective colleges. While a few superstars grow into even bigger fish and rule the pond, one of two things happens to everyone else: Students either turn into predators, desperate to survive, or become prey.

At an elite college, the competitive culture encourages the first group—the predators—to view their undergraduate years as a zero-sum fight for status. They treat their classmates as rivals they must wipe out so they can win whatever prized internships and spots in clubs are left after the kids at the top of the class scoop up the best ones. Students in the second group respond to the pressure quite differently. They look at their brilliant classmates around them, feel worse about their own abilities, and lose confidence.

Looking back, Beth realized that being a big fish in a small college pond gave her the freedom to figure out what she really wanted to do in life and to map out a career trajectory that felt right. No one at her undergraduate school treated her like a threat or pressured her to do or be anything in particular. When she got to Harvard, "everyone liked to talk about their credentials," she said. "It was very intense." Many of her classmates were socialized at elite colleges that fostered the shark mentality. They "hoarded opportunity," she told me. "That might have served them well, but it's not the only way to get to elite places." She paused, as if she were going back over every moment of law school, and then added, "I'm an example of that."

Beth earned plenty of accolades at Harvard, not the least of which was selection to the *Harvard Law Review*, generally considered the most prestigious law journal in the country. After law school, she landed a prestigious role in the U.S. federal court system. It wasn't the big-law-firm life that many of her classmates pursued, but she was also able to strike a balance between her career and time outdoors. Beth had discovered a love for hiking in college because she didn't spend all her time on campus constantly clawing her way up to the next rung on the ladder.

When she'd applied to college, Beth had no idea that she'd wind up at Harvard afterward. At the end of our interview, I asked her how much the name of the school on her undergraduate degree had hampered her journey in a world obsessed with status. She answered without hesitating: "At some point, it stopped mattering."

Explore, Then Exploit

But a brand name must matter—right? If it didn't, you wouldn't be reading this book, Beth wouldn't have made her way to Harvard, and every year tens of thousands of students wouldn't be vying for a spot at a top-ranked college. The question is, how much does the brand *ultimately* matter? Not far from where Beth went to law school, I found someone who could try to answer that question.

David Deming is an economist and a professor at Harvard's Kennedy School. He's also part of a team of researchers at Opportunity Insights, a nonpartisan nonprofit based at Harvard. This group has produced a bunch of headline-grabbing studies in recent years, primarily focused on rising income inequality, particularly in higher education—all based on massive amounts of data that group has access to, including anonymized tax returns from the IRS and profiles from Facebook. When you read or hear about any research from Opportunity Insights, you're likely to see its leader—the superstar economist Raj Chetty—out front. Two others who get a lot of press are John Friedman from Brown University and Deming. I chose to go see Deming because, unlike Chetty and Friedman, he didn't get his bachelor's degree from an Ivy League school. He went to Ohio State.

When we met for breakfast in Cambridge, Deming described himself as an immature undergraduate who spent the first two years of college "frankly, just partying a lot and not really taking anything seriously at all." Late in his sophomore year, he figured out that if he graduated from a state school with a B average, he might not get far in life. "I kind of got my act together halfway through college," he said. He added a second major, economics, and "got close to straight A's after that," he said.

As college graduation approached, however, Deming didn't know what to do next. He'd grown up in a middle-class family that moved to the Cleveland suburb of Shaker Heights when he was fifteen. His father was a Methodist minister, while his mother, the family's breadwinner, was an editor at a religious book publisher. When he got a full ride to Ohio State as a National Merit Scholarship winner, there wasn't really a debate about where he'd go to college (he also got accepted to Vanderbilt and Emory).

Unlike many families in places like Shaker Heights today, who meticulously choreograph everything from the student's college search to what they'll major in and their trajectory after graduation, the Deming household had a more laid-back approach. In his late teens and early twenties, he worked in landscaping and construction. He was a waiter. He served as a page in the Ohio House of Representatives. When he graduated from Ohio State in 2002, he signed with a temp agency to work in a D.C. law firm. Deming took the LSAT with the intention of going to law school, but after a few months of seeing a big firm up close, he changed his plans. Up to this point, Deming said, his life was a series of trying things on and figuring out what fit.

It's what computer scientists and psychologists call the "explore and exploit" trade-off. The question we often face in life is, when do we stop exploring new options and lean into something we're already doing? One of the biggest factors in making this trade-off is how much time we have. And undergraduates possess that in abundance, both in the short term (while at college, especially in the early years) and in the long term (over the rest of their lives, particularly early in their career).

Yet, partly as a consequence of their parents' anxiety about the future, students these days generally don't use college—or the time right after it—to explore. Rather, they approach the undergraduate journey, and the degree itself, as a transaction. In an age of high tuition, overwhelming loan debt, and rising living costs, families increasingly see college as a means to landing a lucrative job, rather than a place for exploration.

As a faculty dean in one of Harvard's residential "houses," Deming has observed that students now tend to approach this period in their lives in a far more utilitarian manner than he did at eighteen. "It's kind of sad to come to college and immediately think about the next thing," he told me.

For today's undergraduates, the college experience isn't like a music festival with acts on a dozen stages that can be sampled; instead, it's a concert with a single act, and they're already focusing on what they'll do when it ends. By cutting their exploration short despite all the time they have, students risk pursuing a career that's a bad fit. "Maybe you *won't* be good at banking or consulting," Deming said, picking the two fields where one-third of Harvard graduates initially land.

After Deming realized being a lawyer wasn't for him, he applied to graduate schools in public policy. He got into Harvard, the University of Chicago, and Berkeley. He chose Berkeley so he could live in California and pay in-state tuition there. He found a faculty member who'd take him on as a teaching fellow as well, which helped with expenses. Over time, his professors noticed Deming's penchant for research, despite his struggles in math-intensive classes the first year. "I hated the classes, but then I improved fast," he said. "It turned out to be a lot of fun." At the age of twenty-three, after much dabbling, Deming had discovered a talent he wanted to exploit.

The Extra Lottery Ticket

Nearly a year before we met in Cambridge, Deming and his colleagues at Opportunity Insights published a study that garnered widespread media attention. It found that children from households in the top 1 percent of incomes were overrepresented at elite colleges, even after adjusting for their high school grades and test scores. But there was another part of the study that received a lot less interest—whether degrees from these schools brought success later in life. That finding, I realized, might help answer my lingering question: How much does a degree from a top-ranked school really matter?

This question has vexed scholars for decades. One reason is that it's impossible to have a given student attend two different colleges at the same time and then measure outcomes. As a work-around, Deming and his team compared the earnings of graduates who were accepted from an Ivy-plus wait list with those who were wait-listed but never admitted and thus went elsewhere. In their analysis, the economists considered all the wait-listed students similarly qualified, whether they ultimately were accepted or not.

By their early thirties, those who'd been admitted to an elite college outperformed those who went elsewhere in three key ways. First, the admits were 60 percent more likely to have earnings in the top 1 percent. Second, they were nearly twice as likely to attend a graduate school ranked in the top 10. And third, they were three times as likely to work for a prestigious employer (such as a research hospital, a top law or consulting firm, or a national newspaper).

On the surface, the findings made it seem like going to an elite school was a guaranteed path to a life of luxury. It's easy to imagine that getting into an Ivy League college means the doors are thrown wide open to all manner of celebrated jobs and unimaginable riches. Meanwhile, the counternarrative suggests that going somewhere else leads to a life of limited opportunities and modest success. But deeper in the paper was a conclusion about earnings that should've been the headline: The *average* income of Ivy-plus graduates wasn't that different from those who attended selective public flagships, such as Ohio State, the University of Florida, the University of Georgia, or UCLA.

To explain this finding, Deming offered an analogy. Imagine a group of a hundred friends, each representing a college graduate, divvying up lottery tickets. Each ticket represents a chance at a highly successful career—let's say, ending up in the top 1 percent of earners. The graduates of public flagships each get one ticket, while those who went to an elite college get two tickets.

Your chances of hitting the jackpot are better if you go to a place like Harvard, no doubt. But remember, the vast majority of graduates, regardless of where they went to school, aren't winning that lottery. In other words, attending an Ivy League school does open more doors—that's the extra lottery ticket. But it's not a guarantee of extraordinary success, nor does attending a different school preclude you from achieving great things. The reality is that for most graduates, "things look pretty similar regardless of where you went to college," as Deming put it.

So, contrary to what many of us have long believed, *where* we earn our undergraduate degree doesn't determine everything about our lives. The notion of rising to the top purely by going to a prestigious college is much too simplistic, in part because there's something profoundly wrong with how we tend to define success.

When making it in life is characterized by our earnings and our job titles, we're easily swayed by the outliers. Do Ivy-plus graduates have a better shot of landing in the top 1 percent of income? Sure. Do they more often become CEOs, Nobel laureates, Pulitzer winners, U.S. presidents, or billionaires feted by *Forbes*? Yes, they do, according to a study published by a group of social scientists in 2024. It found that capturing one of thirty "top" achievements, such as earning a Nobel Prize or even hitting No. 1 on the *New York Times* nonfiction bestsellers list, was "strongly associated" with graduating from one of thirty-four elite schools—often Harvard in particular.

If your goal is to move into the executive suite or rake in billions of dollars, then you're probably better off going to the likes of Harvard. But again, not everyone with a Harvard degree makes it to the top of their field, just as not every star student in high school gets accepted to an Ivy in the first place. And many success stories have modest beginnings. In the previous paragraph I mentioned that study on the outcomes of matriculants at 34 elite colleges. It included the names of undergraduate schools attended by Fortune 500 CEOs. The list wasn't highlighted in the paper, maybe because it didn't reinforce the researchers' thesis. But it was in an appendix of underlying data, and that's where I went looking. Duke and Brown each had three on the CEO list. But so did Ball State University, Kettering University, Louisiana State University, Ohio University (not Ohio State), San Diego State University, and a bunch of other schools. In all, 378 different colleges that weren't among that elite list of thirty-four schools had alumni running Fortune 500 companies.

Okay, so it's possible to make it to the top if you graduate from a college outside of the top 25. Still, we know from Deming's research that students at elite schools get two lottery tickets. Why is that?

Let's consider another study by Deming and his colleagues, which analyzed a massive dataset from Facebook to figure out how our social connectedness comes about. In the simplest terms, teenagers from upper middle-class and affluent families not only go to college at higher rates than everyone else but also make a far greater share of their friends *in* college than do lower-income students, who make their friends in their neighborhoods.

I call this the "rubbing elbows" aspect of an elite education. Because social capital is critical to building networks and getting jobs, who you meet in college is important. And given that Ivy-plus campuses have more well-connected students from households in the top 1 percent of income, they improve your chances of connecting with someone who could potentially help you later—particularly right out of school. Graduates from elite colleges often start out in higher-paying jobs, too.

Deming and his colleagues discovered while designing their research study that the employer a graduate has at age twenty-five "very strongly predicts" earnings at age thirty-three. When I asked Deming why, he quizzed me about my first job after college. It was at a newspaper in Wilmington, North Carolina, a job I got because of a friend I met on a summer internship. I could tell Deming seemed disappointed by my answer because it didn't quite prove his theory. He then asked about my coworkers in North Carolina and where they went to college.

As I started to list the schools—the University of South Carolina, the University of North Carolina, James Madison University in Virginia—Deming's eyes lit up. Many of my coworkers in that first job in North Carolina went to college in the South. "If you get a degree in finance from Ohio State, you'll probably get a great job at Nationwide Insurance based in Columbus," Deming said. "Nationwide is a terrific regional employer, but a finance degree from Harvard will lead you to Goldman Sachs."

A small number of nationally recognized firms, like Goldman, provide a pathway for newly minted college graduates into high-earning and high-status occupations—and students at elite colleges get a head start on navigating that pathway by virtue of the brand name at the top of their diploma.

———

Up until now, we've talked about how success stems from your choice of a pond as an undergraduate as well as the outsize role an elite college can play in helping you start out in life. There is one other piece that's fundamental to answering the question about how much top-ranked schools ultimately matter: a graduate's first employer. That initial job out of college, while not a life sentence, is a key marker for young adults as they trek through their twenties.

To better understand which schools employers hire from and why, I reached out to recruiters at companies that bring on significant numbers of new college grads every year. (I also collected data on Fortune 50 companies where recent graduates landed, which we'll get to at the end of this chapter.) I learned from these recruiters that, much like admissions officers filling spots in colleges, their approach is a bit of art and science and varies widely depending on their organization and industry (in Chapter 10, I'll describe some of the skills and experiences they seek).

Hiring strategies are driven by the employer's particular workforce needs and a desire to outflank competitors to snag prized talent. "We have to think about this with a business mindset around where will the effort pay off," said Simon Kho, vice president and head of early-careers programs at Raymond James Financial, who has held similar roles at several big companies. "We don't just open the floodgates and hope they show up."

Like colleges building a first-year class, employers have priorities that aren't always transparent to students or even to advisors at campus career centers. When Kho worked at a global energy company, it graded colleges on a 16-point scorecard to determine if they'd make the cut for recruiting visits. Sometimes employers' priorities are quite specific. Later on when Kho worked at a big accounting firm, its New England office eliminated Boston University from its recruiting schedule because the university's business curriculum was too focused on managerial accounting when the firm needed associates with a background in financial accounting. At Raymond James, Kho's team spends much of its time at schools in the Southeast since two-thirds of its hires are for the firm's St. Petersburg headquarters.

For most of us, the career lottery is a regional game.

Chart Your Job Prospects

When students apply *to* college, the location of their first job *after* college is not usually on their radar. But the reality is that very few schools (read: Ivy-plus) maintain brands with national pull in the hiring process. Usually, employers think about brand names in context. They consider the reputations of certain majors, for instance, and the typical yield of hires who might perform well and grow professionally in their particular organization.

What's more, I consistently heard in my interviews with recruiters that most employers hire new grads from schools in the regions where the companies are located. Why? Colleges' alumni networks are densest in nearby states and cities—and alumni help new graduates get jobs. They broker introductions, write recommendations, and provide quiet support, like making sure that a fellow alum's résumé lands on the hirer's desk. Even national firms like Deloitte and KPMG, which have offices across the country, tend to fill openings locally. Some are looking for regional expertise (for instance, energy in Houston, consumer banking in Chicago, or finance in New York) and turn to engineering or business majors at colleges nearby.

Perhaps most of all, employers want prospective hires who will stay for a while. In job recruiting, as in college admissions, candidates are drawn to cities where their friends live. Take Lenovo, for example. It's the world's largest PC maker, based in North Carolina. Most of its recruiting is from schools east of the Mississippi. "If I go to the West Coast and try to pull those students, a lot of times they aren't committed to living on the East Coast," said Marybeth Caulfield, Lenovo's senior manager of global university recruitment.

Simon Kho at Raymond James shared a similar view. He said he once cultivated a tech-internship candidate who majored in computer science at Carnegie Mellon, but he knew that was a long shot. "We could hire them for the summer, but there was little chance they'd take it," he said. "Or maybe they will because it's Florida, but then they might not join us full-time. These are all things we're weighing." Pay also comes into play. "Sometimes prestige can hurt you," Caulfield said. "An MIT graduate is going to be looking for a Boston salary in North Carolina."

You'll find plenty of exceptions to region-based hiring, of course. Lenovo recruits at schools known for their top-ranked logistics programs, and a few of those, such as Penn State and Purdue, are outside the Southeast. BYU has a well-regarded accounting program, Kho pointed out, "so you can't ignore it no matter where you're hiring." Ithaca College's Park School of Communications has a semester-long program in Los Angeles and, as a result, a deep alumni network that gets graduates hired in Hollywood, despite the location of its main campus 2,600 miles away. To draw national employers, Wake Forest University—another North Carolina school, with one of the best career centers in the country—asked parents of students for assistance in getting their companies to recruit there. Andy Chan, who oversees career development at the university, told me this effort led to a greater geographic reach for graduates.

Handshake, the job-search platform used by Wake Forest and hundreds of other colleges (think of it as LinkedIn for college students) has also opened up jobs to a broader range of students. According to Handshake, a majority of employers posting jobs to colleges are located in other regions. But Handshake officials couldn't tell me if applicants applying to those jobs outside of their region ended up getting hired. So a college will tell you they have employers recruiting from all over, but what you really want to know is who is getting the job.

It's important to recognize during your college search that the list of elite colleges that employers consider when they recruit is much shorter than the list of brand-name schools in any ranking you consult. In the next two chapters, we'll look at how the geography of higher education is shifting as public flagships draw more out-of-state students and as families begin to skip over what was long considered the next tier of prestige when they're shut out of Ivy-plus schools. While these consumers of higher education hunt for what I'll call "quiet luxury," employers' perceptions of and relationships with schools are changing, too. All of that means you need to ask lots of questions about what the job search looks like for graduates of each college you're seriously considering.

Here are some tips to get you started, based on my conversations with recruiters:

- **Visit career services.** Request a list of organizations that have in the past three years *hired* students from your intended major. Counselors should be able to run a quick report for you. Don't just look at who recruited there; be sure to know who actually hires.

- **On LinkedIn, look at early-career paths of graduates in your field of interest.** Say you want to know more about people who majored in psychology at Fordham. Search for FORDHAM on LinkedIn, look under MAJOR, and then click PSYCHOLOGY in that list. When I did this search, it returned more than 9,000 alums. You can filter by graduation year and see their top companies, their skill sets, and how they are connected to other companies and people.

- **Ask what alumni do to help students get jobs.** Alumni offices can put you in touch with recently hired grads who are happy to talk about the support they received. Some schools have cultures where alumni look out for one another, and others don't. You'll never find the perfect culture, but beware of schools where you might be on your own for the initial job search after graduation.

- **Know the hiring calendar for interns in your field.** As Kho put it, understand what the game is. Internships are often critical (as I'll discuss in Chapter 10), and many students understand that. But landing the right one requires knowing when employers start recruiting for these coveted positions. That takes legwork. It's tricky if you haven't settled on a major yet or haven't completed your required classes. In investment banking, Kho said, "we're often asking students to talk about investment banking when they haven't had their core courses yet. . . . It favors kids whose parents are in investment banking."

Look at Who Lands Where

Why do the headlines on student outcomes focus so narrowly on graduates of elite colleges? To be sure, aspirational appeal is a factor. Families pursuing top-ranked schools *want* to see that those grads are more likely to end up in the top 1 percent of earners, occupy certain leadership positions, or receive major career accolades.

But that's not the only reason. It's really difficult to track where the graduates of *most* schools end up in their careers and how they got there. Colleges often list names of companies where their alumni have worked, but the datasets aren't complete. Schools usually hear about the first stop students make after graduation through what's called the First Destination Survey. Most career centers send it out, but not every graduate responds. After that, the tracking gets even spottier.

To clarify some of this murkiness, I reached out to Lightcast, a firm that analyzes job-market data in real time. The company can track what happens with alumni from basically any college and agreed to do so for this book. Drawing on information from multiple sources, including LinkedIn and résumé databases, Lightcast's data covers some 70 percent of the labor market.

I created a framework for Lightcast to compare colleges, which you'll see again in the chapters ahead. It's a set of 1,200 schools sorted into five groups of selectivity (under 20 percent acceptance rate, between 20 and 40 percent, and so on). I wanted to focus on the launch from college because of Deming's findings about the signaling effect of the job someone holds at twenty-five, so we looked only at recent graduates who completed at a *maximum* a bachelor's degree.

Lightcast looked at those five buckets of schools for graduates who work at Fortune 50 companies. Yes, success after college means more than working at a Fortune 50 firm. But if we believe there's a bias in the job market for elite colleges, we can expect it to be evident among the largest and most influential companies in the world. I wanted to test that assumption.

Here's what we found.

First, the likelihood of having alumni at a Fortune 50 company is slightly higher for the most selective colleges, but not by much. Indeed, graduates from schools in the 20–40 percent acceptance band were *less* likely to be working at a Fortune 50 company than those in the acceptance band below them (40–60 percent).

Second, very few Fortune 50 employees attended elite colleges. That makes sense, because those schools' enrollment numbers are tiny compared with higher education as a whole. Every May at graduation, as elite enrollments hold steady and others grow, that gap expands. Your future coworkers are roughly four times as likely to have graduated from a college with an acceptance rate above 40 percent than from a more selective school.

Finally, just as Beth wound up at Harvard Law School after completing her bachelor's at a relatively obscure college, graduates from such colleges do end up in the Fortune 50. As *Figure 2.1* shows, in a sample of three blue-chip companies from a variety of industries, employees come from schools in all five buckets of selectivity. And the less-selective colleges are very well represented.

Figure 2.1

Who Gets Hired Where

Fortune 50 companies hire from a range of colleges with varying levels of selectivity. As an example, here is where Morgan Stanley, Microsoft, and General Motors get their early-career talent:

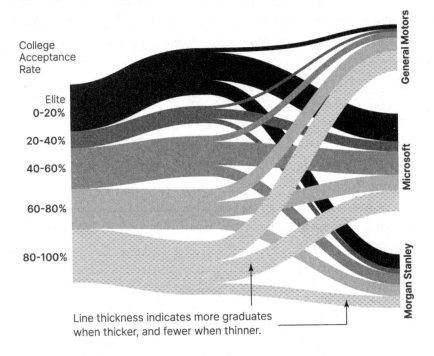

Line thickness indicates more graduates when thicker, and fewer when thinner.

Note: Includes people whose most advanced degree was a bachelor's completed between 2017 and 2023, from 1,241 institutions in these selectivity bands.

Source: Lightcast, 2024

Throughout my reporting for this book, whenever I'd suggest a school outside the top 25 to parents convinced their kids just had to go to an elite college, their response was nearly always the same: "But they'll never get a good job if they go anywhere else." One employer I heard about often in those discussions was McKinsey, the management consulting firm. I asked Blair Ciesil, McKinsey's global leader of talent attraction, about where they recruit from. Ciesil said McKinsey hires anywhere between 500 and 750 undergraduates each year in the U.S., and more than two-thirds are new to McKinsey, meaning they applied directly and didn't intern there. While the top 10 schools McKinsey hires from changes from year to year, in recent years the list has included Kalamazoo, Denison, Chapman, Embry-Riddle, and Occidental.

The belief that "elite college equals elite employer" remains a tough assumption to break, however, because the myths that feed it persist. I know that the rest of this book won't resonate if we don't first debunk those myths. So let's recap what we've got so far:

Myth: Your college determines your career trajectory.
Reality: Alumni from a wide range of institutions find success working in Fortune 50 companies, serving in Congress, furthering their education in graduate school, or running the world's biggest businesses.

Myth: Being surrounded by the "best and brightest" leads to better outcomes.
Reality: Being a big fish in a smaller, less competitive pond can build confidence and facilitate growth.

Myth: Schools with national brand recognition provide crucial career advantages across the board.
Reality: Many employers focus on regional connections and certain majors instead of Ivy-plus prestige.

Myth: Elite-college grads earn much, much more than everyone else.
Reality: They have only a slight earnings advantage, on average. Yes, their odds of becoming multimillionaires are greater, but that's a lottery ticket few people get to cash in, no matter where they went to school.

Certainly, elite colleges often produce outsize outcomes. Think of all the U.S. presidents who had Ivy backgrounds. If we can only get in, we think, we'll be on our way. But as Michelle in Texas observed after her supersmart son left Stanford, life gives us no guarantees. Rather than pick the biggest pond possible and calculate every stroke we take wherever we end up swimming, let's breathe for a moment. There are many ways to get to the other side.

PART II

MAPPING THE
NEW ADMISSIONS
LANDSCAPE

CHAPTER 3

THE RISE OF THE OUT-OF-STATE RECRUIT

What's Driving Teenagers to Cross Borders

Where students end up in college has long been dictated by where they grew up.

To show you the pull that geography has played in our college decisions, let's go on a brief historical tour of American higher education. Picture the map of the United States. We'll start up in the Northeast. This is the land of the small college. Here, compact states are home to hundreds and hundreds of colleges—tiny liberal arts colleges and former divinity schools founded before the American Revolution that are now global powerhouses. In Pennsylvania, where I grew up, scores of teaching academies (once called normal schools) evolved into regional universities. Massachusetts alone has 72 different private colleges. New York has another 181—half of which have fewer than 1,000 students.

Travel to the South, and this is the region of big public universities and small church-affiliated private colleges. Football at the large state universities has produced such strong rivalries and deep ties that families consider it blasphemous for their kids to choose a conference foe in another state.

Meanwhile, in the Midwest, lawmakers pushed to build branch campuses of the public university in every major town. In the 1960s, Ohio's governor, James Rhodes, promised a college within thirty miles of every resident. This is also where land-grant universities provided agricultural extension services in every corner of the state and dominated mindshare almost from the time kids could read their signs. Iowa, a state of just 3 million people, has an Iowa State University extension office in every single one of its ninety-nine counties.

And then we go out West, where vast distances between state schools and relatively few private colleges often kept students from venturing far from home. Private colleges in Colorado, Arizona, and New Mexico—combined—enroll just 35,000 undergraduates. A healthy stock of well-regarded public institutions also kept teenagers close to home, like the University of California, where residents could expect a great financial deal and top-ranked campuses to boot.

For generations, these geographical quirks and historical legacies shaped the college choices available to American families. Most students attended institutions close to home, their options largely determined by their state's educational landscape. But today, that familiar map is being redrawn.

In 2002, the average flagship university—that is, the best-known public university in a given state—enrolled about 70 percent of its students from *within* state lines. That same year, only about 44,000 graduates from the high school Class of 2002—just 1.5 percent of seniors that year—left their home state to go to a flagship elsewhere.

Then we saw a dramatic shift. Over the next two decades, states essentially traded college kids across borders in what's been dubbed the Great Student Swap. By 2022, the number of high school graduates leaving their home state for a flagship elsewhere had more than doubled—to some 94,000 students. Even after we account for growth in overall enrollment during that period, that rise in out-of-staters remains significant. Today, at the average flagship's main campus, nearly 4 of every 10 undergraduates come from other states.

A few small states that have always attracted out-of-staters—such as Vermont and Delaware—have drawn even more since 2002. But even flagships largely filled with residents have grown their out-of-state numbers. Take Indiana University, as an example. While the school still mostly serves Hoosiers, its admission of students who live beyond state borders rose from about 36 percent in 2002 to 43 percent in 2022, or about 8,600 students.

Almost every public flagship has experienced an uptick in its share of students from outside its borders. In 2002, 1 in 4 undergraduates at the University of South Carolina came from elsewhere; now, that's true of 1 in 2 students on the Columbia campus. In that same two-decade period, the proportion of out-of-state students at the University of Oregon went from 28 percent to 56 percent. At the University of Oklahoma, it jumped from 24 percent to 45 percent. The University of Wisconsin gradually raised its out-of-state enrollment cap and then totally eliminated it in 2016. Within six years, nearly half the students on the Madison campus were from other states.

Many flagships were established after President Lincoln signed the Morrill Act of 1862, which gave federal land (or proceeds from the sale of land) to the states so they could build institutions that would educate more people in agricultural and engineering fields. The goal was to meet the country's growing and evolving industrial demands.

Today, land-grant universities are the primary public institutions in states such as Wisconsin, Pennsylvania, and Illinois. In places such as Michigan, Oregon, and Iowa, you'll find not only a land-grant institution (for example, Michigan State) but also a separate flagship (University of Michigan). States built both types of campuses mainly to educate their own residents.

Why, then, have their student populations shifted so much over the past two decades? It's a complicated story, but it starts with money.

Costs Drive Market Behavior—On Both Sides

For public universities, the money part of the equation is about who pays what share of the cost of educating students. To better understand the role money plays in their recruitment and enrollment efforts, let's first pause to consider how college-going families became willing participants in the Great Student Swap.

This game of musical chairs goes back to the two recessions that rocked the U.S. economy in the first decade of this millennium. Each time, state budgets took a big hit, and lawmakers looked to higher education to help close their deficits. Some states slashed existing spending on their universities while others held back on sending new dollars to campuses. As university budgets received less and less from state coffers, they had just one way to make up for lost dollars: charge students more.

In 2004, college students who attended public universities in their own states paid about one-third of the cost of their education. Schools increased tuition for those kids—by 2012, in-state students were paying for more than half their education, on average—but administrators didn't want to go too far too fast and raise the ire of lawmakers who'd hear about it from their constituents. And anyway, they could raise a lot more money much faster by recruiting out-of-state (and international) students, charging them twice the in-state rate, and offering them little, if any, financial aid.

The conditions were almost ideal for public flagships to ride a wave of out-of-state students starting in the early 2000s. High school graduation numbers spiked, but elite private colleges didn't expand their incoming classes to meet the increase in demand. So students who were closed out of top-ranked private schools added big flagships in other states to their lists of options. Those colleges were more than willing to accommodate out-of-state students and their fatter tuition checks by expanding their freshman classes or by rejecting in-state applicants they deemed less qualified.

Then, in the aftermath of the Great Recession of 2008, when families with financial means started to question the value of paying full freight at more obscure private colleges, flagships in other states seemed like a relative bargain. Sure, these families had to pay out-of-state tuition. But that price tag of, say, $30,000 a year at the University of Minnesota at the time looked pretty reasonable compared with the $50,000 or so that a private school like Holy Cross in Massachusetts expected them to pay annually (we'll look more at weighing value in the next chapter).

Choosing an out-of-state flagship over a private college that won't give you much of a discount makes financial sense. But the college decision isn't always such a binary choice for families. Indeed, the biggest growth in applications filed through the Common App since 2014 comes from students applying to a mix of public and private colleges as well as in-state and out-of-state schools. The platform makes it easy for families to cast a wider net and then see what admissions offers and perhaps financial-aid packages they can scoop up. As a result, students are increasingly finding their way to flagships in other states: New Jersey kids go to Penn State instead of Rutgers. Illinois residents head off to the University of Missouri instead of their own flagship in Urbana-Champaign.

Sometimes out-of-state schools offer specific majors or activities that aren't readily available nearby. But more often than not, my research shows, students are opting for Other State U. for different reasons: to get away from home, to avoid being on a campus with their high school classmates, or to experience what they perceive as the "big college" life.

The thing is, if you're basing your choice mostly on atmosphere, you're basically paying twice as much for an experience similar to what you'd get down the road from where you live. Your big state university also has football games, and school spirit, and vibrant Greek life. In a sea of tens of thousands of students, you'll meet lots of new people who have never heard of your high school. And if you're planning to live at school rather than commute, you *will be* away from home, wherever you land.

All that said, Other State U. might actually be a good choice for you for two very practical reasons.

First, you might get rejected from your own state's flagship. While most public universities expanded to take in more students from elsewhere, not all did. According to one study, one-third of the nation's flagships—all ranked in the top 50 and thus popular with out-of-staters—turned away their own state's residents to make room. The researchers calculated that in those schools, for every two nonresident students who enrolled, one in-state student was shut out. That vicious cycle spins in states such as California, Illinois, and Texas: Residents apply to their flagship. They get crowded out, so they go to big public universities elsewhere that have room for them. Then students in those states get pushed aside, so they apply to publics in other states, too.

Second, if you're not being *pushed* to another state's flagship by a rejection at your own, you might be *pulled* by a hefty discount or a boutique academic experience, such as an honors college. As long as your needs and desires intersect with the school's goals, you can both win.

Remember when I mentioned above that flagships like out-of-staters because they pay more in tuition and don't get much financial aid? That's true at universities with big national brands like Michigan or North Carolina or Berkeley, where families pay for prestige. But other flagships are managing recruitment and enrollment a little differently. Stealing a page from the playbook of private colleges, they offer full rides to a select number of academic superstars at high schools where they want to attract more applicants. These high achievers, mostly from private or might-as-well-be-private schools, act as magnets for others who don't mind paying an out-of-state sticker price that, to them, still seems like a steal.

The University of Alabama was the first flagship to follow this strategy. Starting in 2002, the Tuscaloosa campus transformed its student body as it turned the dial way up on its share of out-of-state undergraduates—from just 23 percent to 65 percent by 2022. In those two decades, the school also doubled its undergraduate enrollment to 33,000 students by 2024.

To entice smart kids from the other states, it opened an honors college and made the campus about more than football and Greek life. The average GPA of entering freshmen is now 3.86, up from 3.37 in 2002, and the top quarter of the incoming class scored at least a 30 out of 36 on the ACT.

The university also disbursed a lot of money to lure students from other states who largely didn't qualify for need-based aid. In 2023–24, Alabama spent $185.4 million on merit discounts, more than twice what it allocated for need-based aid to attract students from elsewhere. And it made the rules for getting those discounts very easy to understand for families perplexed by the black box of financial aid at other schools: On its website, Alabama listed the GPA and test score cutoffs for out-of-state students to qualify for automatic merit scholarships.

Then Alabama went fishing for students in two types of places, according to a team of social scientists who studied where colleges recruit applicants. It targeted prosperous suburbs around Atlanta, Dallas, Houston, Miami, and Los Angeles, where university administrators knew that getting accepted to in-state flagships was very difficult for all but the top students.

It also courted applicants from bedroom communities around New York, Washington, D.C., Seattle, Boston, and eventually Chicago, where Alabama's sticker price looked downright reasonable compared with the costs at pricey private colleges and more expensive public options. Do the math: If Alabama has a sticker price of $45,000 for an out-of-state student, and then trims $15,000, on average, off for those getting merit scholarships, paying $30,000 a year looks like a bargain compared to Holy Cross (plus you get football Saturdays).

Over time, these efforts paid off. By 2022, Georgia, Illinois, Florida, Texas, and California ranked among Alabama's top sources of out-of-staters.

Southern Hospitality?

Alabama wasn't the only flagship to adopt this approach, although it spent more money than the others to draw nonresidents. Along with Alabama, four states in particular have brought a disproportionately large number of out-of-staters to their flagships in recent decades: Arkansas, Arizona, South Carolina, and Tennessee. Back in 2002, 4,500 freshmen in total arrived at these five states' flagships from elsewhere.

Two decades later, that number more than quadrupled, to 20,000. That spike is all the more dramatic if you consider it in context. Among out-of-state freshmen at flagships nationwide, today 21 percent are flocking specifically to these five places, up from 10 percent in 2002.

Except for Arizona, these states have one thing in the common, of course: They're in the South. Although the numbers of students heading to Southern flagships had been steadily climbing since the early 2000s, they swelled in the immediate aftermath of Covid. During the pandemic, Southern schools had fewer restrictions on in-person classes and gatherings than colleges elsewhere. Students in many parts of the country were stuck in their childhood bedrooms taking classes on Zoom. Meanwhile, high school kids who conducted their college searches largely online were fed a steady diet of Tik-Tok and Instagram images of football games and sorority parties at Southern flagships.

A few years later, as political protests roiled elite colleges, public universities in the South continued to crank out those pictures and videos depicting what teenagers imagined college life to be. Scoir is a technology platform popular in high schools to help students and counselors keep track of applications. An analysis the company did for me found that applications to public flagships not only out-of-state, but outside seniors' home regions, jumped 24 percent from 2020 to 2024. This coincided with similar data the company compiled showing that applications to out-of-region private colleges fell during that time.

THE RISE OF THE OUT-OF-STATE RECRUIT

The out-of-state enrollment surge to public universities led to a spate of breathless news stories about how Northern kids were decamping to the South for college. In September 2024, one front-page article in *The Wall Street Journal*, headlined "Sorry, Harvard. Everyone Wants to Go to College in the South Now," generated thousands of comments and dozens of social media posts on parenting group pages. A discussion about the article in the Facebook group Paying for College 101 was shut down when it devolved into a debate over state abortion laws and presidential politics.

To what extent did Covid restrictions and the subsequent campus protests change where students ended up going? It's hard to establish cause and effect with any precision, but without question Southern schools attracted more interest than they had before. Post-pandemic, these colleges (both public and private) saw more growth in applications through the Common App than schools in any other region. They received 330,000 more applications in 2023 than in 2019.

By comparison, applications at schools in the Midwest—the region with the second-highest increase in the same period—rose by 260,000. I asked analysts at Campus Sonar, a company that uses algorithms to slice and dice social media chatter about colleges, what patterns they found in the online discussion around Southern schools. Not surprisingly, much of it was about affordability and school spirit generated by athletics and Greek life.

Despite the clickbait headlines, teenagers everywhere are still trying to claw their way into Harvard and other elite colleges. And yet, anecdotal evidence seems to suggest, kids who don't get into those top-ranked schools—the overwhelming majority—are taking a broader view of what constitutes an appealing college. For many teens, stressed out first by navigating Covid restrictions and then by having politics thrown in their face in high school, the Southern flagships provide a welcome release valve.

It's important to recall, though, that these institutions were growing before the pandemic because they favored out-of-state students who were affluent or had better academic stats than many of their own residents. Their campuses had room to expand. Their tuition was modest relative to other flagships. Was their weather better? Sure. How about their football teams? Most years, yes. Their politics? It depended on what you wanted. That's still true, even as views throughout the country become more heated. Overall, the flagships in the South are seen as less politically active. One survey, cited in the *Wall Street Journal* article I mentioned earlier, found that students who moved to the region for school pay less attention than others to politics in general.

But politics can cut both ways. As administrators at these Southern flagships realize, what distinguished their institutions in the past two decades might not in the next two. In conversations with them, I've gathered that growing political polarization, state laws viewed as restrictive, and environments perceived as unwelcoming are certainly among their worries.

Plus, getting students to come to the South from other parts of the country is still a sales job. Not all freshmen on Alabama's Tuscaloosa campus were "predisposed" to even consider the university at first, said Matt McLendon, who oversees its enrollment operation. The school is still known in many places for its ranking in football, not in *U.S. News* (No. 175, most recently). Although parents told me in my survey that *they* don't equate college rankings with prestige, some 60 percent believed that a "very highly ranked" school was a marker of prestige for *other* parents in their community. Only 11 percent acknowledged it as such for their own families—a discrepancy that shows just how much the sticker on the car window *does* matter as a signal to others.

It's that perception that the University of Alabama runs up against as it recruits students from elsewhere, especially as other flagships increasingly sell similar experiences: honors colleges, football, fun, and so on. The merit aid helps Alabama make its case—often a winning one with price-conscious families.

Another way to turn prospects into applicants is to make a lasting impression with the campus visit. "You have to differentiate yourself at the front door," McLendon said. That's why the University of Alabama has spent big money to make its front door look like no other.

When would-be students and their families visit, they start their tour at the Randall Welcome Center. It's reached by taking a long, wide driveway from the edge of campus that ends in a roundabout. There prospective students are greeted by a gleaming white Italianate-style building, topped by a dome and graced with a three-story front porch. The building once housed the state's mental hospital and has earned a spot on the National Register of Historic Places. The university acquired the property in 2010 and, nearly a decade and a half later, opened the facility after extensive renovations.

As you walk in, you're greeted by a giant crimson-and-white BAMA sign—the must-have Instagrammable shot. You'll see something similar on most campuses. The immersive experience that follows, however, is utterly unique. It's a blend of what you'd find in a modern museum display and in the entertaining line queues at Disney World. Floor-to-ceiling screens welcome visitors with their names in lights. As you wind through a series of hallways on the way to the theater for the admissions information session, you pass exhibits with pictures and video monitors highlighting different aspects of the university and the city of Tuscaloosa.

The facility's crown jewel is the "Roll Tide" room, wrapped entirely in video monitors showing scenes from Alabama football games on a continuous loop. The screens above and around you curve inward and out, enveloping you in a rolling wave of evocative imagery.

When I visited campus on a humid weekday in August, I joined a tour with a half dozen prospective students and families. After the information session ended, we boarded a bus. (Campus sprawl is a symbol of growth and progress, and the university doesn't want you to miss anything.) The tour guide, a junior from Texas, wore a flowery summer dress. No Lululemon here (and the men wear ties).

As the bus pulled away, our guide started rattling off key facts about the university (she had clearly studied the thirty-three-page manual to pass her required "script test"). We happened to be there during "rush season." As we passed groups of girls outside the sorority houses, a family seated in front of me asked if I had seen *Bama Rush*, the HBO documentary that chronicled sorority rush at the university. I hadn't, at least not yet.

Next to me, a prospective student busily tapped notes on her iPhone. She told me later that she was a high school junior visiting from Virginia. "UVA is impossible to get into," she said of her state's flagship. She had also crossed two liberal arts colleges, Hamilton in New York and Middlebury in Vermont, off her list. "Too small and too expensive," she said. The week before, she had visited the University of South Carolina. The next day she was off to the University of Mississippi. Sure, the boatload of financial aid that Alabama automatically offered to out-of-staters with her academic stats was a huge draw. But she was on a mission to find out whether the honors colleges at these other schools could give her what she really wanted: a small college experience with the advantages of a big state university.

Creating Community Within a World of Opportunity

While many honors programs can be traced back to the 1960s, such offerings ballooned in popularity around the turn of this century, when they expanded in size, presence, and purpose. Since the mid-1990s, the number of honors colleges at public and private institutions combined has multiplied sevenfold to nearly 200, according to the National Collegiate Honors Council. That growth coincided with the push by many flagships to enroll more out-of-state students. So the honors college became a tool for achieving that goal—in particular, for bringing in gifted students who might have otherwise gone to a private college. Having those kids on campus would, school officials hoped, enhance the academic atmosphere—and, ultimately, improve the university's rankings.

Emily was one of those star students who favored elite private colleges at first. As a sophomore in high school, she'd received a list of top-ranked schools from her grandmother, who offered to pay the application fees for any of them. "She didn't want to see her selling herself short and not going to the best," Emily's mother, Nancy, told me.

Emily had her sights set on the University of Chicago. She had near-perfect stats: a 35 on the ACT, a 1510 on the SAT, thirteen AP courses, and a 3.95 GPA. She applied early decision to Chicago and was denied. When the rejection arrived, Emily's younger sister was in shock. "Was it because she didn't get a 36 on the ACT?" she asked her mom. "No," Nancy told her. "Emily was the best Emily could be—and it still wasn't enough."

By then, Emily had already completed applications to a bunch of other elite private universities, including Rice, Emory, and Vanderbilt. But given the Chicago rejection, her mother wanted Emily to add an academic *and* financial backup option. At the time, Emily didn't have a single public university on her short list. She dismissed her home-state flagship early on and wanted to go farther away in any case. Her mother did some digging and landed on the University of Mississippi as a possibility. It had an honors college and generous scholarships, including some that came with a $12,000 stipend for study-abroad and undergraduate research. "I applied to appease my mom and get an acceptance under my belt," Emily told me. "But I never really seriously considered it." That was, until she started the interview process for the university's top scholarships. "The more I learned about the school, the more I could really see myself going there."

A few days after Emily received her acceptance, her cell phone rang. She saw the Mississippi area code and picked up. An admissions officer was calling to congratulate her. Emily told her she'd never been to Mississippi before. For the next thirty minutes, the admissions officer talked about the city of Oxford, described Saturdays during football season, and answered questions about the university. "I wouldn't just be going to Ole Miss," she realized after the call. As part of her scholarship and major, "there were all these opportunities

I could qualify for, and I was hearing about them before I heard I was even accepted to other schools." Mississippi knew it was competing with much higher-ranked colleges for students like Emily, so it had to be the early bird to get the worm.

By April, Emily had acceptance offers and financial-aid packages from Rice and Vanderbilt. Neither included the full-ride and perks that Mississippi offered. Before making her decision, she wanted to visit Rice again.

Emily and her dad flew to Houston. It was a weekday, but Emily remembers the campus feeling dead. They walked to a nearby park. Emily made a pro/con list for Rice and Mississippi. Then she broke down in tears. "The only thing I could come up with for Rice is that people will know I'm smart because I go to Rice," she recalled. "I only applied to Rice because it was a Top 20 school, not necessarily because it had the academic programs that I wanted, or because it was a good fit."

When I spoke with Emily a few years later, we connected on Zoom because she was studying abroad in Europe. Like many other students I met in reporting this book, she'd found high school a relentless grind and didn't want to repeat that experience in college. "I know how to study. I know how to do rigorous work," she told me. "I didn't need to keep proving that." By going to Ole Miss, she gave herself permission to have downtime, to volunteer, to make meaningful friendships.

Finding great friends matters a lot. In my survey of parents, that's what they most hope college will provide their kids—second only to discovering a fulfilling career. *The New York Times* personal finance columnist Ron Lieber writes that college is about the "search for kinship" and meeting the people "who will stand up for you at your wedding and carry your casket."

It's not that you can't find great friends at Pomona or Yale or Northwestern, but as we saw in earlier examples—William in the Introduction and Beth in the previous chapter—the knives-out culture that pervades elite colleges can make friendships feel transactional.

And such relationships bring little comfort in a loneliness epidemic among adolescents and young adults.

Of course, you're not guaranteed to find deeper friendships at colleges with a less competitive vibe. As we'll explore in Chapter 8, finding a sense of belonging in a college is about connecting with a community that will help you grow as a person and will provide a space for asking questions about who you are, your values, and your place in the world—academically and beyond.

As a student, William, whom we met in the Introduction, discovered his place at a state flagship after trying on an Ivy that didn't fit. Beth, the Harvard Law graduate in Chapter 2, identified hers more methodically, choosing a liberal arts college outside the top 100. Emily carved out hers in an honors college at a public university. Like many kids who enroll in such programs, she wanted to make a big place feel small. It's a common selling point, particularly at flagship universities.

If many honors colleges make similar pitches, how can you distinguish between them in your search? Here's what I recommend:

- **Size up the experience.** Honors colleges range widely in head count from 1,600 students at the University of Wisconsin to 7,400 at the University of Alabama. As a result, student experience varies quite a bit. Smaller programs might offer fewer honors courses each semester or limit them to only freshmen and sophomores. Program size also affects the breadth of special events and offerings for honors students, such as lectures and visiting scholars. But bigger isn't necessarily better. At Alabama, for instance, the honors college consists of several programs, with different benefits and levels of prestige. "If I'm being real here, some students just want the perks—priority registration and access to honors housing—and otherwise they're fine with just being a regular undergrad," one professor told me. Determine what type of honors experience you'd like, and compare programs from there.

• **Scrutinize the value of the benefits.** Most honors colleges offer students a bunch of advantages—particularly hands-on learning opportunities, such as study abroad, undergraduate research, and internships. A few provide stipends for these activities. While the money is nice, ask how much assistance students receive in securing opportunities. Helping a professor conduct research is a great résumé builder. But at many universities, such projects tend to go to graduate students, so you might be left on your own to find a professor who's willing to work with you. Studying abroad is a valuable experience, too, but how much control would you have over the timing? Doing it too early (or too often) in your undergraduate career could come at the expense of developing relationships and getting involved in campus activities. When it comes to honors benefits, more isn't necessarily more. Consider which ones you're likely to use and how.

• **Review the curriculum for fit.** Honors students take certain courses that aren't available to the rest of the undergraduate population. Be sure those courses align with your academic goals. They often explore big questions and connect dots between disciplines. "The students who are the best fit are those who have an intellectual curiosity that exceeds a single major," said Tara Williams, dean of Arizona State's Barrett Honors College. "They don't want to confine themselves to a single lane, so they're engineering majors, but also passionate about music." If you aren't interested in venturing too far beyond your chosen field, honors courses may feel like a waste of time.

• **Ask about the quality of advising.** Intellectual curiosity can complicate a courseload. Students in honors colleges often pack their schedules with extras or try to combine disparate majors and minors. So it's important to have access to good advisors who will help you fit those pieces together and ensure that you graduate on time. Speak with honors faculty and students alike to get a realistic sense of what to expect in terms of support.

- **Check out the honors housing.** Touring the housing options is about more than assessing the spaces themselves. Within residence halls, look for wings or floors reserved for honors students. These "learning communities" are the places, Williams told me, where similarly motivated, ambitious kids from different majors and backgrounds will have the richest opportunities to interact.

One night before giving a talk at a high school just outside of New York City, I met with a small group of parents in the throes of the college search. As the conversation bounced around the table, I listened to their hopes and fears for what college would mean for their kids. These parents talked about dream schools and the frustrations of applying to and paying for college. A few lamented how difficult it had become to get into schools that once seemed like safety picks in their communities (Boston College) and colleges that are now popular as a result (Miami University of Ohio).

Near the end of our conversation, a mother raised her hand and asked sheepishly, "Is it okay to go to SUNY?" The State University of New York is one of the largest public systems in the U.S., with 64 campuses and 367,000 students. Its Stony Brook campus is a member of the Association of American Universities, an invite-only group of prominent research institutions. I rattled off a bunch of reasons why, yes, it's more than okay to go to SUNY. Before I could finish, other parents chimed in with the usual objections: It's too close to home (even though some campuses are hours away). It's too expensive (though the average price tag is around $25,000 including room and board for in-state students). And, of course, the perennial concern: no big-time football, not enough fun.

The discussion that evening about whether it was "acceptable" to go to an in-state public mirrored another category of schools that American parents I met felt they needed permission to consider: international universities. The number of Americans studying for full degrees—not just study abroad—nearly doubled between 2019 and 2024, to more than 92,000, with the United Kingdom and Canada being among the leading destinations. Jessie, a mother from North Carolina, whose daughter is among 1,500 American students at the University of Edinburgh in Scotland, told me that she was attracted to the transparency and simplicity of the selection process at U.K. universities compared to the black box of U.S. colleges: They're very clear about the grades you need to get in, they actually consider your test scores, and have little interest in your list of extracurricular activities.

And while the cost tends to scare families from even looking outside American borders, "it isn't as wildly expensive as you think, and certainly nothing like a private college in the U.S.," Jessie said. Her all-in cost for tuition and housing: $40,000 a year. And like many international schools, her daughter is eligible to use U.S. student loans and grants at Edinburgh. When Jessie tells other parents where her daughter goes to school, it still raises some eyebrows. "They seem to think it's a risky choice," Jessie said. "It's amazing how powerful those unspoken expectations are about where *your* child should go to college."

When we feel uncertain, as we do in the college search, we turn to others for answers as to what we should do. Psychologists call this phenomenon social proof. In looking for colleges, we put an enormous amount of trust in the knowledge of other parents—in our schools, in our communities, and in Reddit and Facebook. We assume that everyone else has a better grasp of what to do. Decades ago, once high school graduates started crossing state borders in bigger numbers to go to flagships elsewhere, kids in subsequent classes followed their lead. When *The Wall Street Journal* says everyone is skipping Harvard to go south, we think maybe we should, too.

Social proof carries a lot of power. And it's problematic.

For starters, following the herd might be wrong for us. As our Instagram feeds show parades of seniors, one after another, skipping out on their own state's flagship for one somewhere else, we have no idea why. Some of these kids might be recruited athletes. Others may have received full-ride scholarships or have chosen their universities for particular majors or honors programs. Perhaps their reasons were more personal, like having an aunt who lives near campus. Or perhaps they were rejected by their home flagship. If we don't know what drove their decisions, we can't reasonably assume that the choices they're making would work for us.

Here's another issue: Social proof can be engineered to nudge us to make choices we wouldn't have otherwise. The psychologist Robert Cialdini lists social proof as one of six key principles of persuasion, and no wonder. Remember, most students still go to college not too far from home. To do something different from those around them, they must be convinced it's worthwhile. So when flagships needed to recruit more out-of-staters to balance their budgets, they fired up their marketing machines to persuade people to pay twice as much, in some cases, as their own state schools would cost. They invited families to visit for special events and to eat together in the dining halls and to cheer together for their athletic teams. They showed people they were far from alone. Many others *just like them* had traveled just as far, for all the same reasons—and you'll continue to travel to campus (and pay for it) long after this one tour if your child eventually enrolls.

And there's one other point worth revisiting from the previous chapter: Where you go to college often shapes where you start your career. Parents may assume their kid will return home or easily find work elsewhere after graduation, but that's not always the case. Thrilling football Saturdays in Tuscaloosa or Oxford could ultimately lead to job opportunities in Memphis or a decision by their kid to raise a family in Birmingham.

According to an analysis by labor-market research firm Lightcast, among the big athletic conferences, the Southeastern Conference—which includes Alabama, Ole Miss, Georgia, and other southern flagships—sends the largest share of its graduates to smaller cities and rural areas. Among SEC schools, only Vanderbilt sends more than 75 percent of its alumni to big city metro areas.

That annual $15,000 merit scholarship isn't just reflected in your bank account—it may be setting the stage for where you'll build your life long after you've packed away your college sweatshirts.

CHAPTER 4

VALUE OVER PRESTIGE

Skipping the Next Tier of Schools to Get a Deal

The response from Bowdoin College was a wake-up call for Frida. The summer after her daughter Abby's junior year of high school, Frida asked the Maine college what her family might get in financial aid if Abby were accepted. That sort of estimate, known as a pre-read or early read, is most common for recruited athletes or at colleges known for their merit scholarships. Neither scenario applied here. Still, during a campus visit, Bowdoin had promised Frida what they called a financial-aid "hard look." After doing her own calculations, Frida wanted to know more about the real costs.

The response wasn't what she'd hoped. Bowdoin expected the family to pay full freight if Abby was accepted: some $80,000 in all, times four. "Many people just told us, you know, pay the $80,000," Frida said when we met a few years later. "And we were just like, yeah, that's not going to happen."

Abby had her sights set on law school eventually. Paying less out-of-pocket now allowed for more financial flexibility for whatever came next. Following advice from Facebook groups and podcasts like *Your College-Bound Kid*, Frida used the net-price calculator to get an idea of what her family might pay. But their income wasn't consistent from year to year, so she worried that the calculations failed to capture the nuances of their financial situation. "We started to get panicked about money," she told me.

College is one of the very few purchases where we choose the seller and commit to buying the product *before* we nail down how much it's going to cost. Imagine ordering from a restaurant menu without any prices. That's essentially what we do when we come up with a list of colleges, apply to them, get accepted to some, and only then find out exactly how much those will cost us.

Abby's list of schools was heavy on what I call "sellers." In *Who Gets In and Why*, I separated colleges into "buyers" and "sellers" to help families assess financial fit. In simple terms, sellers are the "haves" of admissions. Plenty of their applicants can—and, more important, will—pay the full sticker price. That's the eye-popping "cost of attendance" colleges must advertise to prospective students under federal law. Bowdoin is a seller. The buyers are the "have-nots." Although they might provide an outstanding undergraduate education, these schools hand out discount coupons in the form of merit scholarships to meet their enrollment targets.

Tuition pricing works a lot like airline pricing. If relatively few competitors offer a product (think direct flights or lie-flat seats), people willing to pay more (such as business travelers) can be charged more. In higher education, that premium market is dominated by some three dozen schools at the very top of the rankings. Where there is more competition, the typical rules of supply and demand come into play. That sector includes most colleges, which try to differentiate their product (with the majors they offer, for instance, or campus amenities), but in the end are like airlines engaged in a pricing war to fill seats. Similar to airlines, schools don't want to operate at partial capacity. So they offer merit aid to lots and lots of teenagers.

Frida had scoured Facebook groups, including Paying for College 101 and College Talk, for clues about which schools offered generous scholarships and where Abby should "undermatch"—in the lingo of those groups—to "chase merit." She was looking for colleges where Abby's academic stats (3.94 GPA, perfect 5s on seven AP tests, 35 out of 36 on the ACT) would set her apart more than they did at Bowdoin. Colleges where she stood out that needed to fill seats were more apt to give her merit aid. This was a delicate balancing act for Abby because she also wanted a brand-name college. "We knew Abby was a great candidate for strong merit aid," Frida told me, "if she shot at the right targets."

Managing the Donut Hole

Frida and her husband found themselves in what's known as the "donut hole" of financial aid, where their family income—in the mid-$200,000s before Frida lost her job—was too high to qualify for need-based aid, but not high enough to comfortably pay for college out-of-pocket (especially with three teenagers at home). Frida's unemployment during Abby's college search exacerbated the family's financial strain.

Still, compared to most Americans, Frida's family isn't facing day-to-day money worries. Their household income puts them roughly in the top 10 percent of all Americans. (Another way to think about that—nine out of ten households earned less than they do.) In most aspects of life, they are quite comfortable. For families like theirs, it can be shocking and frustrating when college becomes the one cost they can't manage easily.

As the sticker price of college has increased over the years, the donut hole has stretched higher up the income ladder, consuming more upper middle-income families. They're stuck as the one group asked to pay full price without the easy means to do so, even as financial aid reaches more families below them. Surprisingly, the out-of-pocket expenses for lower- and middle-income families have remained relatively flat over the last decade.

To better understand this shifting landscape, we can look at research by Phillip Levine, an economist at Wellesley College. A Brookings Institute study he authored in 2024, using previously unpublished federal data, examined pricing patterns at private colleges for families from different income levels. He found what I just mentioned: Since 2011, net prices at private colleges—the bottom-line number you actually pay—have held steady for families earning up to $170,000 a year. However, around $200,000 that trend abruptly ends, with net prices rising like a hockey stick.

Meanwhile at public universities, net prices have risen for *all* students since 2011, but the increases have been larger for higher-income students, according to Levine. That steep rise at publics starts around the $125,000 income mark.

These trends matter because they're reshaping the college landscape in complex ways. Colleges are engaged in a balancing act. On one hand, they're trying to maximize financial aid for lower-income families—a commendable goal. On the other, they're pushing the limits of what higher-income families will pay, continually nudging up that sticker price. They're creating a sort of optical illusion in the college affordability debate. If you're a dual-earning couple with earnings closing in on $200,000—like many of the people writing for major newspapers that tend to shape our view of higher education or, let's be honest, some of those buying this book—you're in the donut hole. College feels breathtakingly expensive because, for you, it is. Who exactly can "afford" these sky-high prices? And more important, who is willing to pay them?

As we'll explore in the rest of this chapter, wealthier families are deciding that—barring an acceptance to the most prestigious institutions—these prices don't make sense anymore. What I came to realize in this research is that measuring college affordability isn't a simple task. A formula generated by financial-aid software might indicate you can afford a specific college, but it doesn't take into consideration how else you might want to spend your money.

Abby understood this all too well. When we spoke, she said, "I can't think of another time when you would make a $30,000 decision to pay more for something because you liked it maybe a little bit more."

By April of her senior year, Abby had been accepted to Bowdoin and several other selective schools, including Williams College, Northeastern University, Davidson College, Mount Holyoke, and Bryn Mawr. That's when the financial-aid offers started to roll in. The early read had prepared Frida for Bowdoin's letter, but she was shocked by how seemingly arbitrary the offers turned out to be overall. Frida and Abby separated them into three categories: full pay (Bowdoin and Northeastern), roughly half off the sticker price (Mount Holyoke and Bryn Mawr), and two-thirds off (Davidson and Williams).

Because Frida was unemployed at the time, she worried that colleges offering a discount would expect them to pay more the next year if she got a job. With or without additional income, her family couldn't ignore price.

"I wasn't inclined to think that the caliber of the educational opportunity that we were being offered for $79,000 was so much better than what she was being offered for $29,000," Frida told me. "Bowdoin, Davidson, and Williams are very similar calibers, so why would we pay more? Because Bowdoin assessed that we could pay more? It's not rational."

Then there was the outlier: a full-scholarship offer from the College of William & Mary. As a public institution in Virginia, William & Mary had the lowest sticker price of all the schools Abby was considering—and that's what first persuaded her to apply. Measured purely on rankings, the college fell to the bottom of her list. But the financial-aid package changed her perspective. In addition to the scholarship, it included money to work on research projects. As the May 1 decision deadline loomed, Abby continued to weigh acceptances from Williams (ranked No. 1 among liberal arts colleges by *U.S. News*), the University of North Carolina at Chapel Hill (No. 22 among national universities), and Davidson (No. 16 among liberal arts colleges). In the end, she selected William & Mary (No. 53 among national universities), choosing value over top status.

You might be thinking, as I did when I first met Abby and her mom, that William & Mary wasn't much of a pivot. Most students would jump at an acceptance by a school right outside the top 50. But for someone with Abby's academic stats and options, William & Mary was a widening of *her* lens. That's why I included her story here. As I said in the Introduction, thinking more broadly about the range of colleges out there often depends on your perspective and where you start your search. William & Mary is a great school for Abby, but it's not where her search started. Indeed, after Abby made her decision, her high school counselor implied that she had settled. "He suggested I go to William & Mary for a year," she told me, "and then transfer to Berkeley or an Ivy."

At the end of her first year at William & Mary, I reconnected with Abby. She was still enrolled. She'd never considered transferring. She said the small classes at William & Mary make her feel like she matters. (In a survey by *The New York Times* about what's important when choosing a college, small classes were the one thing graduates valued *much* more after college than high school students did when they were looking at schools.) Small classes allow her to get to know her professors, who she has found are interested in her growth and well-being. "The professor I had from my freshman seminar is giving me feedback on an article I'm trying to get published," she told me.

Abby also appreciates having priority registration for courses, a bonus that came with her scholarship. Her friends at higher-ranked schools often can't get into the courses they want. "They're *applying* for their classes," she said. "That's absurd for how much they're paying."

As for the vibe on campus, she described it as living in the moment. While she and her classmates think about what they'll do in the future, they're not constantly clawing for what's next—a spot in a club, a desirable internship, a plum job. For her part, Abby told me she feels a lot less pressure to show her parents their investment was "worth it" than she would have at a college that charged them tens of thousands of dollars more a year.

Abby disagreed with what her high school counselor told her. She wasn't settling for William & Mary. Financial constraints didn't really prevent her from attending some of her more prestigious options— or from trying to crack an Ivy as a transfer. Her family could have stretched if they wanted to and sacrificed savings for law school. Abby just went with the deal where she'd benefit the most all around, thanks in large part to what economists call the "consumer surplus." That's the advantage we gain as consumers if we pay a price that's lower than the maximum price we'd be willing to pay.

For decades, a certain set of private colleges enjoyed a surplus on the provider's side of that market, upping their list prices every year and always getting more than enough affluent families to pay up. Now, the tables are turning. Many consumers who can afford an elite education aren't willing to pay top dollar for prestige. They are bypassing schools they'd have chosen previously, a trend that got its start in Georgia.

Trading In Our Emotional Attachment to Status

In the late 1990s, when I was a reporter at *The Chronicle of Higher Education*, part of my beat was covering the rise of state-based merit scholarships, pioneered nearly a decade earlier by Zell Miller when he was running for governor of Georgia. By promising a new lottery that would cover full rides for academically qualified residents attending the state's public universities, Miller won—and he made good on his pledge. By the turn of this century, a half dozen states, mostly in the

South, including Florida, Louisiana, and South Carolina, had copied the idea to keep smart students local.

Around that time, I visited the University of Georgia in Athens to report on the impact of what came to be called the HOPE Scholarship. One fall afternoon, as I interviewed a professor in his office, he stopped talking midsentence and suggested we take a stroll outside. On a sidewalk near a large parking lot, he pointed to the cars in front of us, noting the makes and models. There were BMWs, Audis, and Acuras. Mostly new. This was the student parking lot. The expensive cars, he told me, started to appear soon after the HOPE Scholarship did. Some of his star students had shared with him that when they didn't get into Harvard or Stanford or another Ivy-plus school, their parents offered a deal: If they went to the University of Georgia instead of a selective, expensive second-tier college, they'd get a new luxury car with the savings from the scholarship.

So that's where they went. Those students defied conventional wisdom, which says you should go to the most selective college you can get into, no matter what you have to pay. The HOPE Scholarship rewrote the rules, and over the following decades, more kids from upper middle-class and wealthy families began arriving on campus in Athens. Today, among public universities in the U.S., the University of Georgia has the third-highest share of students from the top 1 percent of family incomes, just behind its much higher ranked rivals, the University of Michigan and the University of Texas at Austin.

The choice not to pay full freight at a selective school—even if you have the money—has since grown in popularity far beyond the borders of Georgia. In the decade-plus after the Great Recession of 2008, the sticker price of private colleges has increased some 20 percent, even after factoring in inflation, nearing the six-figure mark in some places. Affluent families—usually expected to pay the whole bill—are increasingly saying enough is enough. "Unless you have developed some Enron-level accounting skills, you're not going to get financial aid," a mother of a teenager told *Town & Country* magazine in 2023. "So you're going to have to come up with a pretty big nut every year."

As more families trade in their emotional attachment to status for financial practicality, the result is a new world where students and parents comparison-shop over fine gradations of prestige. To be sure, they often still start the search with an Ivy-plus-or-bust mentality. But then they face a reality check: They probably won't make it past the gatekeepers. According to Opportunity Insights, the nonpartisan nonprofit based at Harvard, the chances of Ivy-plus admission are *lowest* for children from families who earn $158,200 to $222,400 a year. Even if they do get in, they receive very little, if anything, in financial aid.

With that realization, they're now more inclined to *skip over* other schools they'd have applied to and paid full price for in the past. They're chasing merit discounts elsewhere, looking more closely at lower-cost public colleges, or doing a combination of both.

These "skip-over schools," my research suggests, mostly sit one tier down from the most selective institutions. We're talking about liberal arts colleges like Kenyon, Skidmore, and Connecticut College and research universities like George Washington and Brandeis. These colleges and universities once had a lot of pricing power in the marketplace. That's changing.

Creating a simple list of skip-over schools is not feasible, however. Too much depends on the college's trajectory within a turbulent higher-ed economy and the student's relative position within a particular pool of applicants.

Here's what I mean by that: As some institutions rise in the rankings, they can command *more* money. (A good example is Villanova University, at No. 67 in *U.S. News*, where 51 percent of students pay the full bill. That's up from 44 percent in 2012, when the school wasn't even ranked among national universities.) Meanwhile, others drop in standing and struggle to attract full payers.

The consumer side of the market is also far from fixed. If you're a competitive applicant to the most selective schools, as Abby was, your skip-overs might bleed into that top level (Bowdoin, No. 9 among liberal arts colleges, was a skip-over school for her). But if your academic profile isn't as strong as hers, the schools you'll skip and the ones you'll target for merit aid will be lower in the rankings. The matrix below in *Figure 4.1* helps you visualize different types of schools and their relationship to *value* along one dimension and *rankings* and *prestige* along another.

Figure 4.1

Skip-Over Schools: Value Over Prestige

When students can't get into an *Elite Powerhouse* or can't afford one, increasingly they're skipping over the *Next-Tier Elites* they would have chosen and paid for in the past and making a value play for *Accessible Excellence*, schools off the beaten path but with solid outcomes at a good price.

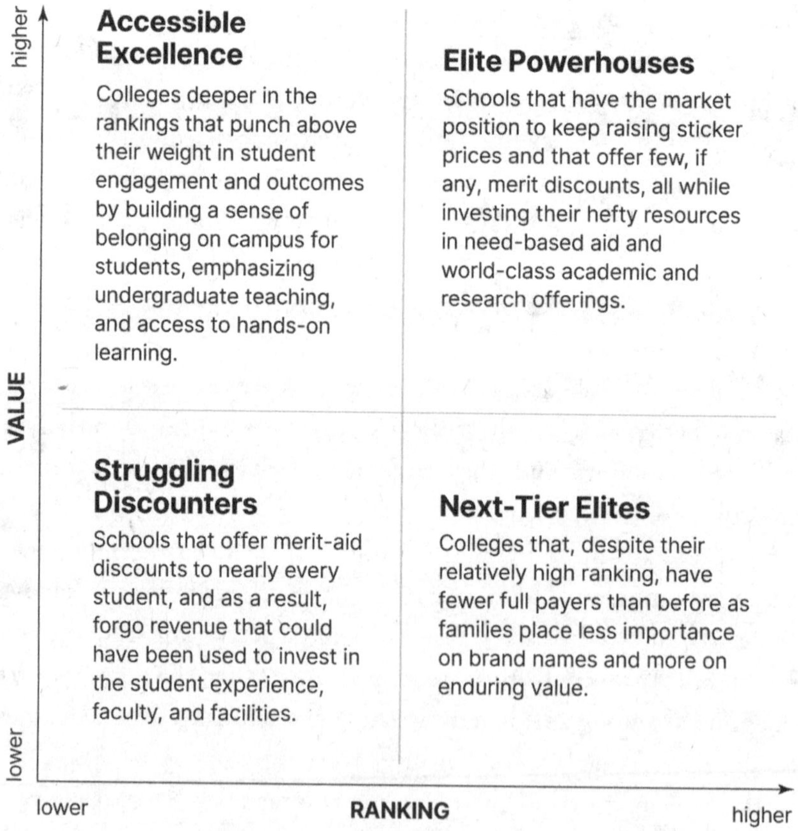

Accessible Excellence

Colleges deeper in the rankings that punch above their weight in student engagement and outcomes by building a sense of belonging on campus for students, emphasizing undergraduate teaching, and access to hands-on learning.

Elite Powerhouses

Schools that have the market position to keep raising sticker prices and that offer few, if any, merit discounts, all while investing their hefty resources in need-based aid and world-class academic and research offerings.

Struggling Discounters

Schools that offer merit-aid discounts to nearly every student, and as a result, forgo revenue that could have been used to invest in the student experience, faculty, and facilities.

Next-Tier Elites

Colleges that, despite their relatively high ranking, have fewer full payers than before as families place less importance on brand names and more on enduring value.

VALUE (higher / lower)

RANKING (lower / higher)

An example of a school that's been able to sit comfortably in the "Accessible Excellence" quadrant is Case Western Reserve University in Cleveland (it makes my "New" Dream School list at the back of the book). It has a solid ranking (51 in *U.S. News*), an acceptance rate that hovers around 30 percent most years, and offers healthy tuition discounts, while not giving away the store. It consistently dedicates about 38 percent of its institutional-aid budget to merit scholarships. The average discount to a freshman in 2023 was nearly $30,000 (Case's price tag was around $82,000 that year).

How Case doles out those discounts is much more sophisticated and complicated than the advice parents often get in Facebook groups, as I learned when I spent time with Rick Bischoff, who has led the enrollment operation at Case since 2009. The nuances of that process is why Case doesn't display simple award charts on its website—in other words, you have this GPA, you get this discount—as I mentioned in the last chapter some public universities do.

When Bischoff arrived at Case, it was "need blind," which meant that it didn't consider a family's ability to pay when making admissions decisions. But often that meant sending acceptances to students with financial-aid packages that "gapped" families, meaning Case couldn't offer enough money to really meet their need, and they'd have to fill the gap somehow—usually by taking out more loans.

Now Case is "need aware" in admissions, meaning at some point it does take ability to pay into consideration in admissions. Doing so has allowed the university to better balance its class income-wise, Bischoff told me, by generating enough revenue among higher-income families by giving them some discount, which then allows for more institutional aid that supplements government grants to lower-income students. As a result, Case is more appealing to donut-hole families "who are often missing on private university campuses because they might be able to do $50K but they can't do $85K," Bischoff said.

How Case discounts is a complex formula that is based on years of data it's collected on accepted students, whether they yield, and then how they eventually perform academically on campus. Each accepted student is assigned a scholarship value with a discount that could range from around $18,000 at the low end to low $40,000s at the high range. A bunch of factors make up that scholarship value. Based on the applicant's high school, their GPA, and intended major, for instance, Case officials know how many applicant pools at other universities the student might be competitive in. If that student is seen as Ivy material, Case might give them a discount in the $40,000 range; if they're more likely in the Northwestern or Emory pool, seen as a step down from the Ivy competition, they might get in the upper $30,000s.

Major also plays a role in discounting at Case and elsewhere. Among its applicant pool, Case has an abundance of highly qualified students who want to major in computer science and pre-med, for instance. So they're likely to get smaller discounts, maybe a few thousand dollars less. Meanwhile, like other universities, Case needs to fill seats in the humanities, and it's often competing for engineering and nursing students with big publics who are seen as less expensive, so the discounts need to be larger.

In the next chapter, I'll discuss how often what is seen as "insider information" is traded and dissected in online communities to gain an advantage. I asked Bischoff whether families can game the system by, say, applying as an English major to garner a big discount and then switching over to computer science.

Not only are such internal transfers to popular majors nearly impossible at most institutions, but Bischoff said there's "too much noise" in how most schools award merit aid for it to be as simple as major in English, get more money. "I know that my ratings correspond to how students will perform here and correspond to how other institutions are going to value that student," he said. "So I may think of one student as more accomplished than another [for the purposes of financial aid] but that may not be the way they're perceived within their high school."

The Overall Decline of Full Payers

In July 2023, a few weeks after the U.S. Supreme Court struck down the use of race-conscious admissions, a group of college presidents gathered at the Department of Education in Washington, D.C. During a discussion of how schools might still enroll diverse classes while complying with the ruling, the talk turned to research showing that elite colleges give an admissions edge to legacy applicants (children of alumni) and applicants from the top 1 percent of American incomes. Then-president of Colorado College, Song Richardson, pointed out that both groups tend to be full payers. "Full-pay students across the country," Richardson added, "are gold."

Richardson said the quiet part out loud. Full-pay students are becoming a rarer commodity everywhere except at elite colleges. When the parents of today's applicants went to college, many more middle- and upper middle-income families paid full freight, even if they had to take out loans to do so. According to calculations by Levine, the Wellesley economist, the share of families making over $200,000 (in today's dollars) who paid full sticker price at private colleges declined from 64 percent in the mid-1990s to 28 percent in 2020. At public colleges, it fell from 79 percent to 47 percent during that time.

Much of that falloff occurred after the Great Recession. To get a sense of where, I looked at selective colleges (those admitting less than 50 percent of applicants) that had a majority of students paying full sticker price in 2012. That list consisted of sixty institutions. Nearly half of those had seen their percentage of full-pay students decline over the next ten years, some substantially as shown in *Figure 4.2*.

Figure 4.2

The Rise and Fall of the Full Payers

How students pay for college varies widely. Many offset costs with grants from federal or state governments or from the colleges they attend. "Full-pay" students receive no grants at all. They might use loans, savings, or family help, but ultimately they're responsible for the entire sticker price.

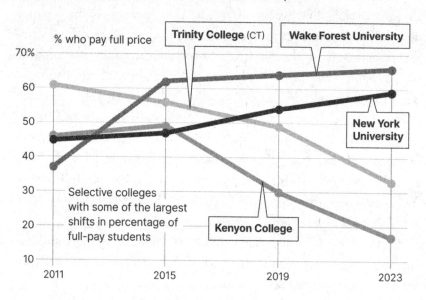

Note: Selective means institutions admitted fewer than half of their applicants in 2012. When colleges mention the overall percentage of students "receiving financial aid," they often include students who received no grants but were offered loans.

Source: U.S. Department of Education, Integrated Postsecondary Education Data System (IPEDS)

The shift in who pays the full price and where reflects a fundamental realignment in how we value and afford college. Financial aid as we think of it today is mostly a modern invention, stemming from the Great Society programs of the 1960s. Merit discounts followed in the 1980s and 1990s as college costs skyrocketed and enrollments ebbed and flowed. Student and parent debt really took off after the Great Recession, as fewer families could use their home equity as an ATM to pay for college.

In my interviews and analysis, I identified another relevant change as well—in the extent to which people prioritized investment in higher education. As Baby Boomer parents (many of them the first in their family to go to college) gave way to Gen X parents (who were more likely to be second-generation graduates), the new crop of families wanted to do something different with their money. A long-running survey by Sallie Mae and Ipsos captures that attitude shift. In the mid-2010s, around 85 percent of parents and students said that college was an investment in the future; by 2024, just 56 percent felt that way. What's more, only 41 percent said in 2024 they were willing to "stretch themselves financially to obtain the best opportunity for their future," compared with nearly 60 percent a decade earlier.

Nowadays, according to that same survey, 81 percent of families with a six-figure income cross a college off their list at some point because of high cost. Only 61 percent did so in the mid-2010s, when six figures went further. Meanwhile, Sallie Mae found, the amount of current income that affluent families spend on college has largely remained flat, while it has risen for lower-income families—another indication that wealthier families are getting more merit aid now but also starting to focus on colleges that cost them less.

There is another reason why wealthier families are skipping over schools that expect them to pay more: Parents know their financial ties to their children won't end after four years of college. As I outlined in my 2016 book, *There Is Life After College*, the road to adulthood is longer and slower now than in previous generations. Fewer than half of young adults ages eighteen to thirty-four say they're completely financially independent from their parents, according to the Pew Research Center.

Spending less on an undergrad degree gives parents more resources later to help pay for graduate school or contribute toward other expenses, like rent and car payments, as their kids get their start in the workforce. Support during that stretch of early adulthood is critical, because research shows that switching jobs in your twenties boosts your chances for more satisfying and higher-paying work in the decades that follow. It's easier for twentysomethings to make those job moves with an eye to the future if they aren't living paycheck to paycheck in the present.

Balancing Money and Brand

In the search for a college that's the right fit, we often don't like the trade-offs that come with it—for instance, between brand and affordability. But let's face facts. Getting a good deal means skipping over big-name schools with minuscule acceptance rates—and, yes, giving up a bumper sticker that signals your kid made the cut. Sometimes I wish those stickers simply said "college," like the generic shirt John Belushi's character wore in *Animal House*.

What are we *really* sacrificing, though, when we opt for a less prestigious brand and reputation? That question—central to this book—nagged at April and her parents in the spring of her senior year. In the spring, April had been invited to Southern Methodist University in Dallas for a weekend of interviews and activities to compete for a scholarship. "They roll out the red carpet for you," she told me. "They tell you they really want you; they show you how well they're going to treat you."

A few days later, she got a call. She had been awarded the coveted scholarship. A week after that, an acceptance letter arrived from what had been her dream school, Cornell University. "They sent me a T-shirt in the mail," April said. "It wasn't as if someone was calling me on the phone, telling me they really wanted me to go there."

Because the most selective colleges have so many star applicants to choose from, they don't need to spend much time or effort trying to reel in each one. What they do instead is point out on tours how much they invest in you once you're there. With their bajillions in endowments, elite schools usually spend *more* per student than their sticker price indicates (I'll have more to say on this in Chapter 9). That money goes to world-class facilities and renowned professors, for example.

April's mom, Kathy, was skeptical of the elite-school hype, however. Her daughter got into Rice University and Colby College, among a few others. Those acceptances arrived with solid financial-aid offers, although they might still require April to take out student loans. "We were very well aware that there were a lot of shiny things available at these schools," Kathy told me. "But we were also coming from the experience of being in a very competitive and intense public-school system with very cool opportunities that only ten students got to do." She couldn't shake her concern that after making significant financial sacrifices, April would find herself sidelined on an elite campus while a select few enjoyed the biggest perks.

At SMU, thanks to her scholarship, April would be guaranteed to be among those few—a small cohort of students with access to paid research with professors, fully funded study-abroad trips, and help preparing applications for top graduate schools and fellowships. And the reality was as promised. During her freshman year, she received funding to attend a conference where she met political leaders. The university also allowed her the curricular flexibility to embark on a trip early on to study abroad (most students don't have room in their schedules to study abroad until junior or senior year, if at all). Then, throughout her junior year, her professors and advisors devoted months to working with April on her application for a post-graduate fellowship. She landed that fellowship, as did a considerable number of Ivy-plus graduates. "I didn't really feel out of place," she said. "It was definitely a thing where I had to explain where my university was, whereas someone from Harvard would be like, 'Yeah, I went to Harvard,' and move on."

Looking back, April acknowledged that her experience at SMU wasn't completely smooth. She'd made trade-offs beyond turning down an Ivy League school. "If you asked me during my freshman year, I would have said that I didn't really want to be at SMU," she said. It was politically conservative and less intellectually focused than April had wanted, and the campus culture centered on football and Greek life. Her study-abroad experience early on helped her sort out what she wanted to do, though. When she returned to Dallas, April chose a new major and found her people (we'll talk more about belonging in Chapter 8).

"I'm glad I went to SMU," April said, "despite the struggles." For her, the full ride and associated extras were a means to an end. "They gave me the support and the experiences to get me where I am now," she said. When the fellowship ended, April secured a job working on a federal grant in environmental research, while a few of the graduates from elite schools who were on the fellowship with her struggled to find what to do next. That's when April realized landing a job had more to do with the whims of the market and the roles people were pursuing rather than the name on their undergraduate degree. She described her new role as one that didn't "pay amazingly well," but it was exactly what she wanted to do, and avoiding the big tuition bills and debt from her undergraduate years gave her the leeway to take the job.

Even so, when April's younger siblings went through the college search, she encouraged her parents to give them the space to better understand the sacrifices they might make if financial considerations ended up rising above everything else. It's a good reminder for all of us. Even when money matters the most, other factors must be weighed as well.

But how much weight should they get? When you have options at different price points, how do you decide when it's worth paying more? And how much is too much for any given upside? What is the incremental value of a school that has a strong program in your intended major? Would you pay a higher price for a college that offers co-ops to all students or for one with a first-rate career center? In responses to my surveys, those are features that parents said they don't want to compromise on. But are any of them worth, say, $10,000 more a year? Are they worth paying $80,000 at a private college rather than $30,000 at a public school in your state—or giving up a full ride?

Five Ways to Maximize Value

April and Abby ultimately went with the best financial offer. While they both ended up at schools that were less selective than their other options, they each got to join an elite community on campus, with a full scholarship to boot. I realize their stories are unique to them, but you can learn from their experiences—and those of other students I interviewed—if you want to maximize value over prestige. In my research, I've identified five action steps (not all of which will fit the circumstances of every student) that will better increase your chances of a good outcome:

1. **Create a search list that reconciles your financial prospects with your ability to get in.** April and Abby had multiple options in the final stretch because they had balanced lists up front. They each applied to a "dream" elite school but targeted as well a healthy mix of small liberal arts colleges with modest application pools as well as less-selective publics both in- and out-of-state. (Abby also got accepted to the University of Colorado, Boulder, and April to Texas A&M, for instance.) Because they had "undermatched for merit" in their searches, they got into schools where their academic stats stood out. That meant their acceptances came with a range of financial-aid offers—including one full ride each. So Abby and April had tangible choices on the table when they had the money conversation with their parents.

2. **Be careful in playing the early decision game.** Highly selective colleges sell early decision as an easier way in—and it is. If you care less about brand name than about overall value, then you should also care less about early decision. If you go all in with an ED application, you're giving selectivity more weight than everything else, including the chance to get a merit-aid discount somewhere else later on. Abby and

April opened up a much wider, richer world of possibilities precisely because they didn't place their chips completely on early decision. Freed from the pressure of finishing an application and making a decision the fall of their senior year, they spent the next several months visiting schools and discovering the types of experiences that would later come to define their best moments of college: small classes, research opportunities, and study abroad. In the end, they had multiple offers to consider, not one binding acceptance at an exorbitant cost. I get it: Early decision is extremely popular. I'm not telling you to not do it, but go into it realizing the trade-offs you're making.

3. **Slow down the search.** Even kids who pass on ED are often tempted to rush the application process. After some whirlwind tours, distinctions between campuses begin to blur—leading many stressed-out applicants to apply to the places people are buzzing about and say yes to the first decent offer. Take a step back. By slowing down your search, you'll have the chance to determine what matters to you. For Abby, it was getting to hand-pick her courses, for example, and form close connections with classmates and professors. For April, it was paving the way for post-graduate study. Both cared deeply about financial stability, too, and received much of what they sought in the way of experience through their scholarship perks. With a slower search, you'll uncover other nonnegotiables, described in Chapter 6. Plenty of campuses—many of which made it onto my Dream Schools list in the back of the book—offer what you want. But you need time to find them.

4. **Start at a community college and then transfer.** "You're too smart to go to a community college." That's what a former

teacher told Sophia when she mentioned the possibility. She went anyway. Her mother, Amy, responded to one of my surveys and later wrote about their experience in *The San Francisco Chronicle*. After graduating from a California high school with a 3.75 GPA, Sophia attended Sierra College, a two-year institution, where she had classes as small as twenty students. Unlike many of her friends at the University of California, she learned directly from professors, not graduate teaching assistants. She met often with her advisor to ensure that her courses transferred to a public university (a key detail, because many courses don't easily transfer, and so families end up paying twice). After two years, Sophia switched to California Polytechnic State University, San Luis Obispo. She saved around $30,000, her mother estimated, and had enjoyed more free time as a high school senior than peers who'd jockeyed for placement in selective four-year colleges. Other parents whose kids took the two-year route to start told me they mostly struggled with the perceived stigma among their friends. That sentiment seems to be dissipating, however, especially among families earning $100,000 or more—who may feel a bit less pressure than others to forge network connections right away at a four-year college. Some one-third of students above that income level now attend community colleges, up from 12 percent in 2015.

5. **Talk about money, costs, and value—but not *too* much.** Parents whose kids eventually chose value over prestige talked openly about money throughout the college search. However, they told me, they didn't fixate on cost savings every step of the way. Rather, they delved into the features of less-expensive options and gradually brought their children around to the idea of trading in a higher-ranked college for a lower-priced one. Remember, teen brains are still developing during each

month of the college search. Their natural, developmentally appropriate impulse will be to push back hard if they sense they're being strong-armed.

The Price of Prestige

The one feature of a college that has historically driven families who *can* pay more to pay more has been prestige, as determined by the rankings.

People tend to assume that prestige is worth the price because of what's called the "Chivas Regal effect," the notion that something *must* be better in quality if it costs more. Economists have observed this phenomenon in markets where prices are primarily determined by consumers' preferences and where brand status is relatively static and secure. Such status gives producers the flexibility to set higher prices without much risk. Think whiskey, wine, restaurants, and fashion.

A team of researchers wanted to know if the same effect extended to higher education. In 2016, they studied what happened with pricing at a group of liberal arts colleges in the *U.S. News* rankings over a period of seven years (before, during, and right after the Great Recession). They found that institutions often *raised* their tuition following a significant *drop* in their rankings. If a close competitor increased prices, so did they, even after a decline in status. Once their *U.S. News* numbers fell, it seems, they tried to retain a veneer of prestige by charging top rates. In a way, it can sometimes feel like schools are colluding on price. When researching an article about pricing at Bates College, for instance, I found that the school waited for peer institutions to announce their tuition so it could set its own within a few hundred dollars.

The Chivas Regal effect has historically kept sticker prices high. And yet, at all but the very top schools, as noted above, fewer and fewer students are actually paying those amounts anymore. "Colleges all now have an opening bid with families," Brian Zucker told me. Zucker runs Human Capital Research Corporation, one of several consulting firms that design sophisticated pricing models to help schools award merit discounts.

The ability of what Zucker classified as "middle-market colleges" to charge full price has collapsed since the mid-2010s. I've already mentioned the falloff of full payers overall in higher education as well as the decline at some individual colleges. But if you look specifically at the relationship between discounts and rankings, the rapid deterioration of full payers has been most acute at small liberal arts colleges that rank between 51 and 100 in *U.S. News*. In 2022, nine out of every ten full-pay students who went to *any* liberal arts college were enrolled at a school *in the top 50*. Who pays what for college has long been defined by how much money you make. Now, the evidence suggests, it's increasingly driven by how much you're willing to pay. With more families questioning the value that certain types of schools promise, the Chivas Regal effect might be loosening its grip on higher education.

Market disruption has a way of creeping up on many kinds of industries and brands. The annals of business are filled with examples. Sears, Roebuck and Co., the first "everything store" long before Walmart or Amazon came along, has shuttered all but a few locations. Kodak failed to pivot to a digital world in time to stay on top, despite having the technology. When I mention these brands to my teenage daughters, they give me blank stares. Like Sears and Kodak, many colleges are losing the market power and relevance they've long enjoyed.

Business history is also replete with newcomers that rose in prominence over time. Consider the automobile industry. To crack the luxury-car market dominated by Germans in the 1980s, Toyota introduced Lexus, at first seen as a poor second cousin to BMW and Mercedes. With a relentless focus on reinventing the segment by copying from lavish brands in other sectors—such as the Four Seasons—Lexus became one of the most successful luxury-car brands of the last quarter century. Or take Rolex, an upstart watchmaker that challenged an established giant, Omega, in the early twentieth century. Now Omega is part of a Swiss conglomerate, with consequent brand muddling, while Rolex is the Harvard of watches.

All sectors of the economy—even those that seem super-static like higher education—experience shifts like these, and it's not always apparent to us. A friend of mine wears a Seiko watch, beloved by watch nerds in the know. Because it's not a smartwatch, people notice it and ask him about it. If you have the ability and money to go to Kenyon or George Washington University but those schools want you to pay full freight, so you choose Furman or Ohio State instead, people will notice that, too. It's a statement, a redefinition of value akin to the "quiet luxury" mindset in fashion, where consumers are investing in minimalist clothing that will last and forgoing purchases that scream wealth.

Quiet luxury is starting to catch on in higher education as well. We're already in the midst of a major shift, brought on by a combination of forces: changing demographics, worries about a job market disrupted by artificial intelligence, and geopolitical and economic uncertainties. That realignment won't knock Harvard, Yale, and Princeton from their posts at the top. But increasingly, students and parents are focusing on value when searching for schools—and finding a good fit deeper in the rankings.

CHAPTER 5

THE AGE OF AGENCY

Why This Is Your Time to Explore

By now, you've got a clear view of the shifting landscape in college admissions. Top-ranked schools have never been more selective. Students are crossing state borders to attend public flagships away from home. Families are beginning to pursue value over prestige, skipping over not-quite-elite institutions that still charge premium prices. And the surprising truth? Most employers don't care about a fancy alma mater anyway.

If these findings have challenged your assumptions about the college search, good. You're ready for what comes next in this book. We're about to cut through the noise from guidebooks, rankings, Facebook groups, and Reddit threads to zero in on what really matters in finding *your* dream school.

Simply put, you have so much more control over this process than you're led to believe.

As a student, if you're feeling intense pressure to apply to elite schools, you may very well be following someone else's dream for what you *should do*, someone else's expectations about what you're *capable of*. I saw evidence of that mindset in my conversations with parents and counselors as I reported this book and gave talks about admissions in high schools:

- A mom told me she was grappling with guilt and frustration because the math pathway she'd chosen for her son in *middle school* had "shut him out" of top-tier engineering programs that wanted him to have "more calculus."

- A counselor suggested during a question-and-answer session that telling parents to break free from the top 50 schools was bad advice because McKinsey and other elite financial and consulting firms wouldn't hire someone from a "second-tier college" (not true, as discussed in Chapter 2).

- A father asked during another Q&A why parents in their town were blindly following other parents in sending their kids off to college right after high school. He told me afterward that he was a union carpenter, earning more than a hundred dollars an hour, and couldn't persuade students in his daughter's high-achieving high school and surrounding community to even consider the trades as a career option.

These stories highlight a common struggle in the college search: agonizing over what colleges will want in your application, what employers will want on your résumé later on, and ultimately what will *become* of you if you don't line up with your classmates and neighbors to apply to elite schools.

But I'm here to tell you that stepping out of that line, at least early on, broadens your perspective and allows you to entertain other possibilities. It reminds me of the queue for a popular Harry Potter ride at

Universal Studios in Orlando. I took my teenage daughters there for a break while writing this book. We waited hours for Hagrid's Magical Creatures Motorbike Adventure, wondering when we'd get on the actual ride. The queue worked its way through several different rooms in a castle so you couldn't see beyond. It was intentionally designed that way—if you could see the entire line, you might make the choice to leave. Instead, we just followed the people in front of us again through each room. The same is often true of the college search (and life on campus, for that matter). You're going to have many choices to make. Don't just keep getting in line because that's what everyone else is doing.

"Many are achieving to achieve," the psychologist Richard Weissbourd told me. "Parents are scared to take the foot off the gas pedal for fear their kids will fail." Weissbourd and I were having lunch at a restaurant just off Harvard's campus, where he's a senior lecturer at the Graduate School of Education. He also directs the school's Making Caring Common initiative, which aims to provide resources and research on "how to raise moral and emotionally healthy children," according to its website. His team was about to put out a report, and Weissbourd was trying to come to grips with its main finding: the rates of anxiety and depression in young adults (ages eighteen to twenty-five) were *double* the rates for teens.

Teen mental health gets a lot of attention, as it should, Weissbourd and I agreed. But he worried about young adults, too, in those formative years during and after college. He meets many of them in his classes. "It's really concerning, the number of young people who are anxious about finding a calling or a purpose," he said.

In recent years, Weissbourd has run an anonymous survey in his classes, where he asks if students exaggerated in their graduate-school application what they wanted to do in their career. Usually half the students say they did. "It opens up a conversation where they ask, 'Why is it that institutions are forcing us to define what we want to do, when what we want to do is come here to explore?'"

This frustration begins in high school, when students are just starting to apply to colleges. But there are many more avenues to life after high school than the few that your parents and counselors have mapped out. In other words, you have agency.

———————————————————

The theory of personal agency, developed by the late psychologist Albert Bandura, holds that people have the ability to influence and even direct the world they live in. That begins with a willingness to break free from what your peers do and what others expect. If you want to enroll in a top engineering program and didn't have the right amount of calculus in high school, you can exercise agency by taking more math classes online or at a community college before applying. If you think McKinsey favors job applicants from top-ranked schools, you may be right—but you can line up internships elsewhere and eventually prove your skills to the McKinseys of the world. If you aren't eager about going to college, your agency allows you to check out vocational training programs at your local community college (where enrollment in those degrees rose 16 percent in 2023 alone, its highest level since at least 2018).

Agency isn't about simply following the rankings and believing those are your only choices in life. Your potential exists beyond the averages, medians, and means that sort students into categories starting as early as elementary school.

In the twelve to eighteen months of the typical college search, you'll need to make many decisions: which schools to add to your list and which to take off, what major to pick on your application, what topics to choose for your essays, where to apply early decision and early action (if at all), which schools to visit and when, how to weigh your financial-aid offers, and ultimately where to go. Saying you're applying to an Ivy-plus school is perhaps one of the easiest decisions you'll make. No one is ever going to question if you apply to Brown or Stanford or MIT. But you don't get to decide whether they take you.

You know how you can have more of a say in where you'll end up? By applying to a school because you met a professor on a tour who seemed to take an interest in what you want to study. Or adding a school to your list because you'd have a chance to participate in a professor's research. Or looking more closely at a college after seeing on LinkedIn that alumni in your intended major had cool internships the previous summer. That's what real agency looks like in this process.

Often agency is "discouraged" by the incumbents in any culture, who already have what you might want, writes New York University professor and author Scott Galloway. "Agency is churn, the essence of upward mobility." In higher ed, the incumbents are the elite universities. They try to protect their status at all costs. That's why they encourage more applications even as they refuse to grow their incoming classes, just so they can boast about their ultra-low acceptance rates.

All those rejections they send out every year are the "dark side" of agency, according to Galloway's theory. It's blaming you, rather than the colleges taking the blame. "In America," Galloway writes, "the view/belief that you can accomplish anything implicitly whispers in your ears that, if you don't, it's your own fault." When smart teenagers refuse to play that admissions game run by the elites, apply elsewhere, and succeed, it threatens to disrupt a system built on scarcity.

You'll have agency throughout your life, but eventually—when you have a job, and maybe a mortgage and a family—you'll have more constraints on your choices. It's true that I'm writing from a position of privilege here, and my kids will have more freedom in their choices than kids with fewer resources. Still, if you're on the road to college, you have greater control over what's next in your life than most Americans without a college degree. Indeed, research suggests that your personal agency is perhaps strongest right now—when you're in your late teens, in the midst of the college search, and in those first few years after you arrive on campus.

Now More Than Ever, the World Is Your Oyster

As Weissbourd observed among his students, the pressure to have it all figured out is immense for teens and young adults. More and more colleges want high schoolers to declare a major on their application. For popular majors with limited spots—such as engineering and computer science—many schools admit by program. But even in other fields, colleges want teenagers to come in knowing what they will study so their advisors can develop plans that allow them to finish their degree in four years.

As a result, students increasingly treat college as a consumer transaction: They're purchasing a diploma so they can cash it in for a job. It's a pervasive attitude, according to scholars Wendy Fischman and Howard Gardner, who led a five-year study that fanned out across ten campuses. For their 2022 book, *The Real World of College*, the research team interviewed more than a thousand undergraduates and another thousand professors, administrators, and parents. Despite having chosen a mix of schools, both elite and less selective, the students were remarkably consistent in how they talked about college: It was completely about jobs, résumés, grades, and a college's reputation.

That view isn't set in stone, however. The researchers actually saw a couple of countervailing trends.

First, it turned out the students were mostly parroting what they'd heard from the grown-ups around them—their parents, counselors, and teachers. "When their institutions embrace this careerism," Fischman told me, "students really interpret *that* as the reason to go to college." In reality, many hadn't given much thought to why they were in college.

Researchers asked them about their goals for their college experience, the role their education played in their future, and their favorite campus activities. "By the end of the interview," Fischman said, "I can't tell you how many students said, 'I wish I had thought about these questions before I went to college,' or 'Nobody's asked me these kind of things before.'"

Second, while around half the first-year students exhibited a transactional mentality, nearly as many freshmen had adopted an "exploratory" approach. They were open to learning and discovering as they embarked on their college experience. Among seniors, the explorers all but disappeared as many students transitioned into a transactional mindset—which makes sense, given their impending move into the job market. But leading up to graduation, a new group of seniors emerged, too: students who saw college as a transformational experience. Even months from graduation, this cohort seemed to prioritize courses, activities, and connections that would feed their development as they prepared to enter the workforce.

The research for *The Real World of College* gives us reasons for both concern and hope. The constant drumbeat of careerism often drowns out individual agency, sending many students on an almost robotic march toward the safest and highest-paying fields. Yes, the astronomical cost of college plays a large role—I won't dispute that, and I explore employment outcomes in detail later in the book. But a path to career success needn't sacrifice what makes college transformative: faculty relationships, intellectual discovery, and the personal growth that comes from engaging with peers. The more exploratory freshmen and the introspective crop of seniors seemed to intuitively understand that.

Like them, you can take charge and direct your college experience. To do so, you need to think more—ideally, before you choose a school—about what you're preparing yourself for.

The Role of Money in Picking a Major

For all the time, effort, and money we spend on the college search, we spend relatively little thinking about what we want to do with our lives. Most freshmen arrive on campus familiar with only a few careers and even fewer actual roles.

Job titles and descriptions are like a foreign language to them. Most students know adults who complain about their jobs and worry about their careers, including their own parents. Unfortunately, they don't receive nearly enough intel on the wide variety of options worth exploring. Here I'm reminded of my wedding rehearsal, when the priest joked with our family and friends, "Don't bad-mouth marriage in front of a couple about to get married." Teenagers should get a realistic sense of any career they're considering, warts and all, but they'll never discover what might interest them if they only hear about the bad parts of a job.

The parents I surveyed seemed to measure a good job more by happiness than by money. When I asked them what they wanted their kids to get out of college, they chose a *fulfilling* career as a top priority three and a half times as often as a *lucrative* career.

But in a separate survey of more than 325,000 undergraduates that I conducted with Vector Solutions, which provides online training to colleges, a different story emerges: Half of them said they felt "a lot" of pressure to major in something that would lead to a job that pays well, second only to the 67 percent who identified getting good grades as a source of intense pressure.

Despite that pressure, how students go about picking a major remains pretty haphazard. Most of the advice they receive comes from family and friends, not counselors in high school or advisors in college. And despite all the talk about landing a job with high earnings potential, it's not clear that they know early on how much different careers pay—nor is it clear that they adjust their paths accordingly when they find out.

In a key study examining the extent to which earnings affected choice of major, researchers asked 500 undergraduates at New York University what they *believed* the salaries of workers with different majors to be. Then they provided the students with actual data from the labor market about earnings by major and followed up with another survey, to see if receiving that information changed their views.

While students better understood what majors paid, what it didn't change was the one they chose. Yes, once armed with the data, the undergraduates agreed that their salaries would be higher if they majored in science or business rather than the humanities or the arts.

But these students felt pretty assured (men even more so than women) that whatever they majored in, their own earnings would grow rapidly as they got older. (One interesting aside from this research: Both men and women said no matter what *they* chose for a major, marrying someone with a higher-earning degree would bring a "spousal return," meaning that, in effect, they would marry for money.)

In general, economists have found that when people make decisions that involve uncertainty about the future—such as choosing a major and occupation—they pick the option that maximizes their "expected utility." We might assume in this case that expected utility means a solid paycheck. But that wasn't the main consideration for the students in this study. Rather, their choice of major was more a matter of "taste," based on whether they liked the courses and subject matter, for instance, and how they perceived work-life balance in careers connected to that major. The researchers found that students were less swayed by money as they moved through college and became more entrenched in their major, in contrast with freshman and sophomores still exploring what they wanted to do.

Here, once again, students feel they have more flexibility early in their college career—when they can exert more personal agency—before their mindset about college and their decisions about majors harden as they approach graduation.

Don't Box Yourself In

While you might be forced to pick a major on your college applications, keep in mind that about one-third of undergrads switch majors at least once. When I mention that statistic to groups of high school parents, some inevitably wince. They worry that switching majors will mean getting a late start, which could impede their kids' success in school and after graduation. They don't want to get out of that ride line.

But slowing down—just a bit—is often a good idea. Even if finances are a chief concern for you and your family, the last thing you want to do is to hurtle headlong into the wrong career and to feel stuck with that choice after graduation.

During the college search and in school, allow some time and room to discover what you want in life. College should include some dabbling and serendipity. In my survey and interviews, I was struck by how many parents whose kids were rejected from their Plan A college later appreciated getting off the hamster wheel at a college deeper in the rankings. Their Plan B allowed them to relax a little. As one parent wrote, "Some of [my daughter's] friends who did get into Ivies are feeling nervous and not looking forward to continuing the intense grind that got them into those schools in the first place." Still, don't conflate rigor with quality. This parent added that her kid, in stark contrast to her friends, "feels genuinely happy about going away to a college where she can enjoy learning, meeting new people, and having new experiences."

Recall from Chapter 2 the "explore and exploit" approach to choosing a job and career. It's similar to an economic theory—"match quality"—used to describe the fit between what someone does and who they are. As David Epstein laid out in his book *Range*, delaying specialization in college is sometimes a critical piece of students' match quality and eventual success. Epstein cited research by Northwestern University economist Ofer Malamud that looked at outcomes for two groups: One were English and Welsh students who had to pick a major before starting college and the other were Scottish students who were *required* to study different fields their first two years.

Poring over data about thousands of graduates, Malamud consistently found that the early specializers in England and Wales were more likely to switch careers as adults than the students in Scotland who specialized later. Yes, the Scots lagged in income at first, because they had fewer specific skills needed for the first few jobs after college, but they quickly caught up. "Learning stuff was less important than learning about oneself," Epstein wrote. "Exploration is not just a whimsical luxury of education; it is a central benefit."

What's more, the students in Scotland more often chose majors that weren't familiar to them in high school, whereas those in England and Wales picked narrower pathways they knew about as teenagers. Epstein likened the English and Welsh system to being forced to marry your high school sweetheart at sixteen. "If we treated careers more like dating," Epstein wrote, "nobody would settle down so quickly."

Earlier I mentioned that in my survey of students they felt a lot of pressure to major in something that would lead to a well-paying job. Yet the research on the NYU students found that the expected utility of the degree wasn't always the paycheck. How do we square those two findings?

It could be a question of timing and whether students' choices are shifting due to the long tail of an economic recession. While the economists who studied the NYU students released several research papers after their initial analysis in 2015, they were all based on their original data collection. That was completed with undergraduates in 2010. I bring this up because it was right after the Great Recession, at a time when students were assessing its impact on their career choices, and before earnings data by school and major were widely available to American high school students.

Over the next ten years, between 2010 and 2020, American colleges and universities witnessed a massive shift in what students majored in. Fields such as philosophy, history, and English drastically declined in popularity. During that decade, the study of English and history in college alone fell by one-third. Overall, humanities enrollment declined by 17 percent. That's equal to about 50,000 fewer students—it's as if the entire enrollment of Michigan State disappeared over a decade.

Where did they go? STEM. Engineering and computer science degrees have now surpassed all humanities degrees combined, both by proportion of all bachelor's degrees awarded and in sheer numbers. Given this change in what students are majoring in, I can't help but think that the proliferation of information about earnings over that decade had some influence on what students decided to major in.

Many students decide what to do in life pretty much the same way they chose a college. They scan an inventory of hot jobs just as they perused listings of brand-name schools. To reassure themselves about those options, they research what those jobs pay much as they scrutinized college acceptance rates. Then they twist themselves into knots to fit certain majors that will get them what they perceive as good jobs, following more or less the same playbook they used in high school—stuffing their schedules with all the right courses and activities—to get into an elite college.

This approach to college and career planning often leads to burnout, unhappiness, and a lack of direction. Nearly three in five young adults in Weissbourd's Harvard study, students near the end of college as well as recent graduates, reported that they lacked "meaning or purpose" in their lives in the previous month.

That doesn't have to be your fate. Use this moment—the college search and those transformative years on campus—to date around intellectually, to explore without committing, to discover what you love before the world tells you what you should do. What do you like to do that makes you lose track of time? Which skills don't feel like work when you use them? What kind of lifestyle do you want? Ask questions like these now so you don't wonder when you're forty how you ended up doing something you hate.

You have time and flexibility now, so take it.

PART III

WHAT TO LOOK FOR IN YOUR DREAM SCHOOL

CHAPTER 6

ON THE HUNT FOR A GOOD SCHOOL

*How the Information Marketplace Fed
Our Obsession with Admissions*

It was early 1989. Congressional aides gathered in the Russell Senate Office Building with their boss, Edward M. "Ted" Kennedy, to discuss a bill that his colleague Bill Bradley from New Jersey had introduced in the U.S. Senate—a bill that would force colleges to publish athletes' graduation rates.

The Senate's Committee on Labor and Human Resources, which Kennedy led, was about to hold a hearing on the matter. Bradley, a member of the 1964 U.S. Olympic basketball team and a former New York Knicks forward, had lined up an ally in the U.S. House of Representatives, another former Olympian and NBA player, Tom McMillen of Maryland. The two lawmakers faced a problem, however. Their chief objective—making public the graduation rates of athletes—would be useless without comparable numbers for all students.

"Wait," one of Kennedy's aides said. "You mean we don't already collect graduation rates?" Terry Hartle, the Senator's top education staffer, shook his head no. Everyone in the room fell silent. How was it that the U.S. government spent tens of billions of dollars on grants and loans to college students and yet no one outside the schools themselves knew whether they were graduating?

The debate taking shape that day in Kennedy's office was a recognition that consumer information about higher education was woefully inadequate. Because more and more teenagers were going to college, families needed better information to make smart decisions. The government also needed basic information to protect taxpayer dollars.

A few weeks later, Kennedy endorsed Bradley's position. Over the next year, a bill expanding the collection of graduation rates beyond athletes made its way through the Senate. That proposal was then combined with a separate piece of House legislation mandating the disclosure of campus crime statistics. On November 8, 1990, in a White House ceremony, President George H. W. Bush signed the Student Right-To-Know and Campus Security Act.

Small changes sometimes ripple through a complex system, triggering larger shifts that we don't fully appreciate until much later. That's what happened with consumer information about colleges. None of the aides in Kennedy's office that day could have imagined that the coming decade would introduce the internet, a game-changing technology that would spawn a whole new information marketplace around the world. A new age of analytics followed, allowing us to generate mind-boggling amounts of data. As time passed, our obsession with data grew as we found ways of slicing and dicing and analyzing it. In settings as diverse as athletic scouting and management strategy, we increasingly made high-stakes decisions by the numbers. Armed with stats they had long lacked, families quickly began to apply this mindset to the college search, organizing their lives and futures around menus of facts and figures, all in the hunt for the perfect fit.

Whenever I give talks about admissions, a request I make of adults in the audience is this:

Raise your hand if you believe that, in applying to your alma mater today, you *wouldn't* get in. Most of the audience puts their hands up.

The prevailing narrative these days is that it's hard to get into college. It's one of the biggest myths of admissions, because in fact, among U.S. colleges, the average acceptance rate is 58 percent. When I divided 1,200 four-year colleges into five tiers of selectivity for my analysis on job outcomes in Chapter 2, there were more than 1,100 schools in the tiers that accept between 40 and 100 percent of their applicants. Most colleges accept most students.

So why do we keep telling ourselves they don't? It's hard to pin the false narrative on one guilty party, but it's largely driven by the panicking class—mostly upper middle-class families in metro areas. As I explored in *Who Gets In and Why*, the decades after today's parents went to college were marked by cheaper air travel and easier communications. That made once far-away schools seem nearby.

Over two generations, higher education transformed from a regional business to a national and international one. As a result, no matter where families lived, they set their sights on elite institutions— and fixated on how hard it was to get into *those*. The truth is that talking about the other four tiers of colleges, where there are plenty of good schools and you can get actually get in, doesn't sell rankings and private counseling services to parents worried about their kids' futures. It's as if these parents don't even consider those other four tiers of schools within the universe of what they mean when they talk about "college."

But there's another piece to add to this puzzle about our admissions anxiety: the information marketplace sparked by the passage of the Right-to-Know Act, which allowed the easy collection, trading, and manipulation of data related to colleges. Starting in the late 1990s, the two trends—government-mandated transparency from colleges and easily accessible information—merged, feeding our anxiety about who gets in and providing families with a new source of decision-making power.

In the decades that followed, the federal government ordered colleges to make costs easier to comprehend (with the net-price calculator) and to regularly report statistics on their students (via the Department of Education's College Navigator). These numbers ended up online for everyone to see. Magazines and countless websites engineered an array of rankings and consumer tools based on the data. Those numbers were like a new currency for families, traded through Facebook groups, Reddit threads, and sites such as College Confidential.

The congressional mandates forcing colleges to release more and more information had shifted the market dynamics in higher education. "The intent was not to regulate the behavior of colleges," Hartle, the former Kennedy aide, told me. "We wanted to make this information public and ultimately let students vote with their feet."

GPSing the College Search

If you're going to vote with your feet, however, you need to have a map to know where to step.

You picked up this book because you're on a hunt for a good college, one you can both get into and afford. When I began my research and asked parents, high school counselors, and admissions deans what was missing in the college search process, they all pointed to different gaps that should be filled. But primarily, people wanted me to name names of good schools. Several encouraged me to come up with my own set of rankings.

I got my start covering higher education as a summer intern in 1994 at *U.S. News & World Report* on its college rankings. There I saw how the sausage was made, and it wasn't pretty. Back then, we still lacked basic data from the federal government. (After the passage of the 1990 bill on graduation rates, it was another *five* years before colleges could report their numbers because regulators had to figure out how to do it systematically. It then took another *six* years to gather that information on a particular class of students because the official rate is measured over a six-year, not four-year, period.)

The rankings, whether *U.S. News* or competitors that have popped up since the 1990s, promote a standardized approach based on scales and weights set by an anonymous group of editors and quants. The biggest weight for *U.S. News* remains the "peer assessment" score. That's when presidents, provosts, and admissions deans rate other schools in an annual survey.

Let's run down a few of the obvious issues here: First, that survey typically has a 30 percent response rate. Second, some colleges try to influence the survey results by copying the playbook of Hollywood studios during voting for the Oscars: They send their counterparts at other schools glossy mailings with campus magazines, annual reports, and even swag celebrating their institutional feats. Or they take out ads in industry publications. No one mentions trying to influence the rankings, of course, because that would appear unseemly.

When a reporter for *Inside Higher Ed* filed a public-information request at 48 universities to obtain copies of the surveys their leaders completed, what they mostly found were haphazard and hasty responses. In many cases, presidents and provosts had passed the survey on to staff members to complete, or deans had spent ten to fifteen seconds on each institution or left a lot of blanks. A few respondents rated most institutions *except for their own* as only "adequate." If you really care what a group of administrators—and a small group at that—thinks about another college, by all means consult the *U.S. News* rankings. But don't expect any degree of precision.

The more I talked with parents and counselors, in particular, and looked through the responses to my survey, the clearer it became. They craved a straightforward answer to a seemingly simple question: *What are some good schools?*

For them, the existing rankings were too much like *Consumer*

Reports: They presented reams of helpful data and rankings, but you still had to evaluate the information to arrive at a bottom-line answer. What people really wanted was something like *The New York Times*'s Wirecutter, which explicitly recommends top picks. But that meant the final pick might be Harvard or Stanford or Michigan—in other words, schools already at the top of other rankings. They wanted schools they couldn't find anywhere else, the so-called hidden gems. A few parents referenced the "Alt-Ivies," an annual list published by *Town & Country* magazine. One asked me in an email for a list similar to that, but "longer" (the *Town & Country* rundown consists of fifteen schools, most of which accept less than 20 percent of students). Another suggested that I "moneyball" it, like a baseball GM placing bets on future stars, to reveal that perfect breakout school for their kid.

A few months before I started writing this book, *The New York Times* released its own college-ranking tool. Unlike most lists, generated by a one-size-fits-all formula, the *Times* rankings allowed you to factor in your priorities. You could move sliders and apply filters to come up with a list of schools tailored to you.

When the tool first came out, I played with it for days to see the various combinations of schools I could create. I thought it was different and useful. But it presented a new problem that I didn't appreciate until I suggested it to parents. To produce results, the tool required them to pick some priorities. The choices—factors like size, academic profile, safety, sticker price, median earnings, and athletics—made sense to me. But many of the parents I spoke with were first-timers in the college search. Although they had opinions, they didn't know how to translate those into the priorities listed or even if they were focusing on the right things. The tool required you to already know something about what really matters in finding a good fit, getting a degree, and launching into life.

Then one day in my car, as I used Waze to figure out the quickest driving route to an appointment in downtown D.C., I realized maybe a similar concept could be applied to creating a list of colleges. Waze uses a mix of established geographic data and real-time input from drivers. That's a rich combination. But when in D.C., I don't follow Waze blindly. I also rely on my intuition from living in the city for nearly thirty years, and that layer of personal insight makes the other information even more useful. I thought, couldn't college rankings work that way? What if I combined stats from government reports (as a proxy for the geographic data in Waze), input from students through national surveys (akin to the real-time driver reports), and my own knowledge from covering higher education as a journalist? Wouldn't that yield a robust list? It sounded like a worthy goal, and a timely one, especially since my own kids would be embarking on the college search in a few years.

Seemed easy enough.

This chapter is the backstory of my research into what makes a "good" college and how the "New" Dream Schools list at the end of this book came together. I wanted to dwell on my own quest because it illustrates how the college search has been hijacked by the quants, appearing to solve your question about where to go to college like a math problem. This information marketplace in higher ed has resulted in a flood of intelligence and advice, some of it contradictory.

Finding the "right" college and figuring out how to pay for it has turned into a full-time job. Parents try to grind it out while doing their real jobs, outsource it like landscaping or housecleaning if they can afford it, or—most often, I find—throw up their hands and let the chips fall where they may. I'm often asked by families when they should start the search or whether they should hire an independent consultant (more questions that don't have precise answers). What I've found is that the information overload leads too many families to overinvest in the short game of the college search—while failing to focus on the long game of what they want to learn and accomplish on campus and beyond.

The Finite Admissions Game vs. the Infinite College Game

Years ago, I saw a lecture by James P. Carse, a religion professor at New York University. Carse, who died in 2020, said two games exist in life: finite and infinite. A finite game has an end, with winners and losers, whereas an infinite game goes on forever with the goal of extending the winning for every participant. As Carse put it, finite players need training; infinite players need education. "To be prepared against surprise is to be trained," he wrote in his influential book on the topic. "To be prepared for surprise is to be educated."

When I heard Carse's lecture, I considered it an analogy for higher education, a way to explain the tension between the practical arts and the liberal arts. In that tug-of-war, schools had begun to put more muscle behind vocational majors on the training side and less behind broader education and the humanities.

But later, as I focused my research on the admissions process in particular, I saw Carse's theory represented in the pathway *to* college. Getting in is a finite game. What happens afterward, the undergraduate experience that empowers you to participate in life, is an infinite game. In trying to master the finite game—obsessing over the information marketplace now at our disposal to crack the acceptance code of our most selective institutions—we've shoved the infinite game aside. My goal in the next several chapters—which delve into the elements to look for in a good school—is to help you play the finite game of admissions more effectively by not losing sight of the infinite game of success in and after college.

If admissions is a finite game, then high school counselors are like coaches, continually evaluated on their winning percentages, especially at top-performing schools. Ivan Hauck, the director of college guidance at the Archer School for Girls in Los Angeles, recalls the first time a parent told him that he had "a really good year." What the parent meant was that seniors were heading off to Ivies and other elite colleges—and Hauck and his staff should get credit for delivering those wins. While Hauck acknowledged that parents expect certain college placement results when they pay tuition at private high schools (or when they move into pricey neighborhoods so their kids can attend private-like public schools), playing the finite game often leads to more homogenous outcomes.

"Finding a good college isn't about trying to find a uniform answer," Hauck told me in his office. "It doesn't work that way. It varies by every kid. You need to identify the core values within yourself *before* finding what fits."

However, students tend to bend their aspirations to match whatever college they think they want to attend. To some extent, they've been coached to do that ("With your stats, you should be able to get into these places."). Hauck wanted to flip that script.

Archer adopted a new approach to counseling, moving away from the usual conversations with ninth- and tenth-graders about what they need to accomplish early in high school to build a strong admissions application later. Now, academic advisors and counselors ask students in their first two years to reflect on their identities, the communities they belong to, and the impact they are having or hope to have. "It opens up all kinds of personal conversation and leads to tangible goals based on how a student is currently navigating high school," Hauck said.

When the college search kicks into high gear during junior year, each student at Archer studies a college and shares their findings with peers. But there's a catch: They can't choose from the seventy-five schools most popular with Archer seniors, and they don't reveal the name of the college until the very end of their presentation. The goal is to expose some hidden gems for a meeting later on with counselors and parents, where juniors present information on three schools of varying selectivity tied to their earlier work on their identities, communities, and impact.

"You can tell a lot of the parents automatically dismiss some schools," Hauck said. "But it's still twenty to thirty minutes of parents just sitting there silently watching their child reflect on certain things that they may not have reflected on before."

This approach of slowing down the college search for teenagers, whose metacognition skills are still developing, is quite rare—a privilege that Hauck enjoys at Archer, which has only seventy students in its senior class and two college counselors.

Families everywhere tend to rush the college search, packing most of it into eight to ten months. Doing so can lead them to overreach in putting together their list. Economists studying uncertainty in markets—which is a good way to think about admissions—long assumed that decision-making isn't swayed by *how* we consume information. Recent research shows the opposite. When we are overloaded with information at once—as we're racing to the finish line of the admissions process, for instance—it turns out we are overly optimistic. We put too much weight on outliers that have a big upside ("Apply to Stanford because you might get in!").

But when we spread out our learning over time, like the students at Archer, we favor options more likely to pay off. That's because we're less focused on admissions 24/7 and—since students tend to tour their reach schools first—we have more distance from the outliers on our list when application time comes.

As I left Archer, I asked Hauck if slowing down the rollout to college has broadened students' lists of schools. His data suggests it has. On average, recent Archer seniors applied to two schools that no one else in their class did. Hauck then pulled up a Google map to show me where last year's graduates went to college. It was an electronic version of the wall maps with push pins you'll often find in high school counseling offices, except this one was interactive: It not only displayed where students enrolled but included their notes on *why*, along with updates now that they're undergraduates. The usual suspects—Yale, Penn, and Williams—still appeared in the mix. But so did Cal State Northridge, Skidmore, and Elon.

"What we're trying to do," Hauck said, "is get parents to talk to other parents about why their daughter chose a less-selective school because it had X, Y, and Z." Those elements—the X, Y, and Z that make up a good college for you—amount to the *why*, not just the *where*, of college. The big push for data transparency in higher education was supposed to help families figure that out. Instead, it has left us awash in stats, and perhaps more puzzled than enlightened about what truly makes a school a good place for us.

Selectivity Isn't Everything

My quest for the elements of a good college led me first to Indiana University's Center for Postsecondary Research on the main Bloomington campus. I met with Jillian Kinzie, who heads up the National Survey of Student Engagement. The survey, known as NSSE (pronounced "nessie"), has been around since the turn of this century. It originated from a meeting the Pew Charitable Trusts convened in the late 1990s with leaders in higher education who worried about the rising influence of college rankings. Their big concern? Rankings measured inputs—think SAT scores and endowments—but not outputs. The output everyone wanted to know was how much colleges contributed to students' (and then graduates') success.

The survey attempts to get to the bottom of that by looking for evidence of "engagement" on campus. It asks freshmen and seniors in a wide-ranging survey how they spend their time at school, how they interact with peers and professors, and what kinds of services and opportunities are provided to students. It also digs into particulars, such as how often they talked about career plans with a faculty member, to what extent their instructors gave feedback on a draft piece of work, and how much their institution helped them manage nonacademic tasks.

The survey is actually a great source of questions to ask on campus tours (you can get the NSSE electronic "pocket guide" for that very purpose). It would be even more useful to know how respondents answered them. Unfortunately, though, NSSE doesn't release the results from individual schools and never has. Colleges "outright rejected" the idea from the survey's early days, Kinzie told me. The implicit threat is that they'd stop participating if the data were ever released. Although Indiana University researchers never suggested that they would circulate the results, many elite colleges have nonetheless used that possibility as an excuse to opt out.

None of this stops you from asking a school for its NSSE results, however. Some colleges already publish theirs online.

While Kinzie and her team couldn't share findings for individual schools, they agreed to mine their treasure trove of data to answer two questions at the heart of this book: Do colleges outside the top 25 offer a highly engaging experience? And what are the differences in student engagement between highly selective schools and those that accept more of their applicants? I provided the set of 1,200 colleges from my analysis of job outcomes that were sorted into five buckets of selectivity (under 20 percent acceptance rate, between 20 and 40 percent, and so on) and Kinzie's team matched them up to schools that had participated in the engagement survey since 2017. They then looked at how those groups of schools performed on 18 engagement measures, including overall satisfaction.

A few months later I received the results, with the names of specific institutions not disclosed. Overall, the most selective colleges—those that accept fewer than 20 percent of applicants—had the highest engagement scores among both freshmen and seniors across many, but not all, categories. Then I looked more closely at the numbers. On many measures, the five tiers were separated by only a point or two among freshmen—a tiny gap that narrowed even more by senior year, as shown in *Figure 6.1*.

Maybe the most notable measure was "higher-order learning" in courses—the sort of critical, analytical, and evaluative thinking that college should be all about. In that category, score averages were highly consistent across every level of selectivity.

Among freshmen, according to the researchers, there was "no statistically significant difference" on any of the measures between

Figure 6.1

Student Engagement: Elite Schools vs. Everyone Else

What college seniors say

Acceptance rate

Elite Colleges[1]   <20%
Selective Colleges   20–40%
Somewhat Selective   40–60%
Less Selective   60–80%
Much Less Selective   80–100%

Engagement Indicators 0 to 60 scale

Higher Order Learning

Extent to which courses emphasized critical and analytical thinking

- 42
- 42
- 41
- 41
- 40

Student-Faculty Interaction

Frequency with which students engaged with faculty outside of class

- 26
- 28
- 27
- 28
- 27

Participation in Experiential Learning Student participation %

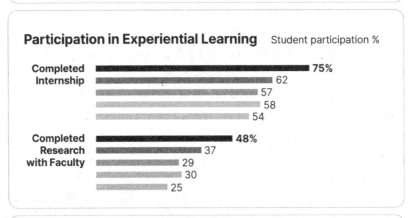

Completed Internship
- 75%
- 62
- 57
- 58
- 54

Completed Research with Faculty
- 48%
- 37
- 29
- 30
- 25

Overall Satisfaction with the College Highly satisfied %

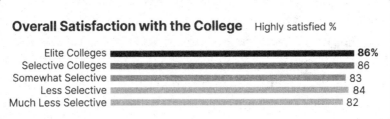

Elite Colleges	86%
Selective Colleges	86
Somewhat Selective	83
Less Selective	84
Much Less Selective	82

[1] Category names by author

Source: Composite findings from the National Survey of Student Engagement, 2017-2023. Includes data from 975 institutions.

the top group of schools and the one right below (20–40 percent acceptance rate). The most significant gaps in engagement—perhaps not surprisingly—were between the top two rungs (under 40 percent acceptance rate) and the bottom one (80–100 percent acceptance rate).

Some of the biggest differences between the very top group and others were in what the researchers classified as high-impact practices: internships, study abroad, research with faculty, and "capstone" experiences. By senior year, a higher proportion of students at the most selective schools had completed such activities. That was particularly true of the all-important internship, where the most selective schools scored significantly higher than everyone else. However, participation in activities like study abroad and internships often depends on financial resources and networks—advantages that many middle-income and most low-income students, who tend to be clustered at less-selective schools, don't have.

The information embedded in the topline numbers, while important, was not the most surprising finding. The researchers sent "boxplots" showing the variability of the scores within each quintile. For the most selective schools, the box was compact, which meant that half of schools clustered around a single score. But at the other levels of selectivity, there was a large spread between the top- and bottom-scoring schools on each measure, suggesting more volatility within those quintiles. More important, though: Those disparities within groups created areas of overlap between groups. In a given tier, the top schools scored on par with—or even a bit higher than—the bottom schools in the one above.

Again, no names were attached to any of these scores. For me, knowing which schools overlapped between selectivity bands would have been like finding a shortcut around a traffic jam. That information would have shown the way to less-selective schools that performed more like elite colleges. But even without the names, the analysis from Indiana researchers confirmed one important takeaway from my own surveys and interviews: Being selective doesn't automatically translate to providing a more engaging experience.

Scoring Colleges on the Return on Investment

For generations, the economic payoff of a bachelor's degree was perhaps its biggest selling point. But in 2010, as the economy sputtered in the aftermath of the Great Recession, once-steady career paths for college graduates began to contract and shift with alarming speed. With tuition prices still rising, students and their parents worried about their return on investment in higher education—the ROI of the degree.

In Washington, the Obama administration took aim at for-profit colleges that had proliferated the previous decade but failed to deliver on promises of larger paychecks for graduates. As with the debates over graduation rates twenty years earlier, however, the federal government didn't know exactly how most colleges were performing on this critical measure. No one could tell consumers if they were getting their money's worth by going to a certain college or earning a degree in a specific major, and they began to demand more information.

Around this time Michael Itzkowitz started as a special advisor to the U.S. Department of Education. The department was at a loss about how to provide data about return on a student's investment. It didn't have wage numbers for all or even most college graduates.

In August 2013, President Barack Obama visited the University of Buffalo as part of a bus tour of campuses to talk about college costs. In his speech that day, the president proposed a plan to rate colleges on access, affordability, and student outcomes, and to allocate federal aid based on those ratings. He said that over the next few months the Education Department would host a series of public meetings around the country to ensure they'd collect the right information about schools.

More details of the proposal came out in the days that followed. It described a "datapalooza" that would allow prospective students to compare institutions on, among other measures, graduates' earnings. "The phones went haywire," Itzkowitz recalled. "No one knew how we were going to do this."

Itzkowitz grew up in Florida, the son of two public school teachers. Money was tight in his family, so there was never any question he'd use the state's lottery-funded scholarship to enroll at a public university. He got into the University of Florida, Florida State, and the University of Central Florida. He chose the University of Florida because his family rooted against Florida State in football. For Itzkowitz, the ultimate decision about where to go to college was rooted in geography, not outcomes.

When the College Scorecard debuted in 2015, Itzkowitz was appointed its first director. The tool was a game changer for the conversation about what people paid for college and what they got in return, which had started to gain steam only five years earlier. And it's easy to use. Sourcing wage information from the Education Department's own database on student loans, as well as earnings information from the IRS, it can tell a high school student, for example, that the median earnings for psychology majors at the University of Oklahoma are $53,516 five years after graduation. It shows them what their median monthly earnings might be ($4,460) along with their monthly loan payment ($230).

The scorecard has its limitations, though. Its data on earnings comes only from students who receive federal aid, including those who take out government-backed loans. That means it omits about one-third of college students, who likely come from families with higher incomes (a strong predictor of what students earn after graduation). In some calculations, the scorecard includes students who graduated in the previous five years, while in others it considers any student who entered the institution ten years earlier, whether they graduated or not. Given the limited time period the scorecard includes, the earnings data can often be a product of geography if most former students work in cities with higher costs of living and salaries (Fordham tops UNC–Chapel Hill). What's more, the scorecard doesn't display occupational data by major, so it's unclear whether students are even employed in the field they studied.

These shortcomings aren't always clear to students and families using the tool. Even so, the earnings numbers from the College Scorecard have traveled well beyond its government-hosted website: The underlying data supply other earnings calculators and ranking instruments, including popular tools published by Bloomberg, for instance, and Georgetown University's Center on Education and the Workforce. The scorecard even feeds the "outcomes" tab when you look up a college on Google.

One regular user of the scorecard data is Itzkowitz himself. He now leads the HEA Group, a research and consulting organization focused on helping colleges provide greater value to more students. He frequently posts to social media comparing the earnings outcomes of various schools. I called Itzkowitz to ask how he'd use the earnings data from the College Scorecard to inform my Dream Schools list—to identify colleges that are accessible and that allow graduates to recoup the cost of their degree relatively quickly.

Together, we developed an earnings-to-net-price ratio—a simple formula dividing the median earnings of a college's graduates across all majors by the combined net price for that school over four years. When we calculated and sorted ratios, two patterns quickly emerged. In line with our expectations, public universities with low tuition rates for residents, namely those in the Cal State and the City University of New York (CUNY) systems, performed exceptionally well on net price, which in turn boosted their ratios. As Itzkowitz found when he applied to college, where you live matters a lot if you want to control the cost side of the equation.

As for earnings, selectivity rates and majors both made a difference. Schools with very low acceptance rates or high proportions of STEM majors correlated with high-paying jobs at graduation. So their ratios were strong as well.

Still, we saw outliers—colleges where students had a reasonable shot at getting in *and* could expect a good return on investment. Take, for instance, Dickinson College in Pennsylvania. The median annual income of its new graduates was $72,568 after six years, compared with $60,000 nationally. Meanwhile, Dickinson's average net price over four years was around $62,000, for an earnings-to-net-price ratio of 117 percent. The median ratio on our list was 69 percent.

How did Dickinson—the type of small, rural liberal arts college that's considered out of fashion these days—end up outperforming many of its higher-ranked peers? What students major in tends to skew the average across levels of selectivity, not just in the top tier. Several of Dickinson's majors, including international and public policy as well as math and economics, earned around or above the college's median. But those majors are pretty common at other schools, too. What seemed to differentiate them at Dickinson was the school's location. The campus is a hundred miles from Washington, D.C., twenty miles from the state capital in Harrisburg, and near several large military bases. So its students often get hired into government agencies and large multinational firms with government contracts. The top employers of recent Dickinson graduates, according to LinkedIn, include the U.S. Army, Deloitte, IBM, and EY.

All that is a good reminder to look beyond headlines that claim— much as Bloomberg did in its 2024 ROI rankings—that one college is a "better investment" than another. Don't simply glance at schools' topline numbers. Use the College Scorecard to check out earnings *within* the academic programs you're considering. Also, weigh each school's location and the types of employers that might hire you. The same goes for graduation rates—another key component of college rankings. Look at those with a discriminating eye. It's easy for Harvard and Stanford to report near-perfect graduation rates when they craft incoming classes with impeccable academic stats and reject everyone with any risk of failing.

The outputs of top-ranked schools—on both earnings and gradua-tion numbers—say more about admitted students' profiles than about the quality of educational offerings. These colleges find the smartest, the most talented, and (in many cases, research shows) the wealthiest and best-connected candidates and offer them spots as freshmen. Then, over the next four years, their job is essentially to avoid screwing them up.

Don't Get Lost in the Haystack

For the Dream Schools list, I wanted to find institutions that out-perform expectations while admitting the vast majority of good students who aren't predestined for the Yales, Williamses, North-westerns, and UC Berkeleys of the world. My plan would come to fruition in early 2024, when a partner at the consulting firm Bain & Company approached me about helping researchers there with their own analysis of earnings and graduation rates at nearly 1,000 schools.

Their approach differed from most mash-ups of earnings and graduation rates that I'd seen. In weighing the outcomes of indi-vidual colleges, they planned to take the students' academic and socioeconomic characteristics into account. They would do that by predicting what a school's graduation rate *should* be and what their graduates *should* earn, in light of certain student body char-acteristics. Their model would include family income, proportions of full-time and first-generation college goers, academic readiness (based on SAT scores), and demographics (race, ethnicity, and gender). Finally, they used a local cost-of-living index to adjust earnings since graduates of a college in New York City are likely to have fatter paychecks than those from schools in Kansas or Iowa.

In many ways, Bain's results weren't surprising. On the whole, the researchers found a "strong relationship" between predicted and actual outcomes. "It's difficult to exceed predictions on student outcomes," they wrote in their report. On graduation rates, for instance, only one in ten of the schools they studied outperformed expectations by more than 5 percentage points.

Still, some colleges punched above their weight. The Bain report, titled "Beating the Odds," included an interactive graphic with bubbles representing each of the schools studied. There was one chart for graduation rates and another for earnings, each with a diagonal line showing what was expected based on their students' academic and financial backgrounds. Schools with bubbles above the line outperformed expectations while those below it underperformed. I started to click on bubbles well above the line for graduation rates (which, in my research, often differ by major and gender, so be sure to ask any college you're considering for the graduation rate for students like you).

One bubble that popped out was Montclair State University, the second-largest public college in New Jersey, with 18,000 undergraduates. Its predicted graduation rate? Fifty-four percent. Its actual graduation rate? Sixty-seven percent. Like a growing number of colleges, Montclair uses technology to track academic progress, identify students in need of support, and reach out to those kids early on. The data crumbs add up over time, allowing Montclair to detect courses or majors where students are getting stuck and look for ways to redesign those offerings. I toggled over to the earnings chart to find Montclair's bubble. There, the university was *below* the line, with graduates making about $3,000 less than predicted. In my hunt for good schools, I often found such contradictions when eyeballing the data. This example was yet another illustration that finding a "perfect school" is a fool's errand.

Looking over the Bain report—after nearly a year of trying to pull together a simple menu of data points that would reveal hidden gems deeper in the rankings—I felt frustrated. It was the end of the summer. The draft manuscript of my book was almost due, and my inbox was filling with messages announcing the latest college rankings. First up was *Forbes*: "38 Great Colleges With Less Admissions Stress." That sounded nice. Then I clicked on the all-important methodology. As I read it, I noted how certain phrases keep appearing: *We ranked, we evaluated, we indexed, we used.* In all, *Forbes* weighed seven categories of data, including its own "American Leaders List," which it claimed set its rankings "apart" from the rest, because it measured "the leadership and entrepreneurial success of a college's graduates."

A few weeks earlier, I'd sent Michael Itzkowitz a draft of my Dream Schools list. I wanted his gut check. "It doesn't appear to emphasize ROI," he wrote back. "I can see some colleges on there where students will leave earning less than they paid." I realized in reading his email and looking back through the notes from our interviews that he viewed colleges through only one lens. Although I appreciated Itzkowitz's perspective, I wrote back that ROI, while important, was one of several elements I was looking at.

That's when I realized I'd spent the past year doing what families do during the college search: acquiring more and more stats about schools and struggling to reconcile them all. I was building what the statistician Nassim Taleb calls a "haystack" of data. As it got bigger, the needle I was looking for got buried deeper inside. "We're more fooled by noise than ever before," Taleb wrote more than a decade ago, adding that the rise of big data has "brought cherry-picking to an industrial level." He saw it coming.

We all cherry-pick—be it *U.S. News*, which emphasizes its own peer assessments, or the parent who likes the dining hall food at James Madison University more than that at George Mason. I was trying to cherry-pick in my own reporting, too. I kept tweaking my own formulas, adding data points, scrapping others. Should I set my selectivity cutoff at a 30 percent acceptance rate, or maybe loosen it to 40 percent? Did earnings averages for a whole institution really mean that much when a student's major drives more of the difference? How should I handle public colleges in my list—where the cost and admissions chances can be wildly different based on where you live?

The information marketplace, just starting when I went off to Ithaca College in 1991, has turned all of us into data-miners trying to make sense of things—and I was getting eaten by it. I was doing what sociologist William Bruce Cameron once warned against: Not everything that can be counted counts, and not everything that counts can be counted.

But then I hit pause, and I'll show you how to do the same thing. In the chapters that follow, we'll keep exploring what really matters in finding a good college for you. It's not a formula exactly, but still, it's a pretty simple framework—one that can be used to cut through the clutter and find the four critical components you need in your Dream School. They are:

1. **A supportive start.** One in four students who start out in college drops out after the first year. Look for schools that have moved on from a simple orientation to a full-fledged "first-year experience," with intro-to-college courses, programming in the dorms, and advisors that overall build "scaffolding" around a student's early undergraduate years and then slowly take it down so the student can learn to function well on their own.

2. **Easy connections.** Students thrive when they feel like they belong. On a campus tour, pay attention to how students find each other. Are faculty accessible outside of class? Do full-time professors teach the intro courses? What percentage of students stay on campus during weekends? These details matter in creating the kind of social and academic environment where students connect—with peers, mentors, and ideas.

3. **Real job experience.** College is more than a degree now. Does the school provide hands-on learning such as internships, co-ops, undergraduate research, or work-study tied to career paths? Does it offer skills-based credentials beyond the degree itself? Does it actively build a "career-ready" mindset—the combination of skills, experiences, and networking that leads to meaningful jobs?

4. **Resources to invest in me.** Students need more than good intentions from a college—they need a school with the financial capacity to support their goals. In Chapter 9, I'll show you how to find financially stable colleges that have the wherewithal to support your journey.

Here's one optimistic note to end on as we get buried under an ever-expanding haystack of data in our college search: We're not hunting for a single needle.

CHAPTER 7

MENTORS MATTER

Finding Colleges That Put Teaching First

When you ask parents what they want out of the undergraduate experience for their teenagers, their hopes are clear: lasting friendships, professors who spark their interests, and mentors who help shape their careers. In my survey of parents, the top feature of a dream school was a commitment to student success—nothing else was even a close second. An overwhelming 72 percent agreed student success was "extremely important."

But how do parents define this sometimes nebulous term "student success"? It's all about one thing: people.

One wrote about finding a place where their son is "valued." Another hoped that their daughter would "experience a positive culture of health and well-being while going to college," adding, "this rarely exists in high school." Another wanted their son to attend a school where he "finds life-long mentors and friends there." In a focus group, one father told me that his biggest fear was that his son would "just sit in his dorm room, go to classes, and nothing else." What did this dad want for his kid? "A college where the adults in the room won't allow him to be a spectator." A mother in the same focus group said her son never learned "great study skills in middle and high school, and the pandemic put him further behind." She added: "He wants to learn; he just needs someone to help create the spark."

As this mother went on to explain that her son was bored in high school, other parents nodded, as if they shared the same frustration. I mentioned that I'd just read Dan Porterfield's book, *Mindset Matters: The Power of College to Activate Lifelong Growth.* Porterfield is the head of the Aspen Institute, a think tank. Previously he was the president of Franklin & Marshall College and, before that, a vice president and English professor at Georgetown University.

In his book, Porterfield argues that a good college engages students by promoting a particular learning mindset. The best professors, he writes, "stoke the flame for discovery" to help turn passive learners into active ones who don't simply answer questions but ask them. A college doing its job (and, by extension, professors doing theirs) will structure the undergraduate experience to teach students new things step-by-step—much as they learned incrementally to ride a bike until they could pedal alone.

As I outlined Porterfield's arguments about the merits of active learning—participating instead of being lectured at and finding mentors who help you connect with your passions and explore ideas—I could see many parents getting animated. *That's what they wanted for their children in college.* "But it all seems so random," one mother said. "Isn't it all about luck?" You're an athlete, and your coach offers encouragement. You choose a class to fill out your schedule, and that professor is the one who awakens your drive. You meet someone on your dorm floor, and they become your best friend.

It *is* partly about luck, but schools can set the stage. Decades of research have shown that the connections students make on campus are essential to their success and well-being, both before and after graduation. What's less clear is how frequently those connections actually happen. Colleges say they create environments that foster them, but not all do—and students often don't know that until they're already on campus. Yes, relationships usually emerge in haphazard ways. And yes, mentoring is a two-way street, and many students are reluctant to engage with professors on a personal level (or even to start conversations). But colleges can and should deliberately encourage the types of interaction they claim to care about.

Think of this chapter and the next as complementary sections on the "people" aspect of your search for your dream school. Here, we'll talk about identifying colleges that help their students develop life-changing relationships with mentors. Mentors come in many forms, but in this chapter we'll focus specifically on college professors because they are often students' first—and most accessible—sources of such guidance. Then the next chapter will be your playbook for choosing a college that makes it easier to find *your* crew and ultimately your sense of belonging.

What the Rankings Pretend to Tell Us

If you liken college to a song, good teaching is the melody. It's central to an undergraduate experience rich in relationships and discovery, especially in the all-important first year. That fundamental expectation hasn't changed much over time. As the authors of a three-volume study on the impact of higher education concluded nearly a decade ago, "Good teaching is the *primary* means through which institutions affect students."

Mentoring is the harmony that adds context to teaching—largely after classes, during office hours, and through activities on the side, such as research projects, extracurriculars, and work-study jobs. The interactions themselves tend to be fleeting, but they can create bonds with long-lasting effects. Sometimes a single exchange or event stands out as a transformative coming-of-age experience, as sociologist Dan Chambliss and his coauthor Christopher Takacs point out in *How*

College Works. One example that came up often in their research was a simple dinner invitation from a professor to a group of undergraduates. That one gesture made them feel as though someone was finally treating them like an adult and for the undergraduates "symbolized the college's commitment to its students."

However, it's not easy to identify schools that carve out the space and time for nurturing such connections. During the college search, we tend to associate rankings with quality of faculty and the richness of student life. Yet, look under the hood of all the different rankings, and you'll find that just a tiny portion of the formulas are dedicated to teaching and mentorship.

Let's start with *The Wall Street Journal*'s Best Colleges list, which in 2024 featured a separate category for the "student experience," deriving the scores from a survey of undergraduates. The top three schools in the category were Scripps College, Harvey Mudd College, and Florida International University. Those are three very different types of institutions: a women's college and a small liberal arts school focused on science and engineering that are *across the street from each other* and a large public university where fewer than 10 percent of students even live on campus. In this category, two-thirds of each college's score focused on satisfaction with campus facilities and social life, including safety and the party scene. Nothing spoke to the quality of interactions with faculty and staff. In the overall rankings—where Princeton University came out on top—*The Wall Street Journal* measured "learning opportunities," drawing on survey responses about "interactions with faculty" and the "overall quality of teaching." But that set of measures counted for very little: just 4 percent of a college's overall score.

Clearly, those rankings fail to gauge the undergraduate experience in any meaningful way. So do those in *U.S. News.* None of the data points that make up a school's overall score reflect student engagement, for instance. Several are pegged to faculty, but not to the quality of teaching. *U.S. News* measures faculty salaries, how extensively professors' research is cited, the percentage of full-time faculty on campus, and the student-faculty ratio. Together, those categories add up to about 15 percent of the overall score. They receive less weight than the peer assessment, in which presidents, provosts, and admissions deans rate other schools. What about the "Best Undergraduate Teaching" ranking from *U.S. News*, touted by many colleges? It relies solely on the peer assessment. As *The Chronicle of Higher Education* put it, "It's not clear how those administrators would even know what goes on in other colleges' classrooms."

In light of how much we pay for college and how much time students spend on their pursuits there, it's shocking how little we know about teaching and mentoring. If a school is highly ranked, we may assume its professors favor active learning over traditional lectures. If it is selective in admissions, we may expect that smart and accomplished classmates will pull our kids along, whether or not the professors are engaging. But those are flawed assumptions.

This may be hard to understand for students coming from high school where the teachers are focused on, well, teaching. In the public's imagination, the central point of being a professor is connecting with students. At most institutions, though, especially highly ranked research universities, faculty members have a different set of incentives. No one wins that lifetime appointment of tenure by ignoring research to focus on becoming a world-renowned teacher. The inverse, though—a remarkable researcher who the department knows is pretty terrible at connecting with undergrads?—that's all too common. In fact, elite schools and those trying to break into that top tier have actually *decreased* their spending on instruction and increased spending on research and student recruitment as they have risen in status.

In my experience and research, I've observed that opportunities for mentoring are actually richer and more plentiful, on balance, at schools deeper in the rankings. Parents tend to blame their kids if they aren't academically immersed. In my survey, one dad shared that he'd begged his son—near the end of a less than satisfying first year at the University of Southern California—to reach out to the faculty for guidance. But his son wouldn't approach any professors to talk about anything beyond what was needed for his courses. When I followed up, the dad asked how he could avoid this fate for his younger daughter, who was in the middle of her own college search. "Don't pick USC," I said, half in jest.

In many ways, this father's dilemma epitomizes the central argument of this book. Finding a dream school often means landing on a more obscure campus where, instead of chasing their next research grant, faculty members focus on preparing for their next class and engaging with undergraduates. Good mentors like these exist at all kinds of schools, but they are easier to come by at colleges that need to prove their educational value—and harder to find at schools resting on the strength of their rankings.

Some parents seem to understand this from their own college experience. "Undergraduates don't require the level of expertise people demand of professors at highly selective schools," one parent wrote in response to my survey. "I went to a middling university myself . . . and then went on to an elite law school, yet I never once questioned my professors' expertise or failed to learn something from them."

Finding a College That Cares About Teaching

When Corbin M. Campbell was pursuing her doctorate in education at the University of Maryland, she worked part-time in its institutional research office. Institutional research functions as a data hub, collecting and analyzing every bit of information about a college's students, faculty, staff, revenue, and spending—and reporting those numbers to government agencies and the various rankings.

One of Campbell's jobs was to study what exactly the rankings measure. And, she told me, she soon came to realize that schools' efforts to rise in the rankings "actively pulled away from the teaching and learning experience."

Take, for instance, the most-cited *U.S. News* ranking category:

National Universities. That grouping is cobbled together solely on the basis of higher education's byzantine system for organizing institutions according to their research expenditures and the number of doctoral degrees they award. These two factors reveal nothing about the quality of undergraduate teaching or faculty mentorship. To even be considered for that list in *U.S. News*, institutions must focus their resources and faculty on research. The more they do so, the higher their rankings. "If you're a great researcher, it doesn't necessarily mean you're a great teacher," Campbell said. "It also doesn't necessarily mean you're a terrible teacher, but basically there's zero correlation between the two."

After graduate school, Campbell taught at Columbia, one of those national universities. "My research was fully supported, but I rarely had a conversation about my teaching," she said. It made her wonder: Where are the best teachers? So Campbell designed a study, backed by the Spencer Foundation and the National Academy of Education, to have graduate students observe more than 700 courses during weeklong visits to campuses. They would look for certain teaching practices, such as discussions, questions asked by students, and whether the course connected students' prior knowledge. They would also survey undergraduates and professors about their classes. Nine colleges—a mix of big and small schools, including both research-focused institutions and liberal arts colleges—agreed to participate.

"If anything, this was a sunny sample," she told me when we met for coffee near American University, where she's now a professor in the School of Education. "They said, 'Yeah, come take a look at our teaching. We're pretty proud of it.'"

What Campbell found was anything but sunny, however. The study's main takeaway? As she later wrote in *Great College Teaching: Where It Happens and How to Foster It Everywhere*, the quality of college teaching is best described as "middling."

In general, higher-ranked colleges scored *lower* than lesser-known schools. The researchers found that regional public universities in particular (think a Western Oregon) fared better than public research universities (think a University of Oregon). Although both had large classes, the size detracted more from learning at the flagships, where faculty tended to lecture rather than, for example, break classes into smaller groups and engage students in discussions. Across the board, teaching was strongest at liberal arts colleges, both higher and lower in the rankings, with one significant caveat: Underrepresented students experienced more discriminatory practices in courses at the liberal arts institutions than at other schools in the study.

In a full-circle way, Campbell confirmed in her research what she'd learned as a graduate assistant years earlier: Faculty at flagships are hired and mostly compensated for their scholarly output, not the quality of their teaching. Indeed, she noted that the professors consistently refer to the number of courses they have each year as their teaching "load"—a burden from which they sometimes ask for "release" time. In fact, at top research universities a typical teaching schedule for tenured professors might be 2-1, meaning they teach two courses in the fall and one in the spring. In other words, they spend the majority of their time doing something else besides teaching.

Also, faculty members aren't specifically trained to teach, even at schools that don't fixate on research. Campbell's team found, for example, that unlike elementary and high school teachers, most college professors are "one-trick ponies." They rarely vary their approach from week to week and mostly teach as they were taught.

The public, it turns out, holds a radically different view of what makes a university great. When Campbell added a question to a national public opinion survey about what defined the best university, the results were unambiguous: "Excellent teachers" topped the list at 80 percent, with "students who learn a great deal" following close behind at 72 percent. The message was clear—Americans value teaching and learning in higher education. Yet Campbell told me that when she shared her findings with the participating colleges, the response spoke volumes: Despite receiving detailed results about their teaching effectiveness, the prestigious institutions that were part of the study didn't even bother to ask how they might improve.

It seems we know what we want as higher-ed consumers. The important question is: How do we find it? The proxies that the rankings use to measure teaching quality—factors like class sizes and faculty salaries—fail to capture how effectively professors teach and mentor students or even how much each college prioritizes good teaching. Nevertheless, we can gather valuable insights by doing the following three things during the college search:

1. **Find out how the school hires its faculty.** When prospective faculty members visit campus to meet with potential colleagues and interview with the search committee, they also give what's known as the "job talk." At a school that cares mostly about research, this talk is attended by faculty members and graduate students so they can see if the candidate is someone they'd want to work with. Ask your tour guide if there's more to the hiring process, and if, as is likely, they don't know, ask to be connected to the college's teaching and learning center (hopefully they have one). There you can ask if faculty give teaching demonstrations when they're hired, and if so, are undergraduates invited? If prospective professors actually have to show they can teach as part of the vetting process, teaching counts for something on that campus.

2. **Ask current students about their professors.** Undergraduates are often your best sources for understanding what the teaching is really like. Don't just rely on the tour guide, who will give you talking points. Seek out students in your intended major by reaching out on LinkedIn or ask the department chair or admissions office. I get that this requires work and risks deeply embarrassing your kid. But if you were

buying a home and saw your prospective neighbor while touring the house, would you seek their feedback about the street or just trust what the Realtor told you? In selecting a college, you're making the same investment as you would buying a house, so try your best to connect with students and ask: What courses are taught by the best professors? Who are their favorites in their major and why? Inquire specifically about freshman year, when students are more likely to drop out of college or to encounter courses designed to weed them out of their major. For example: Did they have teaching assistants or professors for first-year courses? How good were they? Overall, did the faculty members seem to care about teaching? How about mentoring? Did any of their first-year professors invite them to a group dinner or a special event to help them find their footing early on? By asking detailed questions like these, you can move past boilerplate answers. College campuses are teeming with students if you visit during the school year. While your kid is off buying something in the bookstore or grabbing a bite to eat, ask some of these questions out of their earshot. Or find out from your high school counselor or friends if they know any current undergrads at the colleges you're considering.

3. **Sit in on a class, preferably in your major.** Before visiting, ask the admissions office if you can attend a class. If you don't get an answer, or the answer is a blanket no, it's worth politely trying again once you're on campus. Although admissions offices often discourage it, some professors are happy to have you drop in if you ask them before class begins. At the very least, talk to some faculty members about their teaching. What do they like about it? How does the school support them in the classroom? Do they feel that the college cares more about their research than about their teaching when

it comes to granting tenure and promotions? Be direct, and listen closely. You want the real story.

Don't be surprised if questions about the quality of teaching are greeted with vague answers or even silence. In her Substack newsletter on teaching, Michelle Miller, a psychology professor at Northern Arizona University, called this a "bait-and-switch" maneuver. Tuition-paying parents discover *after* their child enrolls that "education is simply not that important in the grand scheme of things" to the school. That's why you want to talk directly to students and professors, not just admissions officers and tour guides trying to sell you on the school.

On campus tours, guides show off the bells and whistles to prove the school cares about good teaching. They'll walk you through state-of-the-art buildings. They'll talk about hands-on learning opportunities. They'll recite a menu of stats that they believe demonstrate the effectiveness of their professors—but in reality tell you little or nothing.

For instance, you might hear about low student-faculty ratios and small classes. While intimate classes can facilitate closer interactions with professors, they don't automatically deliver first-rate teaching. The fact remains that most professors weren't ever taught *how* to teach when they were in graduate school. Or maybe you'll hear about some of the college's big-name tenured professors. But don't confuse tenure with teaching quality. Research has shown that tenure doesn't affect the academic rigor of a course or the expectations in class. The vast majority of college faculty aren't even eligible for tenure, which is essentially a lifetime job guarantee. While some faculty members work under long-term, full-time contracts, most are adjunct professors or lecturers who teach a course or two, earning just a few thousand dollars for a sixteen-week class. And among all those types of professors, colleges don't make it easy for prospective families to distinguish who's who.

A tour guide might also tell you that students rate their professors very highly in course evaluations. Schools do use evaluations—often exclusively—to measure classroom effectiveness. But these tools are far from reliable. Undergraduates typically give higher marks to courses with lighter workloads, classes in the humanities, and even those where the professor brings in cookies or chocolate. They give lower ratings to larger, introductory courses, science classes, and those taught by women or faculty of color. In all, evaluations are a blunt instrument to determine quality, especially since professors whose jobs depend on positive reviews may feel pressure to ease workloads or curry favor with students.

A Little Structure, A Little Serendipity

Your search for your dream school is full of promises. Years before you were ready to apply, colleges began making and marketing *their* promises—to provide *the* best place for your growth as a student and to invest in your success beyond graduation. Now, those assurances are piling up thick and fast as emails flood your inbox and glossy brochures litter your kitchen countertop.

You'll make promises to yourself as well, about how you'll grow and where you want to end up. But those take longer to sort out, or at least they should. Remember the prevailing, transactional view of college as a means to a good job, discussed earlier in Chapter 5? That perspective has its limits. Few teenagers know exactly what they want to do in life. Even students who declare a major on their application are, in most cases, guessing about their future.

Finding the right college is never as simple or straightforward as schools make it out to be in their recruitment materials. What you need is a place that recognizes complexity and accommodates growth. You're looking for a school that has erected what psychologists call "scaffolding."

In construction, scaffolding is the temporary frame that lets workers reach heights they couldn't otherwise and then comes down as the building is finished. In college, scaffolding works similarly. You're looking for campuses that have supports around the first two years—building in opportunities to meet professors and other mentors who will stir your curiosity, challenge your thinking, and guide your intellectual development. This support might sound abstract, but it takes concrete form across campuses: mandatory first-year seminars that introduce students to the rigor and rituals of college, required check-ins with academic advisors, connections to upper-class students who can be peer mentors, and some sort of assessment about your interests to help point you in a direction for a major and a career.

You're still the primary architect of your experience, but early on, your college should provide that basic bit of structure to help you along. Then, as your undergraduate experience evolves over the next few years, the scaffolding slowly comes down allowing you to develop your own independent approach and getting you ready to launch into life after college.

For Charles Miles, that began to happen the summer before his senior year at Furman University, on a basketball court in the campus gym. Miles had just spent several weeks working as an intern at the South Carolina university, helping to design and organize leadership education programs for freshmen and sophomores, when he heard about a group of faculty and staff who played pickup games at lunchtime. During the academic year, the games were usually off-limits to undergraduates. But this was summer, and the group was short a player.

One of the regulars, a friend who'd graduated a few years earlier and worked on campus, knew Miles was captain of the university's club team and asked if he'd join them. Miles jumped at the chance. He knew one of the other players, a professor he'd had for several math classes. And another player was a faculty member in the education department who Miles had heard was a really good teacher. "It was a totally different place to get to know professors," Miles told me. After that first pickup game, he played a few more and then left—for his second internship—to teach math in a summer program in New York City.

That fall, back on campus as a senior, Miles was working on a research project about teacher shortages in South Carolina for one of his courses. He came across some articles that might be of interest to the education professor he'd met on the basketball court and decided to share them. Although Miles wasn't an education major—he studied math and communications—the professor responded to the research thoughtfully. "He actually cared about me," Miles said, "even though I wasn't in his class."

In 2013, Gallup kicked off one of the largest studies of college graduates in the U.S. In a series of surveys that have since spanned more than a decade, Gallup has asked over 100,000 alumni of all ages about the connection between what they did in college and their success later in life. Despite all the data previously collected on schools and their graduates, there was still "a lot that wasn't knowable without asking people directly," said Stephanie Marken, who heads up what is now known as the Gallup Alumni Survey.

The primary measure of success that Gallup analyzed was well-being (that is, being happy, comfortable, and satisfied) across five dimensions: social, financial, sense of purpose, connection to community, and physical health. The polling firm also looked at how engaged the graduates were in their work.

The survey results "unpacked the magical ingredients of college," Marken told me. The most critical ingredient of all? Mentoring and internships provided the "biggest lifts," according to Marken. Graduates who said that someone in college cared about them as a person and encouraged them to pursue their dreams were twice as likely as other participants to be engaged at work after college and thriving in life generally.

Yet fewer than a quarter of the alumni surveyed said they'd had a mentor. Among those who did, the majority—some two-thirds of respondents—said that mentor was a professor. Graduates of large research universities were less likely to have mentoring relationships with their professors, Marken said, a finding that wasn't surprising given the studies on teaching mentioned earlier. And people who had majored in the arts and humanities were significantly more likely than those with majors in business and engineering to have had a mentor.

Gallup's early alumni surveys caught the eye of Elizabeth Davis just as she was arriving to take over the presidency of Furman in 2014. Furman, like most colleges, made promises to would-be and current students about opportunities they'd have to meet mentors, scrub in on faculty or graduate research projects, take part in internships, and study abroad. "Many of our students *were* getting them," Davis told me, "but not everyone." Furman relied on its relatively small size (2,300 undergraduates) to foster relationships and its eighteen sports in the NCAA's Division I to give the school community a bigger feel. "There wasn't a lot of intention to what we were doing," she added. For undergraduates, "there was too much waiting around for something to happen *to* them, and the entire experience wasn't coherent for students."

In other words, Furman needed to erect a scaffolding for its students.

By the time Miles had arrived as a freshman in 2019, Furman had started building that support structure. It established a program called Pathways, aimed at helping first- and second-year students focus on what they valued coming into college and decide what they wanted to keep while also giving them other ideas to explore. Freshmen at Furman now start out in a small breakout class of fifteen students—it was described to me as the college version of homeroom—where they meet weekly to learn a mix of practical skills (for studying, time management, and so forth) and to engage with broader topics related to their particular values and interests.

Mentoring is a central component. Juniors and seniors join these groups to serve as peer mentors, often sharing their own experiences in adjusting to college as well as their survival tips and their strategies for finding fulfillment. Pathways also connects each freshman with a professor. That person might become a mentor, or not. The hope is that students will discover early on that faculty members are approachable and available.

Many schools have tried to do something like Furman does, especially in the first-year transition to college. Sometimes these programs are more marketing than reality, sometimes they don't work for all students, but they demonstrate a commitment to helping undergraduates.

The small breakout class the first semester is a difference maker, according to Beth Pontari, Furman's provost, who helped design Pathways. At most colleges, students are assigned an advisor and "maybe you meet with that person four or five times a year to talk about scheduling, maybe more if you're the type of person that seeks them out," she said. "Now imagine you're in a class with your advisor, you're seeing them every week for fifty minutes, and then add to that you're in a cohort of students who are experiencing similar struggles as you, and you might not have known it otherwise."

As freshmen, Furman students take CliftonStrengths, a personality test. "It was one of my favorite things," Miles said, "because it helped me understand not only who I was but how to talk about it." While students can usually describe their college activities, they often struggle to explain what they learned and how it relates to job skills. Miles's personality assessment found he was an "achiever" and a "strategic thinker" skilled at communications with a "restorative mindset," in other words, a persistent problem-solver.

The results, Miles said, gave him a "baseline" for understanding what he was interested in, and even good at, as he started to pinpoint a major and get involved in campus activities. He applied and was accepted into a two-year leadership program on campus, which gave him a chance to meet peers and adults across campus.

Initially, Miles chose communications as his major, but in meeting with his advisor he discovered he could take on a second major because of his Advanced Placement credits from high school. Both of

Miles's parents are teachers, and he thought he might want to follow in their footsteps and become a math teacher. He declared math as a second major. "The major was relatively small at Furman, so it was really easy to form a relationship with professors," he said.

Once students declare their major at Furman, usually in their sophomore year, they spend the next two years in more focused pursuits: advanced coursework, undergraduate research, internships, and study away (either abroad or in the U.S.). That's when the scaffolding of the first two years slowly starts to come down. Miles recalled when the math professor from the basketball games—who'd since become a mentor—asked him early in his senior year if he had a job lined up for after graduation. Miles told him he didn't. So the professor set up a call with a Furman alumnus whose employer was looking for data analysts.

Though that job didn't work out, Miles learned—through conversations with his mentor and the former student—about the growing demand for data science skills well beyond the tech industry. That year, more than one million job postings across eighty-one occupations called for skills in data analytics. The mentor suggested that Miles could lean into his aptitude in math.

During a career fair on campus, Miles struck up a conversation with a recruiter from Mercer, a global human resources consulting firm. "That's when [his whole undergraduate experience] all started to come together," he told me when we met up in Washington, D.C., where he now works for Mercer. Furman "didn't get me *the* job," he added. Rather, he said, it created space for him to meet mentors early on, better understand his passions and where he might excel with them, and gain confidence in the real world through his internships.

I asked Miles how much he attributed his success to his own initiative and how much to the opportunities and encouragement Furman gave him along the way. He paused. Like some parents who shared their own college experiences with me, Miles came back to the people around him, especially the faculty. "No matter who you were," he said, "they expected a lot but were also there to help you. They were all driven by that same idea." Psychologist David Yeager calls this the "mentor mindset." It holds young people to high standards, but not without giving them the support they need to meet those standards.

None of this is a guarantee, of course, even at Furman. Before Pathways, some students at Furman were able to find good mentors. And even with it, some students surely fail to connect with faculty members. Surveys of freshmen over the first few years Pathways was rolled out show a small increase in the number of students who strongly agreed that professors cared about them as individuals. "The campus culture has to accept it," said Davis, Furman's president. "You really have to get everyone on the same page with what we're trying to accomplish—that every student will be taught by professors who want to teach undergraduates, who see themselves as mentors, and who are invested in providing opportunities."

Adam Weinberg, the president of Denison University in Ohio, made a similar point when we spoke about creating the conditions that facilitate such relationships. At Denison, he said, "we're super clear that we want faculty and staff members who want to be mentors." That desire should be palpable even to prospective students. Weinberg suggested talking to as many different people as you can when visiting a school to see how often they mention the importance of making connections. You can even look at faculty job postings to see whether it's emphasized as a core commitment to students.

Like Davis at Furman, Weinberg was influenced by the Gallup surveys as well as the book by Dan Chambliss, who became one of *his* mentors. "It's one of the few givens in higher ed that if you get the relationships right, everything else follows," Weinberg told me when I first met him on a 2017 visit to Denison.

Since then, I've interviewed Weinberg several times, and we've served on a board together. Each time we spoke, Weinberg told me how Denison isn't leaving relationships to chance. The university started a class for freshmen like Furman's, to get students in a cohort early on—taught by someone who could become a mentor. It also expanded orientation to include short off-campus trips for every student to get to know a small group of classmates. And the school redesigned its career services. Now the "career development" office focuses on capturing the time between semesters (40 percent of the calendar year for undergraduates, Weinberg noted). In addition to coordinating internships, the university runs short courses both online and in person so students can develop professional skills, earn credentials for them, and meet more people in areas of interest.

As I was writing this chapter, Weinberg and I connected once again, and he mentioned that his youngest daughter is now an undergraduate at a public research university in the Big Ten. "It will be a pleasant surprise if she gets to know faculty members there," he said, adding almost nonchalantly, "but that's not why you go there." I was surprised by the comment, given our conversations over the years about how much relationships matter in college. But he reminded me that relationships can take many forms, in many types of institutions. It's all about fit. His daughter wanted a business school, a big campus, Greek life. "Her peers are pushing her to get super involved," he said.

Yes, relationships matter, Weinberg said, but "no college can be all things to all people." It was a reminder yet again that in the college search we seek the Easy Button. We want simple answers and a single best fit, but ultimately there is no formula. When Gallup says relationships matter, we might start off looking for a place where mentoring is central to the experience, like Furman or Denison, only to land at a Big Ten school or somewhere else entirely. The college search and the undergraduate experience are both more random than any of us would like. But paradoxically, they become less so as we get to know more people—and ourselves.

A Place That Loves You Back

A rejection from a dream school stings. Some people fixate on the "what ifs" and have trouble fully embracing the next school on their list. One family I met moved their freshman into a dorm at Arizona State University in the fall of 2023, only to pack up again within days, after coming off the wait list at the University of Michigan.

Other students welcome their Plan B. What allows them to move on, while others brood about what might have been or switch colleges at the first opportunity? To sort that out, I asked parents to tell me about their kids' Plan Bs. I wanted to see if the families that got over their disappointment had adopted a particular strategy or if the colleges they eventually chose had anything in common. Hundreds of people responded.

> My daughter was a National Merit Scholar with a 35 ACT. Her resume was packed with impressive extracurriculars and honors. She set her sights on Vanderbilt—and was waitlisted. We visited Vanderbilt, and they barely acknowledged her presence. Plan B was the University of Oklahoma. She toured OU multiple times. Each time, the university figuratively rolled out the red carpet. She was treated like royalty. Our common conversation centered around "Which college wants you to succeed? Which college is invested in you?" I am not sure she was convinced when May 1 rolled around, but she committed to OU. The admissions rep considered my daughter to be her #1 recruit—and she was thrilled to have her finally commit. In my daughter's time at OU, she flourished. Her professors cared about her. She got to know the president, who ended up writing a recommendation for her. She received one-on-one coaching to apply for a Truman Scholarship. Plan B allowed her to do so much. OU cared about her success.

This wasn't just a story about a backup plan working out. It was about how early signals from a college—the way they introduce prospective students to faculty, the time professors spend with visiting families, the personal attention from staff—predicted the depth of relationships students will form over four years. At Oklahoma, each campus visit revealed another potential mentor, another future advocate, another person invested in a single student's success.

I asked the mother whether her daughter might have found similar connections at Vanderbilt or another elite institution. "Probably," she admitted. But Oklahoma showed her family that relationships were their priority. "Literally every time we went to OU, it was like, 'What department can we show you? Which professors would you like to meet?'" She paused, her voice growing serious. "Vanderbilt couldn't wait to get rid of us. They had a million kids lining up for *whatever* they'd offer. OU showed us that relationships mattered."

CHAPTER 8

FINDING YOUR PEOPLE

How Belonging Shapes Your Undergraduate Experience

In August 1991, my parents dropped me off at Ithaca College for the start of my freshman year. Although I'd been on campus twice before, for an admissions tour and a two-day summer orientation, I felt like a visitor in a foreign country. Only about half my high school graduating class in Northeastern Pennsylvania went to a four-year college, and no one could recall anyone else ever going to Ithaca. I was the first in my family to go to college more than twenty miles from home.

I remember sitting on the bottom bunk in my dorm room when my two roommates arrived in quick succession, acting as if they already knew each other. One look at them told me: They were linebackers on the football team. They sized me up as well: At five-foot-seven, 120 pounds, I was clearly not one of them. Nonetheless, we squeezed into our "nonstandard triple," a 193-square-foot cinderblock box on the seventh floor of the East Tower.

The first few weeks, I couldn't seem to find my place anywhere I went.

Week one, when floormates started talking about summer camps, I pictured day camps like those run by my hometown YMCA, only to discover they were reminiscing about extended sleepaways in New England.

Week two, I tried out for a reporting spot on the campus television station. I had come to Ithaca with my heart set on becoming a journalist and seeing the world as a correspondent for a major TV network. As I waited in the basement of the communications building, I struck up a conversation with a student next to me. He told me that he'd been working as an intern at a local station in Syracuse since seventh grade. (That student, David Muir, would go on to anchor *ABC World News Tonight*.) I felt deflated.

Week three, I got a C on a macroeconomics exam. When the professor handed back the tests, I overheard two classmates talking about how they'd covered the material in AP macroeconomics—a course my high school didn't offer.

The beginning of my first semester at Ithaca wasn't what I expected. In high school, I thrived through frequent interactions and close connections with friends and teachers. I figured college would be more of the same. But when it wasn't, nobody told me that my experience during those early weeks, and really the first few months, was pretty normal. In the early 1990s, the mindset was still very much "look to your right, look to your left—one of you won't be here by the end of the year." Back then, you were expected to take charge of your own success. If you didn't do well, that was just how it went.

In November, things started to change for the better. My macroeconomics professor suggested dropping by during office hours, and I quickly learned how seeking advice from faculty members could help me not only sharpen my study skills but also navigate college life. I joined the student newspaper and realized I was better suited to print journalism than to broadcast reporting. One of the editors, a junior, put me in touch with a professor who was hiring peer writing tutors for a new type of computer lab on campus. I got a job there. And I began to find my crew at the newspaper. One of the freshmen on staff became my new roommate in the spring—freeing me from that non-standard triple with two football players.

I didn't know the technical term yet, but over the course of that first semester, I found my sense of belonging.

Why Belonging Matters

"Belonging" is a buzzword you'll hear frequently during the college search. You might be tempted to dismiss it as a touchy-feely label that schools use to showcase what they do to help you make friends and feel comfortable. But there's more to it. Belonging, or feeling accepted, is not just a psychological luxury. It's essential to your success as a student because it shapes your undergraduate experience: how you learn in the classroom, the opportunities you have on and off campus, whether you stay in school, and even your mental health and overall well-being.

"Good" colleges no longer let you sink or swim. They now provide a deliberate infrastructure for fitting in—right from the start of freshman year. None of the rankings measure belonging, however, even though that's what marks the right "fit" in a college. At a dinner gathering in Chicago one night in the spring of 2024, I was seated next to Marie Lynn Miranda, the chancellor of the University of Illinois Chicago. Miranda had previously been a faculty member at Duke University and provost at Notre Dame. Her daughter, a recent college graduate herself, was seated next to her, so I asked the chancellor what advice she gave her own kids in the college search. She said she told them that there isn't such a thing as fit. "You shouldn't have to fit what a college wants in its students," she said. "A college should be able to serve all kinds of students. They should be able to fit *you*."

In my national survey of parents for this book, two of the top four outcomes they said they want for their kids relate to belonging: finding great friends and discovering a sense of purpose in life. Six in ten parents said finding great friends was "extremely important."

As for their biggest concern in choosing a school, fit was second only to affordability. "I want to know where they could thrive, make connections with professors, be active and involved in campus, and not fall through the cracks," one parent wrote. Responses consistently relayed a struggle to block out the cacophony of voices pushing prestige on their kids and to focus instead, as one parent said, on "selecting a college based on what they are actually interested in and having college support them in their interests."

In the absence of clear signals of fit, survey participants told me, they often gravitate toward brand names as a proxy. They assume that a high school student who excels at academics and is socially skilled will continue in that same lane at a highly selective college. But these days top schools accept fewer and fewer of their applicants, and even those students find that the race to get ahead doesn't stop at the door of the admissions office.

Remember William from the Introduction? He started at Columbia but never found his people there amid the relentless scramble to join clubs and even secure internships in that first semester. Although he transferred to the University of Minnesota and was happier for it, he's an exception, not the norm. Studies show that students at highly selective colleges typically don't try looking for campuses that might be a better fit when their experience doesn't turn out as expected, because they feel resigned to accepting things as they are. Once their Plan A school accepts them, they are reluctant to change course.

But what happens to students and families whose first choices fall through? After being forced to pivot to Plan B schools in their applications, how do they feel about where they end up? Pretty good, it turns out. Maybe it's a form of rationalization on their part, but responses to my survey and follow-up questionnaires reveal a surprising sense of relief. Parents said that the move away from the pressures of prestige allowed their teens to flourish in a less stressful environment. This shift, they noted, opened up new opportunities for personal growth and development that might not have been possible at a top-ranked college.

Their experiences square with larger trends that suggest fit should outweigh prestige in the school search. For one, a poor fit can lead to loneliness—a widespread problem on campuses. In a Gallup survey, almost 40 percent of college students reported feeling lonely the previous day.

Former U.S. Surgeon General Vivek Murthy called loneliness an "epidemic," a public health threat comparable to tobacco and obesity. In 2023 Murthy visited a half dozen campuses to spread this message to college students. "Building relationships is not something you do at the end of a long to-do list," he said during a stop at Drexel University. "This is just as important as anything you may learn in the classroom or any skill you may gain online. This is a core part of the foundation of being."

Belonging is also a critical part of getting to graduation. Every year, about a quarter of college freshmen don't return for their sophomore year—to any college. (Another one in ten transfers to another campus.) Many parents shepherding their kids through the application process don't think they'll be among those dropout statistics a year later. But students are most vulnerable to dropping out their first year. The seeds are planted in those first few months of the fall semester if they don't find their crew, even when other things, like grades and finances, are fine.

Cumulative Effects Add Up Fast

The desire for belonging isn't unique to college students. It's a basic human need for all of us, everywhere. Some of the science behind it dates to World War II, when British psychologist John Bowlby conducted extensive research on the effects of children being separated from their caregivers. Bowlby's "attachment theory" was later adapted to various settings, including K-12 schools and college campuses, where educators found that the more students felt socially connected, the more they thrived.

Belonging isn't static; it changes with context and experience. A freshman who excels in science may feel comfortable in a biology class, for instance, but lack that confidence in a history course. And a senior may adapt more easily when trying something new.

Our sense of belonging can also shift during a period of considerable upheaval—such as the transition to college—as it did for me at Ithaca. In 2007, two young social psychologists, Geoffrey Cohen and Gregory Walton, coined a term for this jarring shift: "belonging uncertainty." It happens when we face a series of unsettling circumstances and then become unsure of ourselves. If I sense that my dorm floormates are quietly snickering at me when I say I'm unfamiliar with sleepaway camps, I'll hesitate to strike up another conversation with them the next day. If other students auditioning for a TV show seem to have more experience in front of a camera, I might skip future auditions. If I feel totally out of my depth in a macroeconomics course, I'm less likely to raise my hand. When such episodes happen one after another, as they usually do in new situations—whether we're first-time parents, new employees, or freshmen in college—a negative narrative emerges in our minds and colors how we interpret everyday events going forward. We become more defensive and less willing to take on challenges that might result in failure.

Cohen and Walton wanted to know if there was a way to head off—from the start—a student's belonging uncertainty. So they designed what social psychologists call a research intervention. They exposed college freshmen to reassuring messages, delivered by upperclassmen, that it was perfectly normal to feel as though you didn't belong in college and that those worries dissipated over time. The study was small. But compared with classmates who didn't participate, the students who did ended up earning better grades on average and achieved a higher graduation rate.

A decade later, Cohen and Walton, by then both faculty members at Stanford University, expanded on their earlier work. In this new study, the intervention was brief: a ten- to thirty-minute reading and writing exercise. But it was conducted on a much larger scale than the previous one: Nearly 27,000 incoming freshmen completed the assignment at twenty-two colleges, including both top-ranked and less-selective institutions, such as Dartmouth, DePauw University, and Southern Oregon University. The assignment was delivered online and, more important, embedded within a cluster of tasks students completed as part of the enrollment process for their first semester.

In the exercise, students were given the results from a survey where upperclassmen deemed everyday worries about belonging— such as feeling homesick, having a hard time finding friends, and struggling to interact with professors—as normal in the transition to college and likely to improve with time. Each school also shared its own set of stories from older students of various backgrounds. These highlighted their excitement about starting college and some of their challenges—like comparing new friends to those back home or getting the worst grades of their life—which turned out to be common concerns among freshmen. The incoming students reflected on the survey results and the stories in writing. The aim of the intervention wasn't to make them think college would be easy but to reframe their expectations.

The students who participated in the study went on to complete their first year of college at a higher rate than a control group of freshmen who didn't participate. And researchers discovered the belonging-intervention effect lasted over time. These students were more likely to take "microrisks" of meeting someone new or going to office hours, and those had kind of a snowball effect over time. Another follow-up study of these students, in their late twenties, found these young adults had greater well-being and job satisfaction.

Among the authors of these studies was Shannon Brady, a graduate student who worked with Cohen and Walton at Stanford. For Brady, doing the research was like looking in the rearview mirror at her own life. Brady grew up in rural Montana, the daughter of two schoolteachers. In 2002, she graduated high school and left for her freshman year at Lewis & Clark College in Portland, Oregon.

What Brady knew about college was mostly from the movies, she told me when we first met, and "this hippie liberal arts college" was nothing like the movies. In one of her courses first semester, she recalled a class discussion about Plato's allegory of the cave. "I did not understand it at all," Brady said. "I remember one student raising their hand and saying, 'Well, when I was in ninth grade . . . ,' before launching into a thoughtful analysis, all while I sat there thinking that I didn't know who I could even possibly call to ask for help."

The social-belonging interventions that Brady researched later were planned and deliberate. But as she told me about her own journey as an undergraduate, it struck me that many of the seemingly random connections we make at college produce effects similar to those in the carefully orchestrated Stanford study.

For Brady, one of those lucky breaks came during a class at Lewis & Clark, when a professor mentioned in passing that undergraduates worked with him on research. The idea piqued Brady's interest, so she went to see him during office hours. She remembers standing outside his office, rehearsing what she was going to say "for what felt like an hour." She finally mustered the courage in a moment that changed her life course. "It helped me see what you could be other than a small-town teacher with a college degree," Brady told me. Working with that professor, she got hooked on research. Eventually, she also figured out how to survive at college. After graduate school, she landed a job as a faculty member in the psychology department at Wake Forest University.

Brady's research on social belonging shaped the advice she now offers to her undergraduates. She tells them that the simple act of participating in college matters. Although more than 100,000 students were invited to take part in the Stanford study, only about a quarter of them completed the assignment. "Those students who chose not to do it missed out on one little opportunity at the beginning of college that potentially could have changed the trajectory of what they'd end up doing," Brady told me.

Yes, you have a runway in college to figure things out. You don't have to do everything all at once at the start of that first year. But early opportunities tend to have cumulative effects. Going to office hours that first semester makes you more comfortable talking to professors your second semester, which results in an undergraduate research gig your sophomore year, and so on. "A little bit of trajectory shift in the beginning can end up mattering," Brady said.

We often assume belonging relates only to the social aspects of college. It doesn't. Students benefit from its cumulative effects in three domains of undergraduate life: academic, residential, and extracurricular. Finding a school that will help you fit in across all three should be central to your college search.

Three Domains of Belonging

When researchers ask what it means to belong in college, they often hear many of the same words and phrases: *comfortable, fitting in, home, truly be yourself, meant to be there, welcomed.* But how do students actually experience belonging across the three domains on campus? In other words, what does it look like to *fit in* when you take a college class? To feel at *home* in a dorm? To be *welcomed* into a student club?

There is no perfect formula for understanding what belonging means at the colleges you're considering, because fit happens differently for different people. It depends partly on your gender, race, or ethnicity, for instance, or whether you're the first in your family to go to college. Also, finding a sense of belonging in one area (in your classes, for instance) doesn't necessarily translate to another (such as your dorm). That said, I've found in my research that certain elements do support belonging across the three domains.

ACADEMIC: HOW YOU CONNECT IN AND AFTER CLASS

In December 2023, a social media post by a professor at the University of Wisconsin–Madison went viral. Sami Schalk wrote that "this has been the worst semester in terms of students' ability to get work in on time. I've never seen anything like it." The post received more than 88,000 likes and nearly 10,000 reposts. The response from faculty everywhere was essentially, "Yes! We know."

Over the previous year, Beth McMurtrie, a senior writer at *The Chronicle of Higher Education*, had been sounding the alarm in multiple articles on student disconnection, which many faculty members considered a post-Covid epidemic for undergraduates who missed out on the concluding years of high school. When McMurtrie asked professors to share their experiences, they described common challenges: Far fewer students show up to class. Those who do avoid speaking when possible. Many skip the readings or the homework. They have trouble remembering what they learned and struggle on tests.

The pandemic certainly complicated schools' efforts to connect with kids academically, as students' learning, financial, and mental-health needs radically changed and expanded. But it's also partly up to you, the student, to set yourself up for success. There is no greater indicator for finding your place in your courses than simply showing up when the semester starts. One study of belonging among first-year business and economics students at three universities revealed that a significant majority—some 85–90 percent—found their place within the first seven weeks. What led to that sense of belonging? Attending class, participating in discussions, and meeting with professors.

Getting to know faculty members in that first semester is critical, yet about a quarter of incoming freshmen expect to have difficulty interacting with them. Students need to summon the courage to visit their professors during office hours, like Shannon Brady did. It helps if they're accessible, so while visiting campuses look for faculty members hanging out after class or coming to the classroom early to chat with students. And go see if professors show up for posted office hours (or ask that question on a tour, since some colleges limit access to academic buildings for nonstudents).

Beyond being "present," picking a major promotes academic belonging, too. Students with a declared major feel a greater sense of connection than those who are undecided, according to the National Survey of Student Engagement. The survey also found that the degree of belonging can differ by major. By senior year, students majoring in health professions, education, business, and social services are most likely to feel valued by their institution, while those in arts and humanities, engineering, physical sciences, math, and computer science report the lowest scores on this measure. Of course, finding your academic footing also has implications for what you do next. It often seems to inspire seniors to pursue a graduate or professional degree.

At some colleges, especially small liberal arts schools, you can't declare a major until the end of your second year. Does that mean you should avoid these colleges? Not at all, but make sure they provide another academic "home" for freshmen.

One possibility is a unified "first-year experience," which stitches together elements that were usually separate when today's parents went to college—for example, orientation, freshman seminars, and a common set of readings.

At St. Olaf College in Minnesota, where students declare a major in their sophomore year, incoming freshmen take two required classes in a smaller cohort: a seminar and a writing course. Those courses and the students in them are connected as well to an extended orientation that runs throughout the year, in which peer mentors advise freshmen on the basics of academic life—everything from the impact of sleep on performance to study skills to course registration to career center essentials. Diane LeBlanc runs the school's first-year experience. She told me that the number one concern of St. Olaf freshmen is making friends—and that concern is as much academic as social. She said that the first-year experience gives students a built-in crew from the moment they arrive on campus and easy access to upperclassmen. Both types of connection make a difference. Peer leaders report that students are more comfortable sharing fears and problems with someone closer in age than with professors or staffers who are older.

While more than nine in ten colleges provide some sort of first-year experience, I highlighted St. Olaf here for a reason: It is among a small number of less-selective schools (acceptance rate: 52 percent) that are on a par with higher-ranked colleges in terms of engagement and satisfaction scores on the National Survey of Student Engagement, as I outlined in Chapter 6. St. Olaf also makes all of its NSSE findings public—the good and the bad. Not every school does. Ask colleges you're considering whether they participate in the survey and, if so, where they publish their results. If they don't release those numbers, consider it a red flag.

Students and parents often assume that small colleges are better for belonging because of their size (3,000 students, in St. Olaf's case). But even at small schools, students can fall through the cracks without a network to support them. No one person on a campus can meet all student needs. St. Olaf engineered its current advising system after seeing its student engagement scores lag on that front. The school piloted a successful program to help first-year athletes learn more intentionally about being in college and then rolled out the system broadly.

St. Olaf now takes a team approach to first-year guidance that is becoming increasingly popular on campuses nationwide: Students are paired with an academic advisor (ideally a faculty member who is teaching one of the freshman's fall classes), a professional success coach, and a peer advisor. Pay attention to how advising works at the colleges that you're interested in. "Good advising may be the single most underestimated characteristic of a successful college experience," Richard J. Light, a Harvard University professor, wrote in 2001. That observation is even more relevant now, given post-pandemic realities and the complex bureaucracies students must navigate on today's campuses.

There are two other important elements that lead to academic belonging: active learning and feedback. Until the pandemic, too much of college teaching was stuck in the chalk and talk days where professors largely lectured. But even after the mass pivot to online learning during the pandemic, faculty members have largely returned to previous ways of teaching rather than making information relevant to students and giving "them an experience instead of just being an audience," in the words of Eva Zygmunt, a longtime professor at Ball State University, who uses Lego exercises to build a sense of creative belonging in her classes.

So when I encourage you to sit in on a class during college visits, preferably one in your intended major, ask yourself afterward: Is that something I'd want to sit through for fifteen weeks as an undergraduate? Also, when talking with current students, find out what kinds of feedback they get on their work, and when. Frequent and timely feedback reveals a college's commitment to active learning, which keeps students engaged and feeling like they belong.

RESIDENTIAL: HOW AT HOME YOU ARE IN YOUR DORM

When Laura Hamilton first began studying a group of undergraduate women who lived on the same dorm floor at Indiana University, her research focused on what happens in college when first-year students from different states and economic backgrounds are brought together. As a graduate student in sociology at Indiana, Hamilton started following these fifty-three young women in 2004.

Years later, in multiple books and studies stemming from her interviews with this cohort throughout and beyond school, Hamilton and her coauthors investigated long-term outcomes and concluded that a student's social class when they enter college is perhaps the biggest determinant of what happens to them later in life. To put it in blunt terms: The wealthiest undergraduates turned out fine no matter what they majored in or how hard they worked in college; the low-income and working-class students more often dropped out or struggled to find good jobs, even though they lived on the same dorm floor as the wealthier kids.

Relationships did benefit both groups. But the gains weren't evenly distributed between them.

Hamilton is now a professor at the University of California, Merced, and the women in her study are in their late thirties. In my research for this book, I wanted to know how she thought a college's selectivity played into the relationship-building that happens in dorm living. After all, we tend to view going to a top-ranked school (in part) as buying into a network that starts forming in your freshman-year dorm, where you meet future friends, coworkers, or even romantic partners. One often-quoted study, conducted among freshmen at Dartmouth College, seems to back up that assumption: It found that your roommate has a significant impact on how much you study, your GPA, and your social life, particularly whether men join a fraternity. All this was especially true for freshmen who didn't arrive on campus with a strong penchant for studying or much preference for what activities they'd participate in during college.

But in my conversations with Hamilton, I realized that the story we like to tell ourselves about the enduring value of residential life on campus isn't as simple or universal as we tend to think. As I laid out in the Introduction, what drives the fascination among the "panicking class" with selective schools is parents' belief that such places will help secure and maintain their kids' socioeconomic status in life. They're partially right to think that, Hamilton pointed out. But kids from wealthy or upper middle-class families are more likely than others to reap that benefit at a top-ranked school, like Dartmouth, because such colleges enroll a relatively high proportion of undergraduates from the top of the economic ladder.

"They end up only hanging out and socializing with people similar to them," Hamilton told me. That results, she said, in "extreme exclusion" at Ivy-plus schools: If you're not at the top of the social hierarchy coming in, it's difficult (if not impossible) to climb up while you're there.

At less-selective colleges with more socioeconomic diversity, students typically find it easier to build relationships with people from different backgrounds. Still, Hamilton told me, they can go "either way"—up or down the economic ladder. That's one reason why "helicopter parents" from affluent and upper middle-class families continue to hover when their kids go off to a college deeper in the rankings. Hamilton's research shows that these parents help manage students' social lives, push their kids to take advantage of academic services (such as tutoring or the career center), and secure internships for them because they "know the potential to make a misstep—and the costs of doing so—may be higher than before."

Here's the bottom line: Don't expect the freshman-year dorm to provide an instant sense of belonging for your kid that will ensure success in college and afterward. But don't plan to monitor your kid in college, either, as parents did in Hamilton's study. It's both impossible and developmentally inappropriate. Instead, center your search on colleges that emphasize how they create communities in their residential experiences and that downplay the bells and whistles, such as apartment-style living and fancy amenities like pools and dining halls that serve sushi.

If you think about it, private kitchens and bedrooms encourage students to spend time alone rather than mingling and developing friendships in dining halls or lounges. After building one of the country's most expensive student-housing projects, a $168 million complex of apartment-style residences called University Commons, in 2007, Georgia State University leaders worried about the impact of pricier housing on students' ability to earn a degree. The university's residence halls built since then have followed a simple mantra: good, modern, but cheap. And those are the dorms that fill up faster than other housing. Thomas Carlson-Reddig, a partner at Little, an architectural firm that designs a dozen campus projects a year, makes a compelling point: "If you can get the cost down, students will live in a closet."

The dorm is a key stop on any campus tour. Many colleges even set up a sample dorm room for you to walk through. Rather than worry about the colors of the walls or the height of the ceilings, however, ask how residential life programs cultivate belonging. Colleges attentive to this question have designed living-learning communities (floors, wings, or entire dorms for students with shared interests), house systems (think Gryffindor and Hufflepuff in Harry Potter), and "neighborhoods" of dorm buildings to make larger schools feel small. These were hot topics at the annual conference of the Association of College and University Housing Officers-International, where I gave the keynote talk in 2024.

During your search, request findings from colleges' latest "campus climate" surveys (or search for them in student newspaper archives) for insight into which schools are closely connecting the academic side with residential living. That's happening at Elon, Iowa, Michigan State, and other campuses where they're bringing faculty into the dorms (to meet with students and sometimes even to live), creating themed dorms, and designing intimate residence "villages."

One final observation on residential belonging: Ask how roommates are assigned. Gen X parents like me who experienced rotten freshman matchups might think random assignments build resilience. Maybe they do, but there are better ways. Research shows that bad roommate relationships can lead to more stress and lower grades. Colleges are increasingly giving students far more control over the selection process—through social media or online matching services—and that's a good thing.

EXTRACURRICULAR: HOW WELCOME AND ENGAGED YOU FEEL IN YOUR ACTIVITIES

As I mentioned at the beginning of this chapter, when surveying parents, I asked what they hoped college would accomplish for their kids. I asked them to choose from a list of thirteen outcomes (and they could also add their own).

More than anything else, parents expected college to do two things: help their child launch a fulfilling career and make great friends. While education for its own sake matters—ranked No. 5 on the list of outcomes—parents chose "making great friends" as a top priority two and a half more times than they did finding a sense of "intellectual curiosity." In the end, parents care more about prospects for jobs and kinship. Classrooms and dorms can provide those to some extent. But the third domain of campus belonging—the extracurricular experience—is perhaps the most vital to building lasting connections.

Activities do the most to expand our personal and professional networks. If we think of those networks as maps of interconnected cities of possibility, college activities such as sports and clubs provide some of the first "roads" that can help us navigate the rest of our lives. That isn't to say the people we meet through activities will be our best friends for life. We don't need them to be. In 2022, when researchers analyzed the networks of 20 million people on LinkedIn, they found that strong ties—immediate coworkers, close friends, and family— actually helped *the least* in finding new jobs. Who helped the most? Acquaintances who share few mutual connections. Those so-called weak ties expose us to new ideas and opportunities.

This idea that it's not who *you* know that gets you the job, but who *they* know, isn't a new one. Sociologist Mark Granovetter first developed the theory, known as "the strength of weak ties," in a seminal 1973 study. But the more recent LinkedIn research provides powerful new evidence. Over the five-year period analyzed, the platform's "People You May Know" algorithm created 2 billion new ties that led to 600,000 new jobs.

What extracurricular activities in college do is expand our field of vision beyond our major and our dorm floor. I think back to the summer after my freshman year, when I stayed in Ithaca to work as an editor on the summer edition of the newspaper. I needed a second job to make things work financially, so the advisor to the paper introduced me to the head of summer orientation, who was looking for an office assistant. Working in that office over the summer, and living on campus with other student workers from a variety of majors, allowed me to significantly grow my network beyond journalism and the communications school. Some thirty years after I graduated, I still count several people I met that summer as good friends, and two in particular have helped connect me to work in my career.

That summer I found what author and academic counselor Ana Homayoun calls "multiple nonoverlapping circles of connection." In elementary and middle school, Homayoun told me, kids typically have a similar network structure, with different friends from different places—their school, the neighborhood, the soccer team, summer camp, etc. As teens transition to high school and then college, however, their friend groups become smaller (and overlap more). As a result, Homayoun said, "when something doesn't work out in some way, shape, or form, it becomes a be-all end-all." In college, students often become comfortable with a group of students early on and "do not venture out over four years." Homayoun added: "When they go to graduate, their network is super small."

This concept of multiple identities is crucial to success *in* college, but even more so *after* college. If you're a great runner, you can still take pride in winning a 5K race despite your boss reprimanding you at work. If you're an actress in a local theater, a mom, a book club leader, a volunteer at school—if you have multiple identities, no matter what they are, you have more to buttress you when you hit a wall in one.

Extracurricular involvement helps you develop your identities, and, research suggests, is linked to academic success and student well-being. It builds a sense of purpose, fosters social integration, and provides meaningful interactions outside the classroom. Simply put, "activities engage students in ways academics can't," Ernest T. Pascarella told me in 2022. Pascarella spent more than three decades studying how college affects students. He identified involvement in extracurriculars—particularly those that occupied undergraduates for at least two hours a week—as a key element in the college experience.

When looking at colleges, find out how accurate their laundry list of clubs really is. In the aftermath of the pandemic, many campus organizations disappeared (or became "ghost clubs," with no one actively participating). When members graduated, their replacements never arrived, because students were learning virtually. So don't assume that extracurricular offerings are as robust as advertised. Also, ask current students how easy it is to join a club, especially one outside your area of study. As William learned at Columbia, the competition to get into clubs can be surprisingly fierce.

Finally, ask about the process for starting a group of your own. When Alexander Jones met the new "vibrant campus community coordinator" (yes, that is her title) at orientation at the University of Virginia's College at Wise, she encouraged him to channel his love of video journalism into reviving the college's old TV club. "If I never had that interaction," Jones told reporters for *The Chronicle of Higher Education*, "I feel like I wouldn't have had as much motivation to really show off my talents here because I wouldn't have really known how much they really wanted that." Wise wasn't Jones's first choice. He was wait-listed at the University of Virginia's main campus but was guaranteed admission if he went to UVA-Wise for one year. The ease in getting involved and taking on leadership roles at Wise persuaded Jones to stay put. Plan B turned out better than Plan A.

When Plan B Is a Better Fit

When we don't get into a first-choice school, it takes time, sometimes years, to get over the pain from being rejected. But we do get over it—and often we find the right fit in unexpected places.

"You want to feel like you're sending your child off to somewhere really good, and you get into your head that only these twenty schools meet that criteria," Catherine, a parent, told me when we first met over Zoom. For Catherine, that list of twenty schools was shaped by her own college experience (she graduated from Williams College), her husband's (he went to Vanderbilt University), and her son's competitive high school in New York, where people talked nonstop about Ivy-plus ambitions.

But when her son Ethan's college rejections started to arrive, Catherine realized—albeit slowly at first—that the right fit needed to go beyond No. 12 on the *U.S. News* list. That was the ranking in 2022 for the University of Chicago, which rejected Ethan in early decision. "I knew in my head that the idea these schools were the only good ones was false," she said. "Like, I knew that intellectually. But I needed to do some more work on the emotional side to really convince myself that that was the case and that really there's a much wider range of schools out there."

Ethan told me he wanted college to "challenge" him and surround him with people who would do the same. He thought that place was a small or midsized campus, like the University of Chicago, with 7,400 undergraduates. Or if not, Vanderbilt. Or if not, Georgetown. Or if not, Claremont McKenna. It turned out to be none of those schools. After the ED rejection came in from Chicago, Ethan was denied admission to three other schools in regular decision. Ethan's backup plan, the University of Texas at Austin, ended up being everything those places mostly weren't: big, public, and in the South. And at No. 32 in the rankings, it was hardly a consolation prize at all. Indeed, I'm not telling you Ethan's story here so you might feel sorry for him that he's at UT. You probably don't. While UT was Plan B for Ethan, for many other seniors each year it's their top choice by far.

Here's why I found his story compelling: After I met Ethan at the end of his sophomore year at UT, he confessed that his approach to choosing a college was flawed. He had equated fit with the prestige of private, brand-name colleges, thinking they'd offer the challenges and the respect for achievement he craved. He limited his focus to academics, overlooking the other aspects of college life and the local community—thinking that the outcomes of his college experience would emanate solely from his academic pursuits.

Two years after enrolling, Ethan's perspective on fit has evolved significantly. He now sees that it is way more complex than he initially thought. He recognizes that most students at UT are deeply committed academically. And he's surprised and delighted by something he hadn't even looked for: the impact of "shouting for this school"—in a football stadium on a Saturday afternoon with 100,000-plus fans—on his sense of belonging.

Austin's rich array of cultural offerings, from jazz clubs to expansive parks, has made him feel at home, too. Even within his major of international relations he has discovered a range of specialties, such as national security, human rights, and Latin American studies, adding layers he'd never considered to his academic experience. And on the political front, Ethan, who describes himself as moderate, doesn't feel he's always trying to mute himself in classes given the more conservative voices that UT attracts.

When I interviewed other students like Ethan, they, too, talked about gaining a more nuanced understanding of what makes a good college fit after enrolling at a Plan B. They'd latched on to brand names at first because those seemed vaguely dependable. But after the search was over, once they set foot on campus, they came to care less about how they could trade on their degree in the outside world and more about how the college experience was transforming them on the inside. As time went on, a sole focus on academic fit seemed stifling. And progressing through their undergraduate years, they felt freed from that focus—and less stressed, and happier. They settled in and explored other domains of belonging.

They also realized that belonging changes over time. "You don't really know who you are when you're eighteen years old," Ethan told me.

As these students matured, many saw that where they landed suited them well. On balance, they fared better than kids who got into their first choice. In *The Real World of College*, which I mentioned in Chapter 5, Wendy Fischman and Howard Gardner found that, over the course of four years, students at the most selective schools experienced a larger decline in their sense of belonging—in relation to their peers and to the institution—than those at schools lower on the selectivity scale. Prestige meant everything to these high-achieving students when they were seniors in high school. Eventually, though, the luster wears off.

CHAPTER 9

THE DOOM LOOP OF COLLEGE FINANCES

How to Make Sure a College Will Continue to Have the Dollars to Invest in You

When Birmingham-Southern College was selected as one of forty schools in *Colleges That Change Lives*, in 1996, administrators saw an opportunity: The designation in this high-profile list could accelerate the Alabama school's rise to the ranks of nationally known liberal arts institutions. As the best-selling book—written by a former *New York Times* education editor, Loren Pope—became a seminal guide for generations of college counselors and parents, Birmingham-Southern rode the wave of its newfound popularity.

Over the following decade, the school moved its athletics teams to the big time in Division I. Its endowment ballooned to $114 million, enrollment grew to 1,500, and leaders spent lavishly on the 190-acre campus. They added state-of-the-art buildings—a science center, dorms, sports facilities—and took on significant debt in the process.

G. David Pollick, the college's president at the time, described the prevailing mindset like this: "If dirt isn't flying on campus, you're losing a lot of advantage."

All signs of progress on the surface, however, concealed troubles bubbling below. Moving sports to Division I resulted in a $6 million deficit. Rosy enrollment projections, fueled in part by inclusion in *Colleges That Change Lives*, never came to fruition. By 2010, mistakes in the awarding of financial aid, major accounting errors, and too much spending from the endowment led to massive budget cuts. Moody's Investors Service downgraded the college's credit rating six times, eventually relegating its debt to "junk bond" status.

In 2011, a retired Marine with virtually no higher-education experience was brought in as president to stanch the bleeding, but it continued. Each year, though the sticker price went up, the college offered prospective students bigger and bigger discounts to fill seats in classrooms and beds in dorms. But the college kept losing more money: Those discounts were paid by forgoing revenue, and not from its endowment, which was shrinking nonetheless. The college operated with a deficit nearly every year. With less money to invest in marketing, recruitment, student advising, and career services, the school brought in fewer new students, and many of those who enrolled ended up transferring.

By the time the Covid pandemic hit in 2020, Birmingham-Southern was on life support. Federal aid to colleges nationwide extended a lifeline, but in March 2024, after the Alabama state treasurer twice denied what would have been an unusual loan to a private school, the college announced it was closing at the end of the academic year. Its enrollment had dwindled to around 700 students—who then had to scramble to find a new home within a few months.

Right up until the end, Birmingham-Southern was featured in *Colleges That Change Lives*, which over the years expanded into an organization that hosted college fairs and a website that touted the benefits of the small liberal arts schools profiled in the book. The recurring listing gave prospective students the impression that everything was okay, even though the school was stuck in a spiraling doom loop. Sure, Birmingham-Southern's financial troubles were covered extensively in the press, but how were families supposed to distinguish between a school that was simply struggling and one about to go out of business?

Today, Birmingham-Southern stands as a warning to students, families, and counselors: Buyer beware. The problem is that the finances of a typical school aren't usually as well-known as Birmingham-Southern's. They remain obscured by a thicket of reporting requirements that can be tough for the most seasoned accountants to navigate. Even if you're able to peek at a college's balance sheet, it probably won't show what matters most to you as an applicant: Does this school have the financial wherewithal to invest in your undergraduate experience?

When we talk about money and college, we tend to talk about *our* finances, not those of the colleges we're considering. We never needed the latter discussion before the Great Recession of 2008, when a decline in undergraduate enrollment and an uptick in college closures cast a shadow over the higher-education landscape.

In 2013, a study by the consulting firm Bain & Company found that one-third of colleges were on an "unsustainable financial path." A decade later, a follow-up report by Bain painted a darkening picture, concluding that the number of schools in "precarious financial positions" had increased from about 17 percent of the market to 29 percent in the previous ten years. Making matters worse for many colleges is a demographic downturn that portends a steep drop in the number of high school graduates in the latter half of the 2020s. Bottom line: Schools don't have much time to improve their balance sheets before there are fewer eighteen-year-olds to recruit.

When you're looking at a school, you need to familiarize yourself with signs of fiscal distress hiding in plain sight. This chapter isn't designed to make you a financial wizard capable of dissecting university ledgers. Rather, it explores critical questions that help determine whether a college can deliver on promises made in glossy brochures and well-crafted campus tours: Why is a college's revenue as important as securing a substantial tuition discount? Can the endowment withstand lean times? And what does the school's mix of academic programs tell you about the sustainability of your own major?

The first thing to know is that while college closures generate headlines, what happened to Birmingham-Southern remains unusual. It's hard to put a college out of business. Since 2000, only 136 schools have closed—about 6 percent of the total number of four-year colleges. And while the trend has accelerated since the pandemic, as enrollment across higher education fell by more than 1.3 million students, we're not going to see hundreds of colleges close anytime soon.

Experts in higher-education finance predict if the worst-case scenarios come to pass, an additional 80 schools will close *each year* over the next decade, about double the annual average over the past one. An equal number will merge or be taken over by stronger players. Most of these campuses will be either private colleges with fewer than 1,000 students, unable to operate at that tiny scale, or smaller regional public universities with a limited recruiting reach beyond their home state.

What's more likely for many colleges is that business as usual continues, with this as the most probable scenario: They focus cuts on low-enrollment academic programs with faculty who aren't tenured or are near retirement. We've already seen this at the University of Montana, West Virginia University, and the University of North Carolina Greensboro, all of which have slashed majors, mainly in the foreign languages and the humanities. It's a blueprint for modest change that more colleges will follow in the decade ahead.

Then one of two things will happen. The college rebounds and invests its savings in previously under-resourced areas and perhaps even expands. Or, more likely, they'll continue to limp along because the cuts they've made won't solve their long-term problems. They'll eventually resemble malls with vacant stores—bringing in just enough money to keep going, but not enough to maintain their buildings, pay competitive wages, or, more important, provide the kinds of services (in academic advising, the career center, and elsewhere) that add up to a good student experience.

Their Net Revenue *vs. Your Net* Price

There was a time when Birmingham-Southern might have been a turnaround story. In March 2014, Moody's upgraded the college's debt, citing a strong fundraising campaign that brought in nearly $16 million. Even so, the debt was still considered below investment grade, and the Moody's analyst issued this warning "Serious challenges remain including stagnant net tuition revenue." A year later, in another Moody's report, analysts noted that while a larger entering class increased enrollment by 13 percent, "the discount rate continues to move upward, limiting net revenue growth."

So how can a college increase enrollment but still bring in less of the revenue needed to spend on those students? Let me explain. Most colleges operate like a typical business—your neighborhood hair salon or coffee shop—where cash is king. Only 140 colleges have endowments over a billion dollars, and some of those spin off enough cash *each year* to cover a quarter to a third of the university's annual budget. That helps pay for generous scholarships and star professors. Some 40 percent of Harvard's annual budget comes from its $50 billion endowment. At Princeton, the endowment contributes $1.6 billion *each* year to the bottom line, which covers, among other things, *all* costs for students whose families earn less than $100,000.

But outside of a small set of very wealthy institutions, the scholarships you're likely to get are what Moody's calls "unsponsored discounts." Most colleges, unlike Harvard and Princeton, don't have the money sitting in a pot somewhere to pay for their merit-based awards. Their scholarships are more like "Kohl's Cash." Schools are simply saying, "Our sticker price says we charge $80,000 all in, but we're going to give you a $30,000 presidential scholarship." For other students it might be a $25,000 or $35,000 coupon that comes with another special-sounding scholarship name attached to it. This pricing strategy is more akin to a hair salon offering 10 percent off for new customers or that coffee shop giving you a punch card to get your tenth cup free. It's an incentive—but it doesn't make money appear from thin air.

The money that *is* real is the school's *net revenue*: the difference between what the sticker price would have brought in, in an ideal world, and the discounts given:

Sticker Price × Enrollment = Total tuition - Discounts = Net Revenue

According to a 2024 Moody's analysis, net revenue is falling at 36 percent of private colleges and 27 percent of public universities. Why is that? The two key levers colleges can pull to lift their net revenue are both stuck. One is government assistance. But only low-income students are eligible for Pell Grants (which max out at $7,395 a year), and any undergraduate who borrows from the federal government is limited to $31,000 in loans over four years. The second lever is you. But after decades of being asked to pay more out of pocket, take out their own loans, borrow against retirement, and dip deeper into other savings, most families have had it and want to pay as little as they can—unless they're stretching their finances to pay for a brand name.

While that hunt for lower prices is utterly understandable, it might also be reinforcing the financial doom loop that many colleges can't seem to escape. Here is why: The *net price* you pay includes the government assistance that you're eligible for. Remember, that aid has a hard cap. With pressure to keep giving you a better deal year after year, the only choice colleges are left with is to keep cutting into their revenue with bigger discounts to you.

The CFO of a small liberal arts school told me that each year its freshmen contribute *less* toward net revenue than the previous incoming class. His only hope to generate additional revenues is through higher charges for room and board. That's why many private colleges require you to live on campus—they turn a profit on your living expenses that subsidizes other operations and services. Colleges that guarantee housing also see that as a differentiator. Fast-growing public universities usually can't put students up for all four years, leaving families to navigate the whims of local landlords and rental markets.

I'm saying this not to steer you toward a college with a higher net price but, rather, to clarify how college finances actually work. It's a system that defies logic. The CFO of that small liberal arts college likened its pricing strategy to the discounts a Four Seasons resort offers off its rack rate (the top, nondiscounted price for its rooms). Everyone wants a deal on what they consider a luxury brand, he said, including parents of college kids. The problem with that comparison is that the Four Seasons has enough people paying the rack rate to hire top-notch staff, buy fresh flowers for the lobby every day, and keep the grounds from looking stale. When basically everyone gets an unfunded discount at a college, the student experience will suffer, the Four Seasons will become the Days Inn, and parents won't realize it until their kid is already on campus.

Good Deals, Troubled Finances

"Most of the schools that give the best merit are in financial straits," Ann told me matter-of-factly when we first met. A mother of three and a vice president of digital marketing in the Northeast, Ann had been researching colleges for her children since they were in middle school. She and her husband, a teacher, make around $270,000 a year; with three kids in college at the same time, securing the lowest net price for each was crucial.

Ann graduated from Colby College, ranked among the top 25 liberal arts colleges nationally by *U.S. News*. But her kids were interested in professional degrees—in engineering, environmental science, and biology—so her alma mater didn't appeal to them, even if it might provide a strong foundation for graduate programs or jobs later. It was a big stretch financially anyway. Having spent considerable time following discussions in the Paying for College 101 Facebook group, Ann knew that selective colleges like Colby mostly give out need-based aid. While such schools are generous with that money, the changing formula for FAFSA (Free Application for Federal Student Aid) would no longer give a boost to families like hers, with multiple children in college at the same time. "Merit aid was more predictable," she said.

As we talk now, with all three of her kids in college, Ann pulls up the spreadsheets she created for their college searches. They have multiple tabs, labeled by month and year, showing how each child's academic stats and their college lists evolved throughout high school. My eyes immediately focus on the categories across the top. The column headers include GPA and test-score ranges for accepted students, application deadlines, retention and graduation rates, percentages of students who stay on campus on weekends, internship and job placement links, average salaries of graduates, and so on. There are nearly fifty columns in all, filled with information from various sources, including *U.S. News*, Niche, and the Common Data Set.

The spreadsheet illustrates how awash we are in college data—and how challenging it is for families to figure out what's most meaningful. As I lean in to look more closely, Ann seems taken aback by my curiosity. "I stopped really going into detail because people get anxious and irritable," she says.

Ann then directs my attention to one column in particular, for net price. She explains how she used the net-price calculator on college websites. The calculators that asked for academic stats were more helpful than those that didn't, she says, because the number they eventually spit out was more likely to include merit aid. (Tip: Take screenshots when using these tools so you can easily refer to the estimates.) Alongside the net prices she calculated with and without academic stats, Ann included a column for actual financial offers that arrived later on with admissions offers.

Here's a look at that section of one of her kids' spreadsheets:

"We set a target of what we could afford to pay," Ann tells me. "In-

School	Net Price Calculator (school didn't ask for academic stats	Net Price Calculator (academic stats entered)	Net Price (as listed on financial aid offer with acceptance)
University of Vermont		$33,974	$28,117
University of New Hampshire		$38,332	$24,276
Clark University		$31,800	$31,720
UMass-Lowell		$23,741	$23,227
Syracuse University	$37,196		Waitlisted
UMass-Amherst	$28,573		$33,478
Colby College	$21,000		Waitlisted
Northeastern University	$34,392		Deferred
Worcester Polytechnic Institute	$35,731		$34,529

itially, we were hoping for $25,000 a year, per kid," she says, pausing. "But as I ran some of the calculators, $35,000 was more realistic."

Scanning one of her daughter's spreadsheets, I notice that just two of the figures from the net-price calculators are below Ann's initial target of $25,000. Then I quickly click through the other spreadsheets to see how the final awards compare with early calculations: Less than a quarter of the eighteen schools her three kids applied to extended an offer within $1,000 of the estimate.

Why is that important? Cost is a significant factor for most American families deciding on colleges. The net-price calculator is supposed to tell you what a school is likely to cost. But if that number is off by, say, $5,000 a year, as it was at the University of Massachusetts at Amherst for one of Ann's kids, how helpful is it? With estimates that rough, you might take certain pricey schools out of the running, although in Ann's case, a couple of those ended up being much *less* expensive than what she originally calculated.

That's why families don't immediately eliminate schools based on price. We're told throughout the college search that schools are more affordable than we think—we just need to wait a few months until financial-aid packages arrive. So teenagers fall in love with campuses only to discover later that those are out of reach financially.

By setting a price limit, as Ann did with her kids, you can shape the list of options, much as you do when buying a house or a car and letting what you can afford determine which neighborhoods you visit or which dealer lots you roam. Ann's kids were given a boundary. They knew that some highly ranked private schools, such as Providence College, were off-limits pricewise, as were some out-of-state public universities.

As I study Ann's spreadsheets, I ask if she wishes she included any other information, now that her kids are *in* college. "The financial viability of the college," she says. "But that's really hard to figure out."

One of her kids ended up at a small school that was subject to increased financial oversight by the federal government because of concerns that it might run out of money. Another enrolled at Clarkson University, and during their sophomore year, the school announced cuts to several liberal arts programs, in part to close a reported $7 million deficit. The same year, Moody's revised its outlook for Clarkson to negative. The analyst noted the school's "steadily rising discount rate and softening net tuition per student," market troubles that "add significant obstacles to sustainably returning to fiscal balance." Elsewhere in the report, Moody's warned of a "rising age of plant" and "reliance on supplemental endowment draws." Translation: Older buildings will need upkeep and the college is already dipping into its endowment for extra cash.

The week I met up with Ann, a headline on *The Washington Post*'s home page, "Colleges Are Now Closing at a Pace of One a Week," caught my attention. I asked Ann if she was worried about her own kids' colleges shutting down. She shook her head. What concerned her more was whether the schools could keep up with better-resourced institutions or would just fall further behind year after year as they brought in less and less revenue. The small school one daughter attends had contaminated water because of old pipes, and a few professors left after her first year. At Clarkson, the situation is "less severe," but still Ann is worried that funds for student clubs might be cut. The dorms are also in "tough shape," she admitted.

Might her family have made the same decisions if they'd known more up front about each school's financial outlook? She can't say for sure. But it would have been helpful to balance that information against her desire to get a good deal.

Ways to Measure a School's Financial Health

When buying a house, we can order an inspection to know what we're getting into financially. There isn't a similar process for choosing colleges whose degrees will hold their value, even though we want them to have staying power. So we're left trying to read market signals that are often ambiguous and difficult to fully understand.

No single indicator of financial well-being puts a college on stable ground, just as no single academic accomplishment ensures an applicant's acceptance. In my conversations with CFOs of different types of colleges, they talked about many factors that can make a difference—where a college sits in the higher-ed pecking order, the size of the institution, its location, and its student profile. But the question I kept coming back to was this: If *their* kid were applying to some other college, how would they assess its financial health? That is, what numbers would they look for, and where?

That framing sharpened their focus and mine. Their insights as administrators and parents—and my own observations from being in boardrooms and on college campuses for nearly three decades—pointed me toward three key sets of metrics:

1. BOND-RATING REPORTS, WHEN YOU CAN GET THEM

The best way to determine how a school is doing financially—beyond getting access to internal balance sheets and budgets—is to look at its bond-rating reports. Three major agencies rate colleges: Moody's, Standard & Poor's, and Fitch. Most of the underlying information is publicly disclosed on the agencies' websites, although access to the reports often requires a subscription.

Ratings actions from Moody's land in my email inbox almost daily. Much like credit reports for people, bond ratings assess the risk of lending money to the school. While individual borrowers receive a credit score, colleges are assigned a letter or letter/number combination. For families looking at colleges, the actual rating is less important—as long as it isn't in the territory of junk bond status—than the larger outlook (positive, stable, or negative) and the narrative around it. There you can find clues about issues you might want to check out, like a pattern of deficit spending or an aging campus.

Analysts for the ratings agencies are like financial detectives, and I was curious to hear how they go about their investigations. One September morning, I met up with Susan Fitzgerald from Moody's. We were both in Denver at a conference about public-private partnerships in higher education. These partnerships are a popular way for colleges to acquire capital to start new projects as well as offset the costs and risks of ongoing operations. The most common type of partnership is one that directly affects your bill and your campus experience: Colleges are increasingly using private developers to construct and manage residence halls on school land. According to a 2023 article in *The Wall Street Journal*, housing is "one of the biggest drivers of rising college prices," jumping 45 percent since 2002. While schools "often boast of keeping tuition in check as a sign they're sensitive to students' financial concerns," the *Journal* pointed out, "they rarely rein in costs for living on campus."

Moody's and the other agencies study every bit of data a college generates as it does business—for instance, its selectivity and yield (to determine popularity among students), its revenue mix from different sources, its fundraising numbers, and how much cash the school has on hand. Fitzgerald oversees the higher-education practice at Moody's, where she has worked for more than two decades. Because nearly every Moody's report I read mentions "net-tuition revenue," I asked Fitzgerald about its significance. She told me it was one of the most significant pieces of information they collect. "Many colleges have hit their peak on tuition revenue." While college leaders will tell Moody's analysts about plans to raise revenues, whether from alumni donations or from real estate deals (Ohio State once sold its parking garages to generate $483 million), those strategies are often more aspirational than grounded in reality.

Since 2019, at least a quarter of private colleges and half of public universities rated by Moody's have seen their net-tuition revenue grow less than 4 percent annually—pretty anemic, given the inflation rates and the ever-rising list price of tuition. If you're considering a college that has year-over-year declines in net-tuition revenue or even if it remains flat for an extended period of seven to ten years, that's cause for concern, especially at a school struggling on other financial fronts.

Take, for example, Muhlenberg College in Pennsylvania, to which Moody's assigned a negative outlook in April 2024, explaining, "Net tuition revenue will decline for the seventh consecutive year . . . contributing to a materially deeper operating deficit." Or John Carroll University in Ohio, which had its outlook changed to negative, with an "enrollment decline of 14% between fall 2019 and fall 2023 . . . [that] has contributed to declining net tuition revenue and deepening budget deficits."

But net tuition doesn't always tell the whole story about a college's financial health. Consider Northeastern Illinois University, which Moody's classified as "stable" in 2023. Despite "multiple years of declines in enrollment and net tuition revenue," the analyst assigned a positive outlook of funding from the state. This is where public universities hold an advantage over private colleges. Despite giving a lot less to colleges now than in the past, states can be a stabilizing force.

Even though bond ratings aren't meant for prospective students and their families, they are quite helpful when a school has been rated recently and you can get the report. That's not as easy as you might think, however. Combined, the three ratings agencies evaluate fewer than 1,000 colleges. Many smaller colleges borrow from local banks and never seek ratings.

If you can't find a rating report, there are two other ways to gauge a school's revenue trajectory. One using the school's Common Data Set (CDS) requires some calculations as seen in *Figure 9.1*. The second way requires fewer calculations but isn't always as precise: Look up the college at the Federal Audit Clearinghouse (fac.gov). Search for "Student Related Revenues" on several years of audits to get a sense of the trends of tuition dollars actually coming in from students. The audits also provide context: In the notes, college leaders can explain significant changes in revenues or expenses, shedding light on their financial strategy or looming problems. These financial records can reveal warning signs that should give you pause. Multiple years of persistent deficits are a red flag—for example, Drew University in New Jersey, Elmira College in New York, and Golden Gate University in California have all posted annual losses for *eight* consecutive years, as have thirteen campuses in the State University System of New York. Another concerning pattern emerges when institutions make increasingly large withdrawals from their endowments year after year to fund daily operations, as seen at Willamette University in Oregon, the University of Hartford, and Wittenberg University in Ohio. No one indicator propels a college into the financial doom loop, but when these factors pile up, they warrant careful consideration before you enroll.

Figure 9.1

Firm Financial Footing

To find out if a school has the money needed to invest in you, look at its net revenue coming from tuition and fees over a few years to be sure it's not falling precipitously. You can do that by searching for its Common Data Set online. Here's how to calculate net tuition revenue for one year using Worcester Polytechnic Institute as an example. Copy this formula for multiple years:

In section H, tally up the institutional aid, both need-based and not.

	Need-based	Non-need-based
	(Include non-need-based aid use to meet need.)	(Exclude non-need-based aid use to meet need.)
Scholarships/Grants		
Institutional: Endowed scholarships, annual gifts and tuition funded grants, awarded by the college, excluding athletic aid and tuition waivers (which are reported below).	$74,100,153	$53,790,160

Total institutional aid: $127,890,313

In section B1, find the total number of degree-seeking undergraduate students.

B1.   Institutional Enrollment: Provide numbers of students for each of the following categories as of the institution's official fall reporting date.

	FULL-TIME		PART-TIME		
	Men	Women	Men	Women	TOTAL
Total degree-seeking undergraduate students	3,416	1,829	73	26	5,344

Total number of undergraduate students: 5,344

Divide the total in institutional aid by the total number of students. That's the average discount. *Average discount: $23,931*

In section G1, look up total tuition (and any required fees). **Subtract the average discount from that number to calculate net tuition revenue per student.**

	FIRST-YEAR	UNDERGRADUATES
PRIVATE INSTITUTION		
Tuition:	$57,960	$57,960
FOR ALL INSTITUTIONS		
Required Fees	$1,110	$910

Approximate net tuition revenue per student: $34,939

2. ENROLLMENT AND ENDOWMENT DATA, WITH CAVEATS

As a prospective student, you're working within a short *and* long time horizon. Most immediately, you want to find a school that has resources to invest in you while you are there so you can thrive at college and graduate on time. Looking ahead, you should also pick a place with a decent financial outlook over the coming decades so your degree will retain its value and continue to pay off throughout your career.

There are tools to help you do both, created in recent years by news outlets and consulting firms. *The Hechinger Report* has a "financial fitness tracker." *Forbes* gives colleges "financial grades." *Bloomberg News* has analyzed the finances of small colleges. Bain & Company has an interactive tool (which I worked on) that gauges a college's "financial resilience." Together, such resources can make the current and future viability of a given institution a bit less murky. They use different publicly available datasets from varying periods, so they're not always consistent in what they conclude about a particular school. If you turn to them for information rather than answers, though, they provide useful perspective.

These tools have one essential data point in common: They look at what's happening with enrollment, and so should you. The best-run colleges typically (unless they're trying to grow) have steady student numbers from year to year. Falling enrollment over a three- to five-year period is a worrisome sign, particularly if the school hasn't announced any plans to shrink. That said, the higher-ed market has been volatile lately, and now campuses are bracing for a decade-long decline in the number of high school graduates.

In the future, few institutions will be able to manage their student numbers as well as they did in the past. Still, you want some assurance that the school you're considering has enough cash in reserve to keep things running if enrollment slips.

Colleges rely on two kinds of "savings." First, they plan their annual budget with a margin—essentially a profit goal—that is usually around 3 percent of the total. Yes, colleges are nonprofit organizations, but this built-in surplus often works like a contingency fund, to be tapped if the school doesn't hit its enrollment numbers or if expenses come in higher than anticipated. If they end up not using the money, the dollars go into their endowment, or into cash reserves, or are spent on campus maintenance.

Bond-rating agencies like surpluses. Fitzgerald of Moody's told me she doesn't "look for any specific margin," but added, "the higher the margin, the stronger the rating, because it speaks to the strength of the business model." Most schools are not racking up huge surpluses one year after another, although certain exceptions come to mind. Take Harvard: When it announced a $114 million surplus at the end of 2017, officials described it as a "high-water mark for the foreseeable future." Then just a year later it announced another surplus of more than $196 million. In its 2023 analysis, Moody's found that the average operating margin for the 229 private universities studied was 5.8 percent. Margins ranged, on average, from 2.5 percent at schools with the lowest bond ratings to 11.7 percent at those with the highest. As you conduct your college search, you're not looking for a particular margin, but you definitely want to watch out for places where deficit spending has become a regular practice.

The other kind of savings that colleges use to manage risk—their endowment—is trickier for families to assess. One of the reasons is that part of the endowment is "restricted" by those who donated the money—meaning school leaders can't use it as a rainy-day fund (the audit will note which portion is restricted versus nonrestricted). Colleges typically spend around 4 percent of their endowment annually. If a school regularly spends more than that—whether to cover ongoing expenses or to make large withdrawals for new projects—it's a red flag.

Another consideration is endowment size. While total size gets the most attention (look at the tens of billions Harvard has!) the amount available per student might be a better metric for our purposes. Some small colleges have an edge here because they can spread out a lot of money over very few students. For example, Grinnell's endowment per student is an enviable $1.4 million. Bigger, better-known schools, like

New York University, have larger overall endowments, but in NYU's case it amounts to only $90,000 per student.

High endowment numbers are a proxy for alumni loyalty and brand strength. At a billion dollars total, a college is probably safe. Most endowment wealth, nearly 80 percent of it, is concentrated among just 3 percent of nonprofit colleges. It's tough, then, to set a minimum for endowment per student. As a guide, you could use the average per student across all college endowments, which is $219,000, but even that is a slippery figure.

Endowment is just one indicator, so try not to overthink it. Here's what I suggest, based on my interviews with experts: Among the colleges on your list, sort by total endowment and endowment per student. If all other things are equal in the end, favor those with higher numbers in both categories because they'll have the resources to weather financial storms and to provide extras in the undergraduate experience.

3. A MIX OF MAJORS WITH HEALTHY STUDENT ENROLLMENTS

Remember General Motors in its heyday? It had multiple brands—Pontiac, Oldsmobile, Chevrolet, Cadillac—each with its own long list of models. That let's-do-it-all product strategy once fueled GM's dominance in the auto market. Retailers took a similar approach when the internet freed them from the space constraints of physical stores; they shifted toward personalization in their desire to please everyone.

Colleges are no different. In their marketing, they often tout a high number of majors and minors as a feature rather than a bug. The volume of options can be overwhelming, though, and it doesn't always inspire confidence in quality. Sure, you want access to several majors that interest you in case you decide to switch at some point. But frequently colleges support many majors with very few students in them, often at a steep cost that the schools themselves don't recognize.

Rick Staisloff, a higher-ed consultant, studies the mix of academic programs at colleges. He previously served as chief financial officer at a college and as a financial analyst for Maryland's higher-education commission. Over lunch in Annapolis one day, he put a chart in front of me showing enrollments by major at a school he'd recently advised. The college had sixty-seven undergraduate majors for 3,000 students. As I looked at the chart, I immediately noticed what Staisloff was about to explain: Half the students were enrolled in just ten majors, and the rest were spread out over the other fifty-seven. Such a high concentration of students in just a few programs isn't peculiar to this school, according to Staisloff. Nationwide, at least 50 percent of students at both public and private colleges completed their degrees in the ten largest programs. The model that's an outlier is the large public flagship institution, like Penn State, University of Nebraska, or University of Colorado, for example. In that type of school, we see a much wider array of well-populated majors: 53 percent of the degrees awarded are spread across an average of seventy-two programs.

The U.S. Department of Education's College Navigator website (nces.ed.gov/collegenavigator) lists the number of degrees awarded by year and program. From those annual numbers, you could infer program sizes over four years. "You'll never see on a college's website that these are our top programs by number of students," Staisloff told me. "Although if a student asked, it's not a difficult thing for an institution to tell you." And you should ask, because enrolling in a small major can be risky. For starters, small programs might offer required courses infrequently and not necessarily when you want them, so you might not (without waivers) get the classes you need to graduate in four years. What's more, smaller majors are prime candidates for cutting if a school needs to trim expenses. There are exceptions, of course. If a tiny program has a strong national reputation, it's much less likely to be eliminated. Some small majors, particularly in the liberal arts, serve dual purposes in that they provide required introductory courses for a college's core curriculum. Unless the core changes, those majors will probably remain.

Even new programs can be superfluous. Colleges love adding majors and minors to signal that they're keeping up with trends in the job market, in hopes of attracting new students and increasing revenue. Not every new program succeeds, and yet many colleges are loath to let them go. An analysis a decade ago by Lightcast, the labor-market analytics firm, found that roughly half of new majors have five or fewer graduates four or five years after they're introduced—just when you'd think larger classes would be cycling through. And get this: Nearly one-third of those new programs reported *zero* graduates five years after they were introduced.

Headlines suggest that schools are beginning to cut majors with low enrollments and will continue to do so. I asked Staisloff why colleges have kept them around. The problem, he said, is that, unlike a retailer or an automaker that can tell you which products are profit centers and which ones lose money, most colleges don't know which majors generate a surplus, or break even, or need to be subsidized by other departments. "The real kicker is that most institutions don't even look at revenue by department or program," he said. That makes it difficult for colleges to figure out where to cut if their overall revenues can no longer support the assortment of majors.

In my effort to sort signals from noise in the world of college finances, I visited one more place—this one a bit unexpected: a small private airfield in Schaumburg, Illinois, not far from Chicago. A few months earlier, Wells College in upstate New York had announced it was going out of business. I noted on social media that Wells had been recruiting students for the following fall right up to the very end. Despite some noise about the troubles Wells was in, the school—much like Birmingham-Southern—hadn't sent clear signals that the end was close.

I waited near the main building of the airport and, at the appointed time, saw Doug Moore emerge from behind his Cirrus SR20 single-prop plane. After posting about Wells on social media, I'd come to know Moore—and nicknamed him "The College Closer." For years, he'd led the closure of industrial sites, until one day, a subcontractor mistakenly opened a gas line. "It nearly killed me," Moore told me. Right around that time, he saw a presentation about the coming demographic cliff in higher education. Then someone asked him to help close a college in Iowa. The college work has only picked up since and is now his full-time gig.

Moore is hired by secured lenders who want to recoup some of their money. He usually gets the call ninety days before closure, when it's too late to save the school. "The die is cast, and it becomes a self-fulfilling prophecy as the media begins to pay attention," he said. I'd told him over the phone that I was writing this book. Now, as we stood on the tarmac, I asked him what he saw as the signs of a distressed college. He rattled off several—not paying vendors, borrowing against the endowment, constant changes in leaders, and others already mentioned in this chapter. He then mentioned one more that surprised me: a high percentage of students playing sports.

The outside bet that struggling colleges are making is adding athletic teams—especially niche ones—to boost enrollment. Division III schools in particular are falling into this trap. They aren't allowed to offer sports scholarships, but plenty of students still want to play and aren't good enough to play at the Division I level. That's who these schools court. Overall athletic participation is growing in college, with Division III seeing the largest growth, adding more than 17,000 athletes in 2022–23 alone.

Adrian College, a liberal arts school in Michigan, has more than doubled its enrollment to 1,600 over the last fifteen years by adding more than thirty sports teams, including synchronized ice skating, bass fishing, and varsity cornhole. Today, 70 percent of the student body are athletes. Fairleigh Dickinson University in New Jersey added two sports after school leaders brought in an outside economist to show that athletics should be judged not only on the costs but also on the potential to drive net-tuition revenue. But as Moore noted, because most schools don't closely track revenue and expenses by program, they can't accurately say how much more tuition money they could net by offering football or field hockey. Nor can they sustain this strategy for growth. "There are only so many sports you can add," Moore observed. "And then what do you do?"

So yes, look at the net-tuition revenue, read over an audit, or track down a bond-rating report for the college you're thinking about spending a few hundred thousand on over the next several years. And then take a minute to see how big the sports programs have become relative to the size of the college. Do athletes make up 60 percent of the student body? Has the college added numerous new teams in recent years? That may not be the sign of strength it seems at first glance. It's sometimes a last-ditch effort to get a few more students to enroll and pay a discounted tuition bill.

As I stood on the airport tarmac thinking about how these hidden aspects of college finances shape the experience for so many students, Moore headed back to his plane. He was off for another visit to another college on the brink of closure.

CHAPTER 10

BETTER THAN AVERAGE

Making Sure the Degree Pays Off

One night during her sophomore year of high school, Katelynn and her dad, Jake, were hanging out in their living room talking about nothing much when the topic of college came up. Katelynn was the oldest of three kids. Jake knew her college search would begin in earnest the following year.

"Where do you want to go?" he asked, somewhat rhetorically.

"Clemson," Katelynn answered, matter-of-factly.

Jake was taken aback. Why pick a public university hundreds of miles away from their New Jersey home when they had a perfectly good one close by?

"It's where all my friends want to go," she said. Then she pulled out her phone. Tilting it toward her dad, she scrolled through the Instagram pages that the senior classes at various local high schools had set up to announce students' college decisions. There were a smattering of Ivies, a healthy number of private colleges, a few in-state publics, and many Southern schools—including Tennessee, Auburn, and Clemson.

"Where your friends want to go is a very blunt tool to assess a college," Jake said, when we met a few years later. He hadn't expected his daughter to simply follow the pack without thinking about other options.

As Katelynn headed into junior year, Jake hoped to broaden her frame of reference, having learned from his own undergraduate days that sometimes, in the long run, you're better off straying from the crowd. Many of his high school friends had gone to Ivies. "Stanford, Penn, Yale, you name it," he told me. "The entire Top 10 Hall of Fame." Jake ended up at West Virginia University. "The words 'West Virginia' and 'elite' don't belong in the same sentence," he joked. But as he and his Ivy League peers swapped stories over the years, he discovered they'd missed out on some great opportunities. As a senior at WVU, he had worked as a teaching assistant and had helped a professor with his research. He wanted his daughter to consider a wider range of schools that might offer similar experiences.

So Jake got to work. The first thing he did was set a budget. Jake, a schoolteacher, and his wife netted around $170,000 a year between their jobs and her side gig as a tutor. With two more children to put through college, they had to be realistic in what they could afford. When he plugged the family's numbers into the net-price calculator on Clemson's website, the estimate it returned wasn't doable. "Look, we can't afford $60,000 a year," he told his daughter. While Katelynn acquiesced on Clemson, whenever she'd resist the financial realities of college costs or cling to notions of prestige during the search, Jake employed a well-honed parental tactic: conversations with his wife, within earshot of their daughter.

In the fall of junior year, Southern schools disappeared from Katelynn's list, replaced by a new fixation: selective private colleges. She and her family toured Holy Cross in Massachusetts and Franklin & Marshall in Pennsylvania. As Jake ran the net-price numbers, he wondered if these schools were really worth the money.

"Prestige doesn't always pay back returns on the investment," he said, "unless you have a career in finance or law." So, with cost still a crucial consideration, Jake began looking at another metric as well: earnings after graduation.

It's smart to think that far ahead as you're homing in on your dream school.

We covered return on investment (ROI) in Chapter 6, in the broader context of understanding higher ed as a long game. Now we'll revisit the topic by looking specifically at college outcomes and the financial forces that shape a degree's value.

Colleges typically use placement rates—percentages of alumni who start a job or go to grad school within six months of completing a bachelor's degree—to measure outcomes. In my survey, this was the top metric parents cited for choosing a good school. Nearly 90 percent deemed it an important factor. Yet when I asked in a follow-up question how assured they felt that a school could actually deliver on that promise for future grads, only 25 percent were "extremely" confident given what they'd seen during the college search. "Stop showing me the rock-climbing wall," one parent commented, "and convince me of the return on my tuition investment." This parent wanted a list of employers that actively recruited on campus, the number of job offers students in each major received, and average starting salaries. "This [information] can be accessed through careers services," the parent continued, "but it's not as readily available as it should be."

Increasingly, families are asking about graduates' earnings, and for good reason. But when we turn to rankings that track outcomes *only* (or even mainly) that way, we still get a skewed list of schools. Many of the usual brand-name institutions rise to the top, along with colleges that have a large concentration of high-paying majors, such as engineering and business. That's why you'll often see obscure schools—like Kettering University in Michigan, the Missouri University of Science and Technology, the Colorado School of Mines, and Bentley University—fare well on this measure. These college-wide metrics look great for places where almost all the students major in those fields. It's like comparing the average dinner bill at a steakhouse to a restaurant with a full menu. No surprise the steakhouse average is higher—they serve only one expensive thing. Highly selective schools also excel on earnings. The geographic location of a college can play a role, too, if many graduates go on to work in nearby cities with high costs of living and wages to match.

Often, then, rankings that heavily weight earnings closely mirror those in *U.S. News*, particularly in the top tier. Yet we know that companies hire graduates from all kinds of colleges. Recall the graphic on page 65 that showed hiring patterns for three Fortune 50 companies: Their hires came from schools that accepted fewer than 20 percent of applicants as well as those that accepted more than 80 percent.

So it's critical to look beyond the top schools in *any* list, rankings based on graduates' earnings included. As you do so, you'll undoubtedly have some questions about where to focus your attention. How else can you find colleges where graduates land good jobs with solid earnings? What are some signs that a school readies its students for a continually changing job market? How do employers hire new graduates, and what skills are they looking for?

This chapter outlines factors you should weigh to choose a school with lasting value and steps you can take as an undergraduate to steer *your* outcomes, no matter where you go. We'll focus mainly on jobs, not graduate school, since most new graduates head right into the workforce even if they go back to school later on.

Dive into the Data, but Don't Lose Perspective

Right after visiting Holy Cross with his daughter her junior year, Jake used the college's net-price calculator to determine what it would cost him. The result—around $41,000 a year—was on the "edge of what we could do." But when Jake ran the figures again before Katelynn's senior year that $41,000 figure suddenly jumped to north of $50,000. Why the difference? The value of their home had risen because houses were being scooped up in the neighborhood, thus according to Holy Cross, at least, Jake could afford to pay more now in tuition.

Jake didn't want to use his home's value as an ATM to pay for college, so Holy Cross would have to come off Katelynn's list. But he wanted to suggest a replacement—another midsized Jesuit college in the Northeast or Mid-Atlantic. He clicked his way through the government data on the College Scorecard website to see how Holy Cross stacked up against other Jesuit colleges on median earnings of graduates. On the Payscale website, he studied salary rankings by major. And he used the earnings projections posted by Georgetown's Center on Education and the Workforce to assess how its researchers measured the value of various schools' degrees.

As he dug into those stats, one unusual suspect kept jumping out in the results: Loyola University Maryland. Unlike Holy Cross, which was ranked among national liberal arts colleges in *U.S. News*, Loyola was relegated to the regional rankings. It accepted most students who applied, while Holy Cross was becoming more selective each year. But on overall earnings (the median across majors) within five years of graduation, Loyola wasn't far behind Holy Cross ($83,000 versus $90,000). It looked like a pretty good deal, especially when you considered that Loyola's net cost was some $8,000 lower *per year*. Loyola even bested Amherst College, a well-known and highly ranked liberal arts college, on earnings overall. When Jake searched for Maryland schools on Payscale, Loyola ranked No. 2 behind Johns Hopkins. Less than $2,000 separated their median earnings even *ten* years out of college.

Jake wanted to see salary figures for Katelynn's intended major (math), but the program had too few graduates each year at Loyola to be included in the College Scorecard (majors typically need to have at least ten graduates a year to be shown). On Payscale, the math major was lumped in with computer science. Loyola ranked in the top 100 on salaries for computer science twenty years after graduation, and above well-known schools, including the University of Michigan, Duke, and

UCLA. That wasn't a perfect window into earnings for math majors, but the *Wall Street Journal* rankings placed Loyola No. 23 nationally and No. 5 for career preparation. Together, these sources of information gave Jake some comfort that he was suggesting a reasonable alternative to Holy Cross.

Before we go on, let's review the key differences in the two sources that Jake consulted specifically on salary outcomes:

- **College Scorecard (collegescorecard.ed.gov):** As mentioned in Chapter 6, the Scorecard data come only from graduates who received federal aid. This is a government site made possible by matching Department of Education data about loans and grants with IRS records showing post-college earnings. Some of its calculations center on students who graduated in the previous five years, while others consider any student who entered the institution ten years earlier. So this tool has its limitations and inconsistencies. What's more, the Scorecard doesn't display occupational data by major (nor does it include all majors), so it's unclear whether people are employed in the field they studied.

- **Payscale (payscale.com/college-salary-report):** Drawing on a survey of more than 3 million college graduates, Payscale provides salary details about majors and occupations that the College Scorecard can't. Because the data are self-reported, however, results can be skewed because research has shown individuals who are satisfied with what they earn tend to inflate their pay.

The numbers Jake found on these two sites confirmed what his gut instinct—and his high school friends' experiences—had told him about the value of certain colleges. "Prestige, brand, and trending on social media kind of glosses over the particulars of a university's output when it comes to their students post-graduation," Jake said.

Right before her senior year of high school, Katelynn made her final campus visit, to Loyola. Meanwhile, her father combed through LinkedIn profiles of math majors from the various schools she was considering. He wanted to know where their graduates interned, worked, and went to graduate school. It's a task I'd recommend. Jake observed that Loyola's math graduates had jobs that weren't all that different from those of math grads from more prestigious institutions on his daughter's list. He also noted that the LinkedIn profiles of the Loyola alumni seemed more "polished and detailed." In his view, they outhustled the kids from elite schools. "In the end," he said, "LinkedIn helped me minimize the importance of prestige and ranking as factors in the college search."

By April, Katelynn had admissions and financial-aid offers in hand from Loyola, Binghamton University in New York, and Rutgers in New Jersey. With discounts, Loyola would cost Katelynn's family around $40,000 a year. The last week of April, however, as colleges nationwide were trying to solidify incoming classes before the traditional May 1 deposit deadline, Loyola offered Katelynn an additional $5,500 for her freshman year if she enrolled. With that coupon, Loyola would be the least expensive option left on her list, even with two public universities still in the mix. On the next to last day of April, Katelynn submitted her deposit to reserve a spot at Loyola.

If Katelynn had applied to college a decade earlier, her father couldn't have easily compared earnings across colleges and majors, and as a result Loyola might never have made her list. "If you go by brand name and word of mouth, it closes off so many hidden opportunities," Jake told me. "If I'd simply been a prestige-monger, we'd never have even looked at a place like Loyola, which turns out to have been perfect for my daughter."

Gone are the days when colleges relied largely on national averages to convey the value of a degree. Prospective students now have access to real, contextual data—and they need it, in light of today's staggering costs. How much graduates earn with a degree in, say, sociology from State U is a critical piece of information when families must take on tens of thousands of dollars in debt to pay for that education.

That said, as with all else in this book, you'll find no Easy Button here. While Jake managed to unearth a school that in some ways mirrored Holy Cross's outcomes, nothing is guaranteed, of course. Katelynn could change her major, graduate into a tough job market, or miss out on learning particular skills that would boost her starting salary (more on that below). In truth, Jake was doing what countless parents do: finding whatever evidence he could to support his hopes and budget. As he scrolled through the salary rankings and LinkedIn profiles, he found enough validation to feel good about his choices—even if that meant reinforcing his own biases.

How, then, should you use the various rankings and calculators about post-graduate salaries in your college search? Here's what I suggest: Use them, as Jake did, to find schools with similar outcomes to those at colleges that aren't affordable or the right fit—or to eliminate schools lower on your list. Then at the end of the process, you can look at earnings data as a tiebreaker if you're weighing two schools that are even on other factors.

As you consult the numbers and note the outliers among majors and schools, beware of those at the bottom—but at the same time, don't read too much into earnings separated by a few thousand dollars a year or even a few hundred thousand over a lifetime. Remember, these are medians you're looking at, and you don't know where you'll end up on the income ladder. So much of this is about comparing the middle of wide distributions and then acting like that's going to be the reality—or more often, that in those dots on a scatterplot of earnings, you'll be one that ends up in the top right and not the bottom left. After hours of looking at all these box and whisker charts of earnings, I realized there was a lot of overlap across majors. For example, even English and history majors who make a little above the median in lifetime earnings for their fields do pretty well compared with typical graduates in business and STEM fields.

What's more, the income advantage that computer science and engineering majors have over liberal arts grads "fades steadily" after the first few jobs, said David Deming, the economist you met in Chapter 2. By the time people hit age forty, their earnings are often more in line with each other. Why is that? Technical skills lose relevance if they're not kept current, while the soft skills often associated with the liberal arts (like creativity, emotional intelligence, and critical thinking) are more enduring.

Still, as parents, we can't help worrying.

How Can Students Move the Needle on Their Own Outcomes?

One evening in the spring of 2024, after I finished an admissions presentation at a public high school southwest of Chicago, I spotted a couple standing off to the side, waiting for a group in front of me to disperse. When they made their way over, they introduced themselves as parents of a junior. A solid student with a 3.7 GPA, their son had several AP courses on his transcript, played in the band at school, and volunteered with their church youth group. They worried, like the parents before them, about getting into a top-ranked school. I asked them why it mattered so much. "It's like an insurance policy," the father said, glancing around the emptying auditorium. He wanted to make sure his son could one day live in a neighborhood like the one he'd grown up in, send his own kids to a school like this.

He went on to explain that he and his wife were first-generation immigrants. Higher education had placed them solidly in the middle class, with a house, two cars, and two kids. But economic anxiety was palpable in his neighborhood. He feared that artificial intelligence was coming for his accounting job. A degree from an elite school, he said, felt more durable in a turbulent economy where entire sectors could disappear more or less overnight.

Similar anxieties permeated my focus groups and parents' survey responses. In particular, people who'd made it to a certain station in life, whether middle class or affluent, wanted to be sure their kids would as well. One parent wrote about their "fear" that "the investment won't pay off, student loans will be high, and a good job will be hard to get." Another wrote about their "anxiety that our child will mention their undergrad institution at some networking event or to a potential employer who replies, 'Where is that?'" A third focused on "how many doors will be open to L. because of school choice, how many opportunities he will have from going to school X that would not be available to him from school Y."

They felt an era had passed. Everybody seemed to know one or more recent graduates struggling to launch after college. Indeed, as parents were taking my survey, this front-page headline appeared in *The Wall Street Journal*: "Half of College Grads Are Working Jobs That Don't Use Their Degrees."

We never know in the moment if we're following the right playbook as parents. Sending our kids to a highly selective college to pursue a STEM or business major *seems* like a winning move to navigate this future we're so worried about. Is it, though? Is our son or daughter's pathway to success really so narrow? What if their dream school isn't at the top of the rankings and they want to major in history or sociology instead of business? Are there steps they can take now to thrive later?

In search of answers to those questions, I met up with Matt Sigelman, whose own résumé many parents would want for their kids: a bachelor's degree from Princeton, an MBA from Harvard Business School, and a first job at McKinsey & Company. In 2002, Sigelman took over as CEO of a small start-up called Burning Glass, which mined and analyzed job-market data from government reports, job postings, online résumés, and professional networking sites. Some two decades later, the company merged with another one in the same business, and Sigelman left to form the Burning Glass Institute, a think tank that studies job-market trends, career moves, and the future of work.

In 2022, as several U.S. governors were eliminating degree requirements for state jobs, I worked with Sigelman on a research project to determine the value of the bachelor's degree and to investigate how colleges—and by extension their students—could make the degree *more* valuable in a competitive job market. A year later, when I started working on this book, we decided to build on our research to identify college characteristics that led to better outcomes for students.

Here's what we found: Not surprisingly, the economic value of a bachelor's degree has, especially in the past few decades, depended on the prestige of the college and the market demand for certain majors. Prestige and major didn't matter *as much* when many of today's parents were growing up. Back in the 1970s and even in the early 1980s, the bachelor's degree was still relatively rare in the job market. So just having one meant you could make more money.

Heading into the early 2000s, as more people earned this credential, the wage premium it commanded (while still substantial over earnings associated with a high school diploma) started to drop. That's when the academic pedigree surrounding a college degree—the alma mater and the major—became a differentiator in talent-hungry settings like big tech, Wall Street, and consulting firms. Higher earnings automatically followed recipients of diplomas from elite schools and people in those three sectors. That generally remains true today.

I'm painfully aware that my advice to consider schools deeper in the rankings doesn't make sense if you look only at overall earnings by college, which are dominated by the elites and those engineering and business schools mentioned earlier. The earnings deck is doubly stacked in favor of highly selective schools where a majority of recent graduates take jobs in finance, tech, or consulting. Nearly six out of every ten graduates from Harvard's Class of 2024, for instance, got a job in one of those industries. But here's the thing: The overall numbers don't reflect what most people in most fields earn. The outliers throw the averages—and our expectations—out of whack.

Even if you don't go to one of those elite schools, you can land a fulfilling job with a steady paycheck after college by pulling two levers while you're there: acquiring the skills employers want most and getting an internship.

Build Marketable Skills While in School

Breaking into the post-college job market requires practical know-how, not only a degree. In our research, the team at the Burning Glass Institute analyzed job postings data to identify particular skills that drive up wages for graduates. They separated their findings into "foundational skills" (those that are broadly applicable, such as project management and creativity) and "specialized skills" (which are field specific).

The biggest wage premium comes with a mix of foundational and specialized skills. Sometimes foundational skills deliver outsize returns. Business majors, for instance, get more of an income boost from knowing how to negotiate and how to influence others than they do from studying accounting. Other times, a single specialized skill provides the biggest wage gains, especially when it's relatively scarce within a field.

The problem is that most colleges don't talk about the "skills" students learn. Professors tend to list on their course syllabi "learning outcomes," like the ability to outline the scientific method as used by psychologists or to classify various marketing strategies. "There's some correspondence between learning outcomes and skills, but they are definitely not the same," Sigelman said. "So there are all sorts of skills that we are teaching, but which we don't claim credit for." Sigelman recalled work he did for the University of Central Florida years ago that compared the outcomes in each of its majors with the skills sought by employers. He discovered, for example, that in preparation for fieldwork, the gender studies majors had acquired extensive experience in project management, a skill that boosts graduate earnings by 22 percent. "But no one in the gender studies department ever called that out," he said.

Advocates of a broad-based education sometimes criticize Sigelman as someone who sees a degree through the reductive lens of marketable skills and as currency for getting a job, rather than as well-rounded knowledge that can be enriching. But when you hear him speak to leaders in higher ed, he emphasizes job-related skills as complements to the liberal arts, not as substitutes. Indeed, he often introduces himself by telling the audience that his wife, Asya, is a classics professor at Bryn Mawr College.

Most colleges stuff their degrees with requirements. But sometimes one skill alone delivers enormous value, no matter your field or school. Take, for example, data analytics, to which marketing majors often gain exposure. The average marketing manager in the U.S. makes $71,000 a year, but one with data analytics skills earns, on average, $95,000. "Think about that," Sigelman said. "You can spend $5,000 to take a course in data analytics and get a return of almost $20,000."

That's what Matt Dvortsyn is hoping. I met Dvortsyn in 2024 at a New York City "datathon," an event designed for college students to practice on real-world projects. Dvortsyn's team from Camden County College in New Jersey placed first, with its analysis of data on homelessness, outperforming competitors from several four-year universities.

A freshman at the University of Massachusetts Amherst when the Covid pandemic hit, Dvortsyn was forced to return home to New Jersey. While taking virtual courses at UMass, he was also working part-time in a warehouse. But his father wanted him to use his brain, not his back, to get by in life, and encouraged him to take certificate classes online in data science to fill his free time. He earned a few certificates from a software company, but he knew he'd also need a college degree. When in-person classes resumed, he dropped out of UMass and enrolled in the data analytics program at the local community college before transferring to Rutgers to finish his bachelor's. Plan A for Dvortsyn was UMass, where he was undecided on a major and a bit adrift. "The pandemic was a curse and a blessing," he said. "It gave me space to reevaluate what I wanted to do." Dvortsyn conceived of and then pursued a course correction, as described in Chapter 1—only later and in an unexpected way.

The term of art for that certificate Dvortsyn obtained is a "micro-credential." They come in various flavors—badges, certificates—and are something many of today's parents may never have thought about. They might credential someone to be a "cybersecurity analyst" or to specialize in "cloud operations" using a specific software platform like Microsoft or Amazon Web Services. Or they could provide a crash course in "health care law" or "digital design" that is targeted at learners outside those fields. Alone, these microcredentials don't do much—but paired with the degree, a microcredential from an industry leader or reputable provider can be like a skeleton key, unlocking new job opportunities.

In a survey of employers by the American Association of Colleges and Universities, almost 70 percent said they would prioritize hiring a college graduate with a microcredential over a graduate without one. I met a recent Lehigh University grad who was told he landed his new job because his knowledge of Salesforce set him apart from the other candidates. He'd picked that up on his own while working for his mother's nonprofit one summer. But at some schools, such as the University of Texas and the City University of New York, students can now earn a "credegree" that combines microcredentials (in skills ranging from finance to user experience design) with a traditional bachelor's program.

Ask the colleges you're considering if they offer microcreden-tials. Relative to quality and value, the schools will have already done the due diligence for you. If the schools you're considering *don't* offer microcredentials—or if you end up at a school that you worry is little-known to employers—look to earn the extra credentials yourself. Before you do, research if the credential will be of value in your intended field (for example, is it something employers ask for in job ads?). You might pursue an industry-based certification like Adobe if you want a career in graphic design, for example, or a certificate in project management if you're interested in technical work. You can also add a second major or a minor, but with both now common on résumés, a microcredential from a trusted provider will be more helpful in differentiating you from the pack, giving employers real proof you have the skills they're looking for.

Put Those Skills to Use

Building in-demand skills as a student is one way to boost the value of your bachelor's degree, no matter where the skill knowledge comes from. Applying those skills—in internships—is another.

Internships used to be nice-to-haves. Now they should be considered *essential* in most fields, especially for students at colleges deeper in the rankings. If your résumé shows that you've both developed and practiced critical skills while in school, you'll move closer to the front of the line for full-time work after graduation.

And yet, in a Strada-Gallup study, not even one-third of college graduates said they'd completed a paid internship, and those who hadn't earned less money later on. The absence of any internship (paid or not) on your résumé puts you at significant risk of what's called "underemployment" after college—meaning you end up in a job where a degree isn't needed. In another study, more than half of graduates who failed to secure an internship as students were underemployed five years after college. Nothing predicts underemployment more than the absence of an internship—not gender, race, ethnicity, or school selectivity. In some majors, internships make an enormous difference, as shown in *Figure 10.1*.

Figure 10.1

Underemployment and Internships

Rate of underemployment five years after college among graduates who did an internship in school vs. those who didn't

● With internship   ○ Without internship

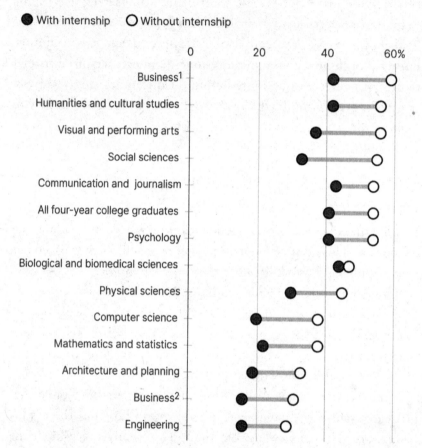

¹ management, marketing, HR   ² accounting, finance

Source: Burning Glass Institute analysis of Lightcast Career Histories Database

Those stats above—they apply to all colleges. But your chances of underemployment are even greater if you go to a school deeper in the rankings and miss out on an internship. Since I'm encouraging the approach of applying to a wider range of schools, be extra sure you leave with an internship or two.

Simply put, elite colleges, which tend to have deep networks with employers, outrun less-selective schools in the race for internships. You might recall from Chapter 6 that in the National Survey of Student Engagement students at brand-name schools were much more likely to have internships; students at less-selective colleges, meanwhile, participated in service learning (loosely defined as community service in the classroom). It's not that you can't secure an internship as a student at a less-familiar college, especially if you have skills that employers need. Odds are, though, you'll need to work harder to get it—unless your school helps level the field.

Here are two key supports to look for in the college search:

- **Built-in internship or work experience:** Study the curriculum for your intended major to see if it includes an internship, and ask what the school will do to help you secure it. Some schools, like the University of Cincinnati and Drexel, have co-op programs that are essential components of the curriculum. Most schools don't, however, so ask if they require an internship, and if so, do they have direct channels to employers to get hired. Increasingly, schools such as Georgetown, Arizona State, and Virginia Commonwealth are building work experiences directly into courses where students work on real-world cases for weeks at a time with companies ranging from Intel to Starbucks. If they don't have required internships in your major, then ask about how they bring hands-on experience to campus.

- **Job shadowing and externship programs:** Look for schools that provide opportunities to visit companies and learn from employees. By shadowing a professional in your desired field for a week or so, you can see what their job is like day to day and get a foot in the door for your first internship down the road. At the Stevens Institute of Technology in New Jersey, freshmen and sophomores shadow alumni at their jobs over winter break. The preparation required is almost as important as the visit itself. Before they show up, students must research the mechanics of the job they're shadowing, create a résumé, and develop questions for a series of informational interviews they will have on-site. When students return to campus, they give presentations on what they discovered about themselves and their career aspirations.

At many large companies, internship programs are designed to feed full-time hiring pipelines. Even smaller organizations with less-structured programs (or none at all) like to hire candidates who've gained valuable experiences as interns at bigger firms. In a typical year, the biggest companies offer full-time roles to two-thirds of their interns. An overwhelming majority of these students (some 80 percent) take the job. In some ways, the process is reminiscent of early decision in admissions: Lots of spots are already spoken for by the time most students apply.

Companies favor hiring from their intern pool because "it's essentially a ten-week job interview," said Simon Kho, who heads up early-career programs at Raymond James Financial. He wants 70 percent of the company's entry-level hires to come through its internship program. Other companies set even higher targets. In my research, I learned that Discover's goal is 85 percent. At KPMG and General Mills, it's 90 percent. "Our internship program is built to fill full-time roles," said Elizabeth Diley, who formerly led campus recruiting at General Mills. "My goal? If you perform over the summer, you will get an offer."

Such tryouts are highly predictive of job performance. "Work ethic is hard to accurately assess in any other way," according to Ryan Craig, author of *Apprentice Nation*. When researchers ask hiring managers what tips the scale when they're weighing two equally qualified candidates, by far they say it's the internship, preferably at their organization but, if not, then in their industry. After that, they look at the student's major, general work experience, leadership positions, and extracurricular activities. The applicant's school ranks near the bottom of factors considered.

In the end, internships count—a lot. Once you've chosen a school that helps students get good ones, you'll need to do your part to line up fruitful experiences. In your planning and prep work make sure to do the following:

- **Pace yourself:** Think of job shadowing and externships as experiences you will build into your first year to prepare for internships later. Some firms hire only juniors as interns, but others consider sophomores, depending on the major. "We have twelve interns who are sophomores this year," said Diley, the former recruiter at General Mills, one of the largest food manufacturers in the world. Half are likely to return the following year, she said, because "they know they want to work in the food industry." The final internship before your senior year is perhaps the most important bridge to your first employer after college. As Adam Ward, former head of recruiting at Pinterest, told me years ago: "He who gets them last, gets them for good."

- **Treat the search for internships (and for jobs later on) like a class:** Finding the right opportunities takes discipline. Block off time in your calendar—an hour or two every week—to look for postings. Set up alerts on job-hunting platforms. If you're interested in a particular employer but you don't see anything about internships on the company's website, do deeper research or call the HR department and ask. Check, double-check, and then triple-check deadlines. Finance and accounting firms recruit interns nearly eighteen months before students are expected to start. To compete for talent, other sectors and companies are moving up their deadlines, too, so most summer interns are now hired before winter break.

- **Engage in college with an eye toward interviews:** Many big companies use some version of structured interviews and case studies when interviewing interns and full-timers. From day one of college in your coursework and extracurricular activities, think about how you'll demonstrate your qualifications when it comes time to do so. Look for examples that highlight specific skills, and work with mentors or alumni in the industry to find ways of talking about what you have learned and how that knowledge can be applied in different settings.

No matter where you go to school, you can use these strategies to steer yourself toward the outcomes you want after graduation.

Matt Dvortsyn's story—the community college student who won the datathon competition against students from four-year universities—remained with me long after we met. It wasn't simply that he'd challenged conventional wisdom about the talents of community college students when pitted against those from four-year schools or that he'd found an unexpected path after dropping out of UMass. What made his story compelling was that he'd discovered something fundamental about success in today's economy: It's not where you start your college journey that matters most but how you take control of it.

A parent who works in big tech at one of the so-called FAANG companies [Facebook (Meta), Apple, Amazon, Netflix, Alphabet] made that point loud and clear in a response to my survey: "I interview new grads. Where they went to school matters far less than what they did while there. The kids who maximized opportunities at lesser-known schools often outperform the ones who just coasted at top schools."

This observation gets at something that's often lost in our collective anxiety about prestige and starting salaries. Yes, money matters. Financial security matters. But the most valuable aspect of college isn't the degree itself or even the first job—it's what you do while you're there.

CONCLUSION

DREAMS

If you started reading this book because your Plan A was to get into a top-ranked college, you know by now that it's a high-stakes game where the rules keep changing. Even if you've never tied your dreams to rankings, college planning is the product of a lot of deliberation, so this is a stressful time, no question.

Navigating admissions—the sheer number of options, the byzantine systems and processes, the promises that all these schools make—can feel quite overwhelming. And no matter where you get accepted, you'll have to sort out how to pay the bill. As you calculate and recalculate your chances of getting in and receiving a decent price break, and perhaps ask others for their predictions about your odds (check out r/chanceme on Reddit), you might find yourself wondering how on earth you ended up where you are: wading through GPA averages, scattergrams of acceptance rates, merit scholarship charts, graduate earnings, and other intricacies of the higher-ed information marketplace. You might also start to lose hope.

I understand the frustration so many people feel about the college admissions process. It's exhausting, and it's not fair.

But let's put the numbers into perspective. They tell an incomplete story. As Todd Rose reminds us in his book *The End of Average*, averages are conclusive only for groups where everyone is identical and stays that way well into the future. (In other words, practically never.) No two individuals who major in, say, psychology at University of Oregon will have the same lives in school or afterward. Nor will everyone who earns a degree in marketing from Marquette pursue the exact same career path—even if the average earnings five years out on the College Scorecard seem so exact: $81,846. Averages are blunt tools for gaining insight and making decisions. They're convenient and efficient, so we cling to them, but they do little to help us find the "perfect fit" in a college.

Unfortunately, as Rose writes, by "substituting knowledge about the group for knowledge about the individual . . . you get exactly the wrong answer." Averages in the college search don't account for you as an individual and the faculty you'll meet, the people you'll live with, the mentors you'll get to know, the work experiences you'll have. They might shed some light on your likelihood of getting into a particular school, but they say nothing about how you'll use your college years. That's something *you* control.

Consider Colleen McAllister, whom I met at an Ithaca College alumni gathering in Los Angeles in February 2024. McAllister graduated more than a decade after I did. She was accepted to that Ivy League school on "the other hill"—as we called Cornell—but chose Ithaca College for its communications school and its financial-aid package. She spent the spring of her junior year at Ithaca's Los Angeles center, where she interned at two companies. McAllister had grown up with a single mom in a blue-collar family in upstate New York. Hollywood felt like a different planet. After mustering the courage to ask to stay on in both her gigs, she spent her last summer before graduation in Los Angeles working as a paid production assistant.

After receiving her bachelor's degree in 2008, during the recession, McAllister eventually made her way back to California. She took on a series of internships, including one at Illumination, an animation studio still trying to gain name recognition. Then a full-time job opened up there. "I had, at that point, done so many different internships and entry-level jobs," she told me. "I was happy to take out the trash, happy to do the coffee run. I was willing to read everything that crossed the desk." She knew the competition would be fierce. She saw a "perfect candidate" come in who went to the same Ivy as her boss (Princeton) and who had other elite bullet points on his résumé, but was late to the interview and "didn't do the homework," McAllister said. "He was sort of above it all." McAllister ended up getting the job. Over time, her reputation as a problem-solver led her to work directly with Illumination's CEO. One of McAllister's projects was as creative producer and Illumination's liaison to the design team at Universal's theme park in Orlando, which was working on a *Secret Life of Pets* ride, based on a movie that she'd helped launch.

It was that experience that McAllister talked about at the alumni event in Los Angeles. The story caught my attention not only because I thought working on a theme park ride was cool but because it illustrated how wildly our lives and successes can deviate from any predictable path we might imagine as young adults. Indeed, McAllister has since jumped off the executive track and started writing for television, returning to a love she'd developed at Ithaca as a creative writing minor. Would she have done just as well at that university on the other hill? Would she have still ended up in Los Angeles? Maybe. Or she might have found herself in an entirely different city, with an entirely different career. Our dreams take shape as we live.

As I reflect on my conversations with families, I'm struck by how often we conflate college dreams with the American dream. That dream was first articulated by the writer and historian James Truslow Adams during the Great Depression. Adams's basic idea—to live a "better, richer, and happier" life than the one into which you were born—crops up again and again in our lives. And higher education has long been seen as a vehicle for achieving that American dream.

While popular culture fixates on the "richer" part, my research revealed something different: What parents most want for their children—and what teens most want for their future selves—is happiness. If you could guarantee only one aspect of the American dream for your future—better, richer, or happier—which would you choose?

We're a nation of strivers. I'm acutely aware, as someone who lives among the "panicking class," that most of us would jump at the chance to get one of those "extra lottery tickets" that go to students at elite schools, as economist David Deming put it earlier, to give ourselves or our kids the best possible shot at success.

But in moments when I catch myself worrying about my own children's futures, I also think about how, just two generations ago, my grandparents worked for coal mining companies and dress factories in Northeastern Pennsylvania. They wanted a better and happier life for their kids. My father got the opportunity to go to college; my mother didn't. But then their three kids did, and now I get to write about the same system of higher education that wasn't even a possibility my grandparents could imagine. My story isn't unique. Most of today's parents of teenagers are only second-generation college graduates themselves. In higher education, the real threats to the American dream aren't rejection letters from Harvard and Yale; they're the barriers, mostly systemic, that keep talented teenagers (and adults) from reaping the benefits of any college at all.

Perspective is important in the college search. In trying to master the finite game of getting in we lose sight of the larger infinite game of life. Our certainties about which colleges matter—and which don't—may look embarrassingly short-sighted over time. Schools like Northeastern, the University of Southern California, and NYU were regional brands just thirty years ago. Today, they're among the most sought-after schools nationally. Your Plan B dream school now might be a next-generation Northeastern, USC, or NYU.

In the end, the right school is one where you, like McAllister, can discover who you want to become. It equips you with the mindset, relationships, and skills you'll need in the decades ahead. Those are the real keys to success.

The good news is they're entirely accessible to you. When you find a place where you can grow, challenge yourself, and build meaningful connections, that college will become *your* dream school.

APPENDIX: THE "NEW" DREAM SCHOOLS—A SELECTED LIST

Colleges That Are Both Accessible and Excellent

As I wrote in the Introduction, finding your Dream School isn't about fixating on a single name or a universally understood brand like the Ivy League. It's about choosing a place where you can thrive, learn, and become the person you're meant to be.

To help you in that endeavor, I've compiled the following list of colleges that might not (but perhaps should) be on your radar. It is not a ranking, nor is it a comprehensive catalog. It's a sampling of schools designed to expand your thinking—and your search. All of the colleges listed here accept at least 25 percent of their applicants most years. Nearly all of them accept way more than that, with many saying "yes" to more than 50 percent.

I'll be honest: If you're stuck on prestige, this list isn't for you. You'll find none of these schools in the top 25 of the *U.S. News* "national university" rankings and barely any in the top 50. To consider a broader range of schools, you need to push past that layer of sameness and look deeper in the rankings. A college's absence from this list doesn't diminish its potential to be a good match for you. There are institutions waiting to be discovered by you beyond these schools by using the advice from this book.

How you go about that depends partly on where you live. If you live in California, then Montclair State—a good regional college in New Jersey that's on this list—probably isn't for you. But if you live in New Jersey and are thinking about Rutgers or Penn State, then Montclair State might be worth more than a passing look. Of course, the type of campus you want matters, too. Let's say you're especially drawn to small, top-ranked liberal arts colleges like Bowdoin and Pomona. In that case, it may make sense to include St. Olaf from this list as you expand your field of vision, but you can most likely skip big, rah-rah campuses like the University of Illinois and Clemson.

And so I organized this list into three groups:

- **Hidden Values.** These tend to be private colleges, many smaller campuses, with strong graduation outcomes and opportunities for fulfilling careers that are often overlooked by high-achieving students because they lack big national brand names. Because of that, many of these schools will also cut you a nice tuition discount. (Examples from the list: Denison University, Santa Clara University, and St. Olaf College.)

- **Breakout Regionals.** Institutions—mostly public but a few privates, too—that tend to draw most of their student body from close by. When compared with more expensive alternatives, these schools have a compelling value proposition for students. (Examples from the list: Florida A&M University, George Mason University, The College of New Jersey.)

- **Large Leaders.** Big universities with the depth and breadth of other large public and private institutions that many students have just missed in the past as they focused on the top of the rankings. But these are campuses where they can thrive and break free of the "elite college or bust" mentality. (Examples from the list: Case Western Reserve, the University of Maryland, College Park, and Michigan State University.)

How This List Came Together

The full story behind this list is outlined in Chapter 6. To recap: I compiled it by examining various existing datasets on schools from 2023 and 2024 and commissioning new research and analysis. There are more than 3,900 colleges and universities in the United States. I wanted to look at a smaller universe for this list, so I started with four-year colleges with at least 1,000 undergraduates. That left about 1,200 schools to consider along the following dimensions:

- **Accessible admissions.** My research team and I divided those 1,200 schools into five buckets of selectivity. I didn't include any schools from the top group, which accept fewer than 20 percent of applicants, because they're too difficult to get into. Since selectivity is a moving target from year to year, I included a few schools that accept 20–30 percent of applicants. But the vast majority of the colleges on this list have acceptance rates between 30 and 80 percent. In other words, they're pretty accessible. Two things to remember: Acceptance rates for public colleges are often lower for out-of-state students than for in-state students, and they differ by academic program. STEM fields, for example, tend to have lower acceptance rates than arts and humanities programs.

- **Financial sustainability.** It's difficult to predict which colleges might close or merge in the coming years. But drawing on the research and analysis described in Chapter 9, I eliminated schools that are or could be financially vulnerable. This is the primary reason I didn't include any colleges with under a thousand students. They aren't necessarily in financial trouble, but as various analyses show, enrollment at such a small scale tends to be an economic disadvantage.

- **A solid earnings-to-net-price ratio.** Working with Michael Itzkowitz, who directed the U.S. government's first College Scorecard (a website that displays earnings of graduates by school and major), we developed an earnings-to-net-price ratio for schools that provided enough data. We estimated how much a degree over four years will cost you in the long run, given the net price of the school and how much graduates earn, on average, ten years after enrolling. Many colleges that are "buyers" when it comes to their approach to financial aid— typically, giving out sizeable merit-aid discounts—made this list and I note that in several places.

- **Outcomes that "punch above the school's weight."** Student outcomes vary widely across colleges. Often, they're tied more to the human beings who enrolled than to any other factor. So a useful way to compare two critical outcomes—graduation rates and earnings after graduation—is to control for student body characteristics, such as family income, academic preparation in high school, demographics, and local cost of living. Using an analysis of federal data provided by Bain & Company, we were able to compare each institution's predicted outcomes with actual results to reveal which schools serving similar populations do the best job helping their undergraduates succeed.

- **Student engagement.** The researchers who conduct the National Survey of Student Engagement (NSSE) identified schools with high student engagement scores across levels of selectivity. NSSE then asked a subset of those schools if they'd be willing to share their survey data with me since the results aren't publicly released. Several of the institutions that said yes are on this list.

- **Job prospects for graduates.** To ensure that I was including colleges that produce talent for a broad range of employers, I consulted LinkedIn data to see where schools' graduates land. In this work, I was also guided by data from Lightcast, a labor-market-analytics firm, and by analysis from Handshake, a job-search platform for college students.

- **Delivery of value to undergraduates.** With the backing of a grant from Lumina Foundation, I partnered with the Burning Glass Institute, a think tank, to analyze data on institutional characteristics and practices. Together we identified which factors were most—and least—significant in driving outcomes.

One last note on the list: It includes two schools where I have personal connections. Ithaca College is my alma mater, and I have served on its Board of Trustees. I'm also a professor of practice and a special advisor at Arizona State University. So, I've seen the outcomes of these two schools up close and personal, but both made the list initially based on the data sources cited above.

Now that you have the "how" behind the list, let's get to the "what": the schools themselves.

HIDDEN VALUES

AUGUSTANA COLLEGE (IL)

The academic experience for Augustana undergraduates is bookended, starting with a first-year "inquiry" program that emphasizes writing and oral communication around a central question, and ending with a senior-year research project. In addition, all students can apply for up to $2,000 in funds to pursue internships, research, or international study. Two and a half hours from Chicago, Augustana capitalizes on its location through the Upper Mississippi Center's environmental research programs while connecting students to employers like John Deere, State Farm, and Northwestern Medicine. The college's new Augustana Possible program meets 100 percent of demonstrated need for qualifying students through a $40 million alumni gift. What's more, nearly a third of the college's institutional financial aid is awarded without respect to need.

STANDOUT FACTOR

With 91 percent of faculty serving as academic advisors, Augustana gives students plenty of face time with professors.

BENTLEY UNIVERSITY (MA)

Located thirteen miles from downtown Boston, Bentley's business-focused curriculum sets students up to capture job opportunities in New England and elsewhere: Graduates earn nearly $112,000 annually ten years after enrollment, placing the university among the region's highest-earning bachelor's institutions. Although it isn't as well-known as nearby competitor Babson College, Bentley is more accessible. High-achieving students majoring in finance can earn both a bachelor's and a master's degree in four years by starting graduate classes as juniors. Nearly a third of institutional financial aid is given out in discounts.

STANDOUT FACTOR

Bentley combines selective admission standards with remarkable completion numbers compared with those for institutions serving similar student populations. Its 88 percent graduation rate exceeds expectations by 7 percentage points.

BERRY COLLEGE (GA)

On 27,000 acres of rural land, Berry College operates the world's largest college campus, turning its grounds into a living laboratory for environmental and animal-science programs. This natural setting provides distinctive opportunities for students to conduct fieldwork in forests, fields, and streams right on campus. Beyond its environmental programs, Berry has built strong offerings in education, business, and nursing while maintaining an intimate student body of 2,200 undergraduates. The college has also redefined the term "student worker" through its LifeWorks program, which places applicants in one of 180 departments to learn practical job skills while earning a paycheck.

STANDOUT FACTOR
Berry College outshines its peers on the National Survey of Student Engagement (NSSE).

BUTLER UNIVERSITY (IN)
With major health care companies like Eli Lilly, Anthem, and Roche Diagnostics headquartered in Butler's hometown of Indianapolis, students have close access to internships and other professional opportunities. Butler emphasizes hands-on learning and small classes while having the feel of a larger university, especially with a men's basketball team that competes in the Big East Conference and has gone to the Final Four. Butler is well-known for its health care programs, and now has started a bachelor's degree in nursing. Some 45 percent of Butler's institutional aid given to students isn't based on financial need.

STANDOUT FACTOR
At 81 percent, Butler's six-year graduation rate matches that of selective private universities, while the school's 82 percent acceptance rate promises greater access.

CREIGHTON UNIVERSITY (NE)
With 4,000 undergraduates and Division I athletics, Creighton provides the advantages of a small college with a bigger university feel. More than 83 percent of students engage in experiential learning—working with start-ups and real-world clients through various practicums, for example, and presenting roughly 400 research projects annually at

conferences. Situated blocks from downtown Omaha, in the heart of "Silicon Prairie," students gain ready access to Fortune 500 employers like Berkshire Hathaway and Union Pacific. Popular majors include nursing, exercise physiology, and finance.

STANDOUT FACTOR

A hallmark of the university is its comprehensive pre-professional advising, which offers guaranteed admission pathways to its professional schools in medicine, dentistry, law, pharmacy, and occupational therapy.

DENISON UNIVERSITY (OH)

Denison transforms semester breaks, which account for 40 percent of the year, into windows for professional development. During these periods, students can earn credentials through specialized courses while building their networks. To foster relationships on campus, the university starts every freshman in a mentor-led cohort class. And to instill skills for the future, Denison's Center for Data Reasoning and Visualization integrates data analysis across disciplines. Strategic partnerships, including workforce preparation programs with Intel's forthcoming chip facility near Columbus, blend career readiness with a liberal arts education. Recent graduates have found success at firms such as PNC, Fidelity, UBS, and Google.

STANDOUT FACTOR

Expanded orientation includes short off-campus trips for every student to get to know a small group of classmates.

DEPAUL UNIVERSITY (IL)

The nation's largest Catholic university, DePaul spans two distinct Chicago neighborhoods—a traditional college setting in Lincoln Park and a downtown Loop campus embedded in the business district. Despite serving more than 14,000 undergraduates, the university maintains small class sizes, typically in the twenties.

The Vincentian mission of the school shapes DePaul's approach to professional preparation, which prioritizes service to others. Finance and marketing graduates often secure positions at Northern Trust, Discover, and United Airlines, while the film/video production program benefits from Chicago's active media industry.

STANDOUT FACTOR

More than 20 percent of undergraduates get institutional financial aid without respect to financial need. The average merit discount is more than $18,000 dollars.

DEPAUW UNIVERSITY (IN)

Thanks to a transformative $200 million gift in 2024, DePauw is restructuring into three distinct schools: Liberal Arts and Sciences, Business and Leadership, and the Creative School. Freshmen choose one of eight first-year discussion-based seminars, which provide exposure to big ideas across disciplines. About 92 percent of students complete at least one internship, often with major Indiana employers like Eli Lilly and Salesforce. Drawing 60 percent of its students from outside the state, DePauw offers a variety of majors—the largest of which include econometrics, speech communication, and computer science. The university also consistently ranks high for study-abroad participation.

STANDOUT FACTOR

DePauw's graduation rate exceeds predictions by 8 percentage points, and more than 40 percent of its institutional financial-aid budget is awarded without respect to financial need.

DICKINSON COLLEGE (PA)

A liberal arts college located 100 miles north of Washington, D.C., Dickinson is known for having a high proportion of students who study abroad (some 60 percent of its undergraduates, compared with an average of just 1 percent nationally). The college offers flexible options for study abroad, ranging from a few weeks to a semester to a year in multiple locations. Popular majors include economics, international business, and political science and government. Recent graduates tend to stay in Pennsylvania or work in New York City or Washington, D.C. Their representation is highest at the U.S. Department of Defense, Vanguard, Deloitte, Capital One, and Merck.

STANDOUT FACTOR

Dickinson has an enviable price-to-earnings ratio for liberal arts colleges like it. On average, its graduates make $72,500 annually ten years after enrolling. With tuition discounts, the school's median net price is around $62,000 for four years.

ELON UNIVERSITY (NC)

Within higher-education circles, Elon University is known as a school that other midsized private universities want to learn from. Elon's longtime president until 2018, Leo Lambert, has authored several books on the importance of relationships in college, and Elon under his leadership became a campus where connections between its 6,500 undergraduates and mentors became a hallmark of the student experience. The university's Center for Engaged Learning brings together international leaders in higher education to develop research on central questions about student learning. The most popular majors are business, communications, social sciences, and the visual and performing arts. Elon is one of the top producers of Fulbright Scholars. Elon operates a cooperative-education program that integrates work into the undergraduate curriculum, and as a result, some nine out of ten graduates complete at least one internship during their undergraduate career. After graduation, the biggest employers of Elon alumni include Bloomberg, Wells Fargo, Fidelity, and Google.

STANDOUT FACTOR

One-third of institutional aid is awarded in discounts without respect to financial need. The average award is $12,510 and Elon's total cost of attendance has historically been lower than its private-college peers.

FAIRFIELD UNIVERSITY (CT)

Straddling Connecticut's "Gold Coast" between New York City and Boston, Fairfield is ideally situated for internships and professional networking. More than 40 percent of students each year graduate with a degree from the business school. Otherwise, the most popular majors at this Catholic university are in the health professions and the social sciences. Known for providing immersive clinical experiences, Fairfield's nursing school attracts strong students from all over, accepting roughly 28 percent of undergraduates who apply. The university's higher overall acceptance rate for undergrads, at 45 percent, reflects a blend of selectivity and accessibility.

STANDOUT FACTOR

Fairfield graduates earn $95,393 annually ten years after enrollment, exceeding predicted earnings (based on school characteristics) by more than $10,000.

FURMAN UNIVERSITY (SC)

Furman structures early student engagement through its Pathways program, where freshmen join fifteen of their peers in cohorts led by junior and senior mentors. Through these groups, students interact directly with faculty members to develop skills and explore interests. As a result of the program, 92 percent of graduates participate in high-impact experiences such as research projects, internships, and study abroad. The university matches its 85 percent graduation rate with impressive student achievements: for instance, four members of the Class of 2022 captured Fulbright awards. Recent graduates have secured positions with a wide range of employers, from Wells Fargo and EY to Michelin, SpaceX, and the PGA Tour.

STANDOUT FACTOR

Furman's graduation rate of 85 percent exceeds expectations by 4 percentage points, in light of the stats for institutions serving similar student populations, and the university maintains an accessible acceptance rate of 67 percent.

GETTYSBURG COLLEGE (PA)

First-Year Seminars at Gettysburg flip the typical undergraduate script, offering freshmen experiences usually reserved for seniors. These sixteen-person classes incorporate field trips, films, and community service projects, which together lay a foundation for the high-engagement culture that defines the institution. This go-get-it ethos carries through to dual-degree engineering partnerships with Columbia, RPI, and other top universities. Gettysburg's location between Philadelphia and Washington, D.C., supports strong placement at firms like Deloitte, Vanguard, and Fidelity Investments. Some 70 percent of classes enroll fewer than twenty students, and more than half of students participate in faculty-led research.

STANDOUT FACTOR

Gettysburg's engagement metrics are stellar. Here's just one example: 91 percent of students discuss academic performance with faculty versus 84 percent at comparable colleges, according to the National Survey of Student Engagement.

HOBART AND WILLIAM SMITH COLLEGES (NY)

Challenging conventional curriculum design, Hobart and William Smith require just one preset course: a first-year seminar. Beyond that, students work with faculty to craft individual academic plans targeting eight core goals—from developing critical-thinking skills to analyzing cultural differences. The colleges' Finger Lakes setting provides a living laboratory, where, for instance, environmental science students conduct research aboard the *William Scandling* vessel on Seneca Lake. But the schools' hands-on approach to learning extends well beyond the region, as 70 percent of students study abroad through more than fifty programs. Recent graduates have landed at financial firms like Fidelity Investments and Morgan Stanley, while the pre-health students have consistently achieved medical school acceptance rates nearly double the national average.

STANDOUT FACTOR

Hobart and William Smith came in fourth nationally for student experience in *The Wall Street Journal*'s rankings, reflecting the colleges' emphasis on personalized education and global engagement.

ITHACA COLLEGE (NY)

With five distinct schools under one figurative roof, Ithaca creates a hybrid university-college model that's increasingly rare in higher education. Its nearly 5,000 undergraduates make it larger than most liberal arts colleges, and yet its offerings are more focused than a university's. Ithaca provides specialized training in communications, performance, and health sciences along with programs in business and the arts and sciences. This structure has proven particularly beneficial in the communications and media fields, where graduates have built pathways to employers such as ESPN, NBCUniversal, IBM, and Google. While sometimes overshadowed by its Ivy League neighbor, Cornell University, Ithaca offers access to world-class facilities and cultural events as well as limited classes on the "other hill," all while its students enjoy their time in a quintessential college town in the Finger Lakes region.

STANDOUT FACTOR

Ithaca is known for providing students with hands-on learning opportunities from day one in studios, on stages, and in clinics.

LOYOLA UNIVERSITY MARYLAND (MD)

The Jesuit approach to education takes tangible form in Loyola's Messina program, where freshmen explore academic, spiritual, and social growth in small cohorts. An emphasis on personalized instruction continues through all four years, with an average class size of twenty students—all of whom must tackle a seventeen-course core curriculum in addition to the requirements of their majors. The Sellinger School of Business and Management has built strong recruiting pipelines to firms like T. Rowe Price, M&T Bank, McCormick & Company, and Stanley Black & Decker, and the university's pre-professional programs maintain exceptional placement rates. Nearly 90 percent of Loyola grads who apply to law school and some 70 percent who apply to medical school are accepted.

STANDOUT FACTOR

The Wall Street Journal ranked Loyola No. 23 nationally and No. 1 among Jesuit institutions for career preparation, reflecting strong outcomes across business and pre-professional programs.

MACALESTER COLLEGE (MN)

Located in St. Paul, Macalester combines liberal arts education with urban opportunities rare among small colleges. In keeping with the school's international character (students are from more than 100 countries), undergraduates must demonstrate proficiency in a second language over four semesters. Nearly 60 percent choose to study abroad. To foster engagement and citizenship, the Action Fund provides up to $2,500 for student-led community projects with Twin Cities organizations. A remarkable 73 percent of students complete internships or research before graduation, aided by 200 internship sites within eight miles. Popular majors include econometrics, computer science, and mathematics, with graduates landing at employers like Target, Wells Fargo, Google, and UnitedHealth Group.

STANDOUT FACTOR

Macalester's six-year graduation rate of 90 percent is 4 percentage points higher than predicted for institutions serving similar student populations.

SAINT MARY'S COLLEGE OF CALIFORNIA (CA)

Among the smallest colleges to compete in NCAA Division I athletics, Saint Mary's fields eighteen varsity teams, including basketball, soccer, cross country, softball, and baseball—fostering an outsize athletic culture within its 3,000-student undergraduate population. The college's location in Moraga provides a traditional campus setting just twenty miles from professional opportunities in San Francisco's technology, business, and cultural sectors.

STANDOUT FACTOR

Saint Mary's graduates earn, on average, over $71,700 annually ten years after enrollment, which is $4,400 more than expected for similar institutions.

SANTA CLARA UNIVERSITY (CA)

Silicon Valley's tech ecosystem has shaped Santa Clara's academic programs—from its bioengineering department, where students develop health care solutions, to its business analytics program, which prepares data-driven decision-makers for their future jobs. At 6,200 undergraduates, this Jesuit institution maintains an ideal size for both personalized attention and comprehensive resources. Major employers of recent graduates include Google, Apple, Cisco, Amazon, and NVIDIA. A completed $1 billion campaign has added 750,000 square feet of new and renovated facilities, enhancing the university's academic infrastructure.

STANDOUT FACTOR

Even within the competitive Silicon Valley market, Santa Clara delivers strong career outcomes. Graduates earn $99,012 per year, on average, ten years after enrollment, exceeding predictions for similar institutions by nearly $15,000.

ST. OLAF COLLEGE (MN)

With a higher acceptance rate than its liberal arts neighbor Carleton College, St. Olaf is a more accessible yet still moderately selective option. It is a Lutheran college located just forty miles from the state's employment center of Minneapolis–St. Paul. All incoming students take two required classes—a seminar and a writing course—in smaller cohorts. Those courses and the students in them are connected to an extended orientation that runs throughout the year to foster a sense of belonging. Popular majors include biology, economics, and mathematics. Representation of recent graduates is highest at Target, UnitedHealth Group, the Mayo Clinic, Wells Fargo, Medtronic, 3M, and U.S. Bank.

STANDOUT FACTOR

St. Olaf's student engagement and satisfaction scores are on par with higher-ranked colleges, according to the National Survey of Student Engagement.

STEVENS INSTITUTE OF TECHNOLOGY (NJ)

Across the river from New York City, in Hoboken, Stevens Institute of Technology combines technical education with entrepreneurship and industry ties. All undergraduates take entrepreneurship coursework and complete a Frontiers of Technology sequence covering emerging fields like AI, quantum computing, and biotechnology. Senior engineering students work with industry partners on capstone projects simulating real-world professional environments. The university's location enables strong connections with employers like Verizon, Citi, and Pfizer. Popular majors include mechanical engineering, computer science, and business administration. For students interested in advanced degrees, Stevens offers accelerated pathways to law school through Seton Hall and medicine through Rutgers New Jersey Medical School.

STANDOUT FACTOR

On average, Stevens graduates earn over $104,000 annually ten years after enrollment, placing them among the highest-earning engineering school graduates nationally.

TRINITY UNIVERSITY (TX)

One of the few liberal arts colleges in the South located in a major city, Trinity leverages its San Antonio setting to bridge intimate academics with urban opportunities. The university maintains classes of fewer than twenty students in 68 percent of courses while engaging 80 percent of students in hands-on learning through research and internships. The Summer Undergraduate Research Fellowship keeps students on campus, advancing faculty-guided projects during the school break. A structured, progressive professional-development initiative, aimed at preparing students for life after Trinity, focuses on skill building and experiential learning. Popular majors include finance, accounting, and political science.

STANDOUT FACTOR

Trinity's endowment of $650,000 per student—triple the national average—fuels both strong financial-aid and comprehensive support programs.

UNIVERSITY OF DAYTON (OH)

With 8,500 undergraduates, Dayton hits a sweet spot between small-college attention and big-school resources. The university forges innovative pathways to advanced degrees: Students can accelerate into master's programs across several majors, saving 30 percent on graduate tuition while finishing within a year of their bachelor's. Local families benefit from a seamless transfer partnership with Sinclair Community College, which accounts for around 150 of 2,000 incoming students annually. Finance, marketing, and mechanical engineering are the most popular majors, and graduates land at GE Aerospace, Deloitte, and Amazon. The pre-med program achieves an impressive 75 percent medical school acceptance rate.

STANDOUT FACTOR

Dayton's transparent financial-aid model guarantees four-year tuition costs up front, with merit aid reducing the average net price to less than half the published rate.

UNIVERSITY OF DENVER (CO)

The 6,000 undergraduates at the University of Denver benefit from their proximity to an emerging tech and business hub downtown, just minutes away from campus. The school's 14:1 student-to-faculty ratio allows for rich discussion and personalized instruction. Beyond the classroom, learning is extended through integrated internships, research, and service projects, and the Rocky Mountains provide a stunning backdrop for recreational activities such as skiing and hiking. Some 41 percent of institutional aid is awarded without respect to financial need.

STANDOUT FACTOR

Denver's 77 percent graduation rate exceeds expectations by 2 percentage points for institutions serving similar populations, reflecting strong student support systems.

UNIVERSITY OF THE PACIFIC (CA)

Among California's private universities, Pacific stands out for its accelerated professional programs, including 3+3 paths to law and dental degrees that trim years off traditional timelines. The School of Pharmacy is among the university's most popular programs. Students also come to Pacific for its School of Business, where they gain experience managing real investment portfolios through the Student Investment Fund. From the Stockton campus, students access internship opportunities in both San Francisco and Sacramento, where major health care employers like Kaiser Permanente and Sutter Health actively recruit graduates. Pacific alumni earn an average of $80,965 annually ten years after enrollment, outperforming expectations by nearly $1,600 given student demographics.

STANDOUT FACTOR

Pacific is generous with merit-based scholarships, awarding about 20 percent of its institutional aid without respect to financial need.

BREAKOUT REGIONALS

BARUCH COLLEGE (NY)

A powerhouse for business education in New York City, Baruch's Zicklin School prepares students for careers in finance, accounting, management, and entrepreneurship. The fourteen-story Vertical Campus in Gramercy Park—which houses these programs and others, in arts and sciences and public affairs—serves as an urban hub from which students can easily forge connections with major employers like Citi, JPMorgan Chase, and Morgan Stanley. Operating primarily as a commuter school in the City University of New York system, with just 3 percent of students living on campus, Baruch capitalizes on its Manhattan location to provide a seamless transition from classroom learning to professional opportunity.

STANDOUT FACTOR

Baruch achieves the highest earnings-to-price ratio among its peer institutions, with graduates earning $77,436 annually ten years after enrollment against a net four-year, in-state price of just $7,744.

BINGHAMTON UNIVERSITY (NY)

As part of the State University of New York (SUNY) system, Binghamton is a big public research school with a smaller-college feel. Undergraduates who distinguish themselves get to work on research projects alongside faculty members. For example, Binghamton's "First-Year Research Immersion" program provides freshmen with research experience in sciences and engineering. Popular majors include Biology, Economics, and Psychology. The university also fields more than twenty varsity sports in the NCAA Division I (although no football). More than 90 percent of freshmen return for their sophomore year—a retention rate similar to that of a public flagship or an elite private university.

STANDOUT FACTOR

The price-to-earnings ratio is strong, especially for in-state students who pay a net price of $77,000 over four years and make that much annually across all majors, on average, ten years after enrolling.

CALIFORNIA STATE POLYTECHNIC UNIVERSITY, POMONA (CA)

As one of only eleven polytechnic schools in the U.S., Cal Poly Pomona integrates technology and experiential learning across its curriculum. This approach is exemplified by the Digital Transformation Hub, where students have worked with real clients—including the World Bank and various state agencies—to solve technical challenges using cloud computing and artificial intelligence. Nearly a quarter of all degrees awarded are in engineering, spanning industrial, mechanical, aerospace, computer, and civil programs.

STANDOUT FACTOR

Within ten years, Cal Poly Pomona graduates earn, on average, an annual salary that's 1.4 times their in-state four-year net price of $47,000. That's one of the strongest earnings-to-price ratios among California public universities.

CALIFORNIA STATE UNIVERSITY, FRESNO (CA)

Situated in California's agricultural region, Fresno State offers programs in agriculture and viticulture that maintain strong connections with the industry. The university's College of Agricultural Sciences and Technology operates the Fresno State Winery, where students engage in every aspect of winemaking from vine to bottle, integrating scientific and business knowledge.

An honors program in engineering endowed in part by Boeing gives students full scholarships and access to individualized learning options and internships. Recent graduates have found success with a variety of employers in the region, including Fresno Unified Schools, Pacific Gas & Electric, and Kaiser Permanente.

STANDOUT FACTOR

On average, ten years after enrollment, graduates earn an annual salary that's 2.27 times the total four-year, in-state net price of $26,976.

THE COLLEGE OF NEW JERSEY (NJ)

The College of New Jersey (TCNJ) is recognized as a regional public university that competes on the same playing field with much bigger players in the space. Its 94 percent freshman retention rate is on par with the stats at many prestigious private institutions. Accepting 64 percent of applicants, the college balances accessibility with excellence: It boasts a low 13:1 student-faculty ratio, extensive undergraduate research opportunities, and favorable career outcomes. Particularly notable is a medical school acceptance rate that is twenty points above the national average.

STANDOUT FACTOR

As one of only eight public colleges in the country with a four-year graduation rate above 75 percent, TCNJ is in the company of institutions such as the University of Virginia, Michigan, and UNC–Chapel Hill.

FLORIDA A&M UNIVERSITY (FL)

At Florida A&M, the nation's highest-rated public Historically Black College or University (HBCU), a peer-mentoring program pairs first-year students with upperclassmen who provide guidance, support, and encouragement to facilitate a successful transition into university life. The school's signature offerings include a pre-pharmacy program and a bachelor of science in chemical and biomedical engineering, both of which prepare students for careers in health care technology. Based in Tallahassee, Florida A&M has established relationships with regional employers like Miami-Dade Public Schools, Baptist Health, and Royal Caribbean.

STANDOUT FACTOR

The four-year, in-state net price of $49,916 is notably lower than the average for peer institutions, and Florida A&M maintains competitive graduation rates for a public university.

FLORIDA INTERNATIONAL UNIVERSITY (FL)

With *The Wall Street Journal* ranking Florida International's student experience third in the nation and first among public universities, this school demonstrates how a large research institution can deliver personalized education at scale. The university's pre-orientation program connects incoming students with peers and campus leaders before classes begin, which may eventually contribute to graduation rates that exceed predictions for its student population.

STANDOUT FACTOR

Florida International delivers an exceptional return on investment. Graduates earn $58,000 annually after ten years—2.3 times as much as the net four-year in-state educational cost of $24,928.

GEORGE MASON UNIVERSITY (VA)

Located fifteen miles from Washington, D.C., George Mason University has evolved into Virginia's largest public research university with 25,000 undergraduates. Its School of Public Policy provides direct pathways to federal agencies, and its cybersecurity engineering program addresses critical security challenges through industry partnerships. The university's economics department features Nobel laureates among its faculty. The location advantage shows in career outcomes—86 percent of graduates stay in Virginia, D.C., or Maryland, working for employers like Booz Allen Hamilton, Deloitte, Capital One, Freddie Mac, and Microsoft.

<u>STANDOUT FACTOR</u>

George Mason's graduation rate of 70 percent exceeds expectations by 2 percentage points, given the rates of other institutions serving similar student populations. Meanwhile, the school maintains a 90 percent acceptance rate, which keeps its programs quite accessible.

GEORGIA SOUTHERN UNIVERSITY (GA)

Georgia Southern has positioned its professional programs to leverage Statesboro's growing industrial base. The College of Business's supply chain program connects students directly to internships with DHL and the Georgia Ports Authority, while the College of Engineering and Computing stands to benefit from Hyundai Motor Group's new electric vehicle plant near campus. The College of Health Professions combines classroom instruction with hands-on exercises in simulation labs. The university's emphasis on industry alignment appears to pay off in career outcomes, with graduates securing positions at major regional employers like Gulfstream Aerospace, Home Depot, and Amazon.

<u>STANDOUT FACTOR</u>

On the surface, Georgia Southern's graduation rate at 53 percent is below national averages, yet it ranks above peers who serve a similar student body, which merits its inclusion on this list. The university is an access campus, meaning it accepts nine out of ten students who apply. If students end up transferring to other universities in the University of Georgia system and graduate, their completion is counted for the new campus, not Georgia Southern.

MARQUETTE UNIVERSITY (WI)

A midsized Jesuit school that emphasizes service along with academics and career skills, Marquette draws students from far and wide: 65 percent come from out of state. The university's Biomedical Sciences program is known for undergraduate research and pre-med preparation, and its

College of Nursing allows students to begin clinical coursework in their first year. The College of Business Administration, which awards about a quarter of the university's undergraduate degrees, connects students to Milwaukee's business community. Located in the heart of the city, Marquette provides ready access to internship and job opportunities. Graduates often land positions at major regional employers like Northwestern Mutual, GE HealthCare, and the financial-services firm Baird. About a third of the university's financial aid is awarded without respect to financial need.

STANDOUT FACTOR

With an 81 percent six-year graduation rate and average annual earnings of $76,417 ten years after enrollment, Marquette produces strong student outcomes compared with those of peer institutions.

MONTCLAIR STATE UNIVERSITY (NJ)

Located just twelve miles from New York City, Montclair State is New Jersey's second-largest public university, with over 18,000 under-graduates. The university partners with Rutgers New Jersey Medical School to provide an accelerated pre-med program where qualified students in biology, chemistry, biochemistry, or molecular biology receive comprehensive support and automatic advancement to medical school. The School of Computing and School of Communication and Media are recent additions to campus, expanding career pathways for graduates. Across all majors, the Office of Student Belonging provides cohort-based experiences for freshmen, transfers, and first-generation students. Recent graduates have found success at major regional employers including Hackensack Meridian Health, Atlantic Health System, ADP, and Prudential Financial.

STANDOUT FACTOR

Montclair State's six-year graduation rate is 13 percentage points higher than predicted for institutions serving similar student populations—a reflection of strong student support.

SAN DIEGO STATE UNIVERSITY (CA)

California's second-largest city provides the backdrop for San Diego State's nationally recognized programs in international business and engineering. The university population extends beyond California residents, with 12 percent of nearly 8,000 freshmen coming from out of state. Business administration graduates find success at major employers like Qualcomm, Amazon, Apple, and ServiceNow, benefiting from the university's industry connections in the region.

STANDOUT FACTOR

San Diego State's 76 percent six-year graduation rate exceeds predicted outcomes for similar institutions by 4 percentage points.

UNIVERSITY OF NORTH CAROLINA ASHEVILLE (NC)

As one of the few public liberal arts colleges in the country, the Asheville campus of UNC takes advantage of its place within a larger research university system. Some 65 percent of students complete original research in their field of study, with class sizes averaging just 14 students. The core curriculum includes first-year seminars and senior capstones. The Art & Art History Department stands out as the most popular major, drawing talented students to a city known for its galleries and vibrant arts scene. Recent graduates have found success at major employers including Mission Health, Wells Fargo, Bank of America, and the EPA.

STANDOUT FACTOR

The $52,276 average net price over four years makes UNC Asheville an affordable pathway to careers in the arts and sciences, with graduates earning about $2,800 more than predicted based on student characteristics.

UNIVERSITY OF PUGET SOUND (WA)

Interdisciplinary thinking defines the undergraduate experience at Puget Sound, where students tackle core requirements organized around themes rather than traditional departments. This holistic approach extends overseas through the university's signature Pacific Rim Program, which sends students on nine-month academic journeys across Asia. With most classes between ten and nineteen students, Puget Sound maintains intimate learning environments across popular majors in business, psychology, and exercise science. The Tacoma setting places students within reach of Mount Rainier's recreational opportunities and Seattle's tech employers, including Microsoft, Boeing, and Amazon.

STANDOUT FACTOR

About one-third of the university's financial-aid budget is dedicated to discounts, with the average merit award nearly $29,000 a year.

WASHINGTON STATE UNIVERSITY, WA

As the state's land-grant institution, the university is known for its programs in agriculture, engineering, veterinary medicine, and hospitality management. The university works closely with the Pacific Northwest National Laboratory, one of the U.S. Department of Energy's national laboratories, which offers internship opportunities to undergraduates. The School for Global Animal Health is named for Paul G. Allen, cofounder of Microsoft, who attended the university and donated the largest private gift in its history. Located in the rolling hills of southeastern Washington, the university is twenty minutes away from Idaho State University. About 15 percent of undergraduates come from outside the state of Washington. Graduates land positions at large state employers, including Amazon, Boeing, Microsoft, and Nordstrom.

STANDOUT FACTOR

Washington State's graduates earn, on average, $5,000 more annually than predicted based on student characteristics.

LARGE LEADERS

ARIZONA STATE UNIVERSITY (AZ)

As one of the nation's largest universities, Arizona State uses its size to create distinctive learning and networking opportunities for undergraduates. The Barrett Honors College serves more than 7,200 students (with an average incoming GPA of 3.81) in a dedicated residential complex. In ASU's "innovation zones," students get to work on projects and research for major employers like State Farm and Amazon Web Services. A light-rail line connects ASU's Tempe campus to Phoenix, where the university's communications, nursing, and public policy schools (as well as others) are located, closer to the state's health care and government sectors. In 2024, the Global Employability University Ranking & Survey ranked ASU second among U.S. public universities (behind the University of California, Berkeley) for employable graduates. Top employers of the university's alumni include Amazon, Intel, Deloitte, Honeywell, and American Express.

STANDOUT FACTOR

ASU's charter, chiseled in stone at the entrance to the main campus, proclaims that the school is measured "by who it includes and how they succeed, not by who it excludes." As a result, Arizona State celebrates its high acceptance rate, while still drawing academically talented students who come in with a 3.5 GPA, on average, with 28 percent of them ranking in the top 10 percent of their high school classes.

CASE WESTERN RESERVE UNIVERSITY (OH)

Undergraduates at Case Western engage in research at rates far exceeding typical universities, with 84 percent of undergraduates participating in faculty projects. The school's seven-story Sears think[box] innovation center functions as a library of tools—from 3D printers to water jet cutters—that support experiential learning across disciplines. Engineering, biology, and computer science are among the top majors, providing strong pathways to employers such as the nearby Cleveland Clinic, the U.S. Department of Veterans Affairs, and Deloitte. Unlike many universities, Case Western has a single-door admission policy, which means students can change majors without reapplying to specific schools. Despite the university's urban setting, 80 percent of students live on campus, with all freshmen grouped in residential communities.

STANDOUT FACTOR
More than 40 percent of Case's institutional aid is in the form of merit discounts, making it a good deal for many families compared to less accessible universities, like Carnegie Mellon and Johns Hopkins. The average first-year discount award is more than $31,000.

CLEMSON UNIVERSITY (SC)
Clemson offers specialized programs that combine academic disciplines with practical applications. For instance, at its 250-acre International Center for Automotive Research, juniors study and apply (through design and prototyping) a blend of mechanical engineering, electrical engineering, and computer science. And at Clemson's business school, students can earn an eleven-credit Leadership Certificate, which adds real-world training and development to traditional coursework. With 41 percent of classes under twenty students, Clemson maintains a close-knit academic environment despite its size. The honors college provides key advantages, including priority registration and separate advising. In recent years, numbers of graduates have gone on to secure positions at Michelin, GE Power, IBM, and Bank of America.

STANDOUT FACTOR
Clemson reports a 94 percent first-year retention rate and an 85 percent graduation rate, indicating strong student outcomes.

COLORADO STATE UNIVERSITY (CO)

In the foothills of the Rocky Mountains, Colorado State stands out for providing research opportunities and specialized environmental programs. More than 5,000 undergrads participate in research, many of them publishing their work in the university's own peer-reviewed student research journal. The College of Veterinary Medicine and Biomedical Sciences anchors the university's strong life-sciences focus, while programs in animal science, plant science, and natural resource management leverage the region's natural assets. Students develop a sense of belonging through residential learning communities centered on particular areas of interest, like engineering and health science. The university's proximity to Denver's tech corridor has created a pipeline to employers such as Amazon, Google, and Tesla.

STANDOUT FACTOR

Colorado State's in-state net price of $74,048 over four years delivers strong value, with graduates earning $58,388 annually, on average, ten years after enrollment. That earnings-to-price ratio sets it apart from most peer institutions.

DREXEL UNIVERSITY (PA)

Drexel operates one of the nation's largest and oldest cooperative-education programs, alternating academic terms with full-time paid work experience. This structured approach to career preparation creates direct pathways to Philadelphia employers like PwC, Deloitte, EY, UBS, and Morgan Stanley. While business programs are prominent, health professions and social sciences also rank among top majors for the university's 14,000 undergraduates, who maintain a 78 percent six-year graduation rate.

STANDOUT FACTOR

Drexel's emphasis on paid co-op experiences sets the stage for average graduate earnings of nearly $80,000 annually after ten years, exceeding predicted outcomes by nearly $2,000 a year.

FORDHAM UNIVERSITY (NY)

"New York is my campus, Fordham is my school" isn't just a marketing slogan. It's how Fordham structures the undergraduate experience across its Bronx and Lincoln Center locations. The university's mentoring program formalizes connections between students and alumni through twenty-four hours of one-on-one engagement each year, leading to opportunities with employers like JPMorgan Chase and Citi. Fordham also maintains a strong global perspective, with 40 percent of students studying abroad through 125 programs in fifty-plus countries. Popular majors include finance, business administration, and psychology, and the theater program at Lincoln Center draws national recognition.

STANDOUT FACTOR

Fordham graduates earn $78,820 annually ten years after enrollment, outperforming baseline predictions, perhaps owing to the school's strong placement rates in New York's financial sector.

HOWARD UNIVERSITY (DC)

As one of the most respected HBCUs in the nation, Howard University has built a sturdy bridge between its deep history of educating African American leaders and today's tech economy. The university's success in placing graduates at companies like Amazon, Microsoft, Google, and IBM reflects its particular strengths in business, communications, and biology. The campus comes alive during Homecoming Weekend, when Yardfest transforms the grounds into a cultural celebration and the Divine Nine fraternities and sororities showcase their precision in the traditional Step Show. Through these events, current students connect with Howard's extensive network of alumni who have shaped U.S. history and culture.

STANDOUT FACTOR

Howard produces strong career outcomes for its graduates, who earn nearly $2,000 more annually than predicted in light of stats for peer institutions.

INDIANA UNIVERSITY BLOOMINGTON (IN)

Indiana combines the resources of a major research institution with surprisingly small class sizes (nearly 40 percent of courses have fewer than twenty students). For many of its undergraduates, the Kelley School of Business and the Jacobs School of Music anchor the academic experience, while the Luddy School of Informatics, Computing, and Engineering prepares STEM-savvy students for tech careers. The university maintains close connections with employers—61 percent of students complete at least one internship while enrolled. Recent graduates have landed positions at major companies including Eli Lilly, Amazon, Salesforce, and Microsoft. While many flagship universities have become increasingly selective, Indiana remains accessible. Its out-of-state acceptance rate is above 80 percent, and it hasn't sacrificed its 81 percent graduation rate. The Common Ground curriculum ensures that all students develop core skills across disciplines regardless of major.

STANDOUT FACTOR

Indiana's graduation rate is 5 percentage points higher than predicted for institutions serving similar students, and the university delivers strong career outcomes at a moderate in-state net price ($56,864 over four years).

MIAMI UNIVERSITY OF OHIO (OH)

While many public universities grow ever larger, Miami of Ohio maintains a size and scale that serves its 16,000 undergraduates well. Its "Miami Plan" core curriculum gives students in all majors the flexibility to take twenty-seven credits across the humanities, the sciences, and global perspectives. The university's Georgian-style campus offers specialized learning communities through housing tied directly to academic programs. Dorm mates take courses together. This integration of living and learning, combined with strong career connections to firms like Procter & Gamble, EY, and JPMorgan Chase, has helped Miami establish itself as a destination for students seeking a flagship university experience with a more intimate feel.

Miami achieves an 83 percent graduation rate while serving a large public university population, outperforming most peer institutions in the Midwest for student completion.

MICHIGAN STATE UNIVERSITY (MI)

One of the original land-grant institutions, Michigan State combines the resources of a major research university with robust support systems for its 41,000 undergraduates. The campus organizes its twenty-seven residence halls into five neighborhoods, each with an Engagement Center providing academic support, career planning, and health services. More than 4,000 students participate in the invitation-only honors college program, which includes independent research projects and priority course registration. Business, communication, and engineering are among the most popular majors. Graduates often launch careers with major Michigan employers like General Motors and Ford, as well as national companies including Deloitte, Target, and Microsoft.

STANDOUT FACTOR

Michigan State's graduation rate is 7 percentage points higher than predicted for institutions serving similar students. The university delivers strong value for graduates, who earn an average of $64,500 annually within ten years against a four-year in-state net price of $43,700.

NORTH CAROLINA STATE UNIVERSITY (NC)

In the Research Triangle of North Carolina, talk about higher education focuses mostly on Duke and Carolina (the University of North Carolina at Chapel Hill). But recently, thanks in part to a deep run into the March NCAA basketball tournaments for both men and women, NC State's name is becoming better known nationally. At this major research university, one advantage that undergraduates have is the opportunity to participate in research across disciplines. The school offers an annual "Speed-Data-ing" event that brings students and faculty members across campus together in a casual setting so the professors can describe the types of research they conduct and the roles available for students.

STANDOUT FACTOR
NC State's graduation rate is five points higher than the national average for institutions serving a similar student body.

OREGON STATE UNIVERSITY (OR)
Oregon State has reimagined the large lecture hall through its Learning Innovation Center, where even 600-seat classrooms bring students close to faculty through "teaching in the round" designs with wraparound screens. The university's commitment to engagement extends beyond architecture: Oregon State funds more undergraduate research than any other institution in the state and brings research directly into daily student life. For instance, its Menus of Change program transforms campus dining into a laboratory for food systems innovation. The university's computer science, business, and engineering programs have built strong recruitment pipelines to Pacific Northwest tech giants and to Fortune 500 companies like Intel, Nike, and Amazon.

STANDOUT FACTOR
Oregon State maintains an accessible 83 percent acceptance rate, and its graduation rate of 70 percent represents a two-point improvement over predicted outcomes for the school's student population.

ROCHESTER INSTITUTE OF TECHNOLOGY (NY)
The university's cooperative education program, among the oldest nationwide, places students in paid positions at companies like Boeing,

SpaceX, and Google as part of the academic curriculum. RIT cultivates expertise and supports achievement across a variety of technical fields. Its College of Art and Design earns national recognition for programs in photography, graphic design, and industrial design. Students pitch business ideas through Tiger Tank competitions for start-up funding, and graduates secure positions at tech leaders such as Microsoft, Amazon, and Apple.

STANDOUT FACTOR

On average, RIT graduates earn $69,250 annually ten years after enrollment. That's about $16,000 higher than expected at similar institutions outside major tech hubs, which speaks to the effectiveness of the school's cooperative-education program.

RUTGERS UNIVERSITY (NJ)

Rutgers is New Jersey's public flagship university. With over 36,000 undergraduates, it maintains a strong graduation rate of 84 percent, nearly matching the stats of many elite private schools. The university provides extensive research opportunities across its sprawling campus system, and its location between New York City and Philadelphia gives students access to internships and jobs in two major metropolitan areas. About 21 percent of students at this major institution in the Northeast corridor receive merit aid without regard to financial need.

STANDOUT FACTOR

Rutgers delivers value. Graduates earn nearly $70,000 annually ten years after enrollment, on average, capturing a 1.2 times return on the net price of attendance.

SOUTHERN METHODIST UNIVERSITY (TX)

Even though "Methodist" is in its name, more students identify as Catholic than as Methodist at this Dallas-based university. The Engaged Learning Fellowship, SMU's most prestigious engagement program, provides both funding and coaching for student research initiatives. Through Research Assistantships, undergraduates work directly with faculty while earning income. Popular majors include finance, economics, and sport management, with graduates landing positions at AT&T, Goldman Sachs, and Southwest Airlines. The pre-health advising program achieves a 53 percent medical school acceptance rate, outpacing the national average of 43 percent.

STANDOUT FACTOR

SMU's graduates earn $5,358 more annually than predicted based on student characteristics, a nice return on the university's investments in career preparation.

SPELMAN COLLEGE (GA)

Although not as large enrollment-wise as other schools in this section, Spelman is typically the highest-ranked HBCU, in part because of its innovative academic programs. Its cosmetic science program brings chemistry and product development together with research focused on ethnic hair and skin care. Through dual-degree partnerships with Georgia Tech and University of Michigan, engineering students can complete a distinctive five-year program spanning two institutions. The "Spelpreneur" initiative connects students directly with successful entrepreneurs through weekly programming that culminates in a *Shark Tank*–style competition. Major employers of graduates include the Centers for Disease Control and Prevention, Delta Air Lines, and Accenture.

STANDOUT FACTOR

Spelman graduates earn, on average, $11,086 more annually than predicted based on institutional characteristics.

SYRACUSE UNIVERSITY (NY)

With Micron's planned $100 billion chip-manufacturing complex practically next door, Syracuse students are well positioned for emerging opportunities nearby. The university's 15,000 undergraduates span ten distinct colleges. For instance, the S. I. Newhouse School of Public Communications prepares students for careers in esports management alongside traditional media paths, and the Maxwell School focuses on public policy and international relations. The five-year architecture program at Syracuse stands among the nation's first. One-third of students join Greek organizations, and campus traditions include a ninety-year-old Winter Carnival celebrating the region's snowy climate. Top employers of alumni include Amazon, Microsoft, IBM, and Google. Some 20 percent of graduates advance to professional or graduate programs.

STANDOUT FACTOR

Syracuse graduates earn, on average, $3,113 more annually than predicted based on student characteristics. The school maintains an 83 percent graduation rate that exceeds expectations by 4 percentage points.

TEXAS A&M UNIVERSITY (TX)

As one of the largest universities in the country, Texas A&M turns its scale into an advantage for its 57,000 undergraduates. The university offers more than 100 majors across twelve schools, with particular strengths in business, engineering, and political science. Despite its size, Texas A&M achieves an 84 percent six-year graduation rate—notably high for a public institution. The university has both professional success coaches and peer success coaches meet with students to help them improve their academic performance and navigate the common challenges many face.

STANDOUT FACTOR

Texas A&M's graduation rate is 5 percentage points higher than predicted for similar institutions. And the yield rate in admissions is 46 percent, compared with an average of 30 percent for other large public institutions, showing just how popular this university is with applicants.

UNIVERSITY OF ALABAMA (AL)

Although known historically for football and Greek life, Alabama has in recent years transformed itself academically through aggressive merit-aid packages and an extensive menu of courses and services that draw 65 percent of its 33,000 undergraduates from out of state. Its honors college—one of the nation's largest, at over 7,000 students—consists of ten distinct programs. Alabama offers more than 100 majors across twelve schools, with particular strengths in business and engineering. But despite its size, most classes have just ten to twenty students. Popular majors include marketing, finance, nursing, and psychology. Graduates land positions at Regions Bank, Deloitte, and Protective Life. The university spends over $185 million on merit scholarships, setting applicants up for success by spelling out transparent GPA and test score requirements for automatic awards.

STANDOUT FACTOR

Alabama's graduates earn, on average, $3,000 more annually than predicted based on student characteristics.

UNIVERSITY OF CALIFORNIA, DAVIS (CA)

Managing 23,000 acres for research purposes in addition to its 5,300-acre main campus, UC Davis has turned its land-grant heritage into a modern advantage. The university's College of Agricultural and Environmental Sciences ranks among the world's best, complementing strong programs in veterinary medicine and nursing. Popular majors include psychology, management sciences, and neurobiology. Located in a classic college town between Sacramento and San Francisco, UC Davis primarily serves in-state students. Only 6 percent of its 31,000 undergraduates come from outside California.

STANDOUT FACTOR

Thanks to $700 million devoted annually to research, students participate in faculty projects through the Undergraduate Research Center and present their work at an annual spring conference.

UNIVERSITY OF CALIFORNIA SAN DIEGO (CA)

Through its unique system of eight residential colleges, UC San Diego creates intimate communities within its population of 33,000 undergraduates, each cohort with its own educational philosophy and general-education requirements. This structure supports the university's research intensity: 60 percent of undergraduates complete projects in their coursework, and 25 percent work directly with faculty on projects outside class. Popular majors include STEM fields such as biology, engineering, and computer science. Despite large lecture courses in some subjects, more than 40 percent of classes enroll fewer than 20 students. The La Jolla location, between beach and city, puts students near major tech employers like Google, Amazon, and Apple.

STANDOUT FACTOR

Like other institutions within the UC system, San Diego prioritizes California residents in admissions. That said, its out-of-state acceptance rate hovers around 30 percent, which makes the university more accessible to students than many schools that are similarly ranked.

UNIVERSITY OF CONNECTICUT (CT)

With roughly 20,000 undergraduate students and a winning Division I athletics program, UConn promises a lively campus experience, but this research institution distinguishes itself in other ways, too. Each year nearly half its freshmen join one of thirty-plus living-learning communities, while 2,200 participate in research and specialized coursework through the honors program. First-year seminars and Learning Community Seminars (capped at nineteen students) help students engage in discipline-specific exploration. The university's location between Boston and New York brings major employers like Aetna, Cigna, PwC, and Raytheon Technologies within reach. Popular fields of study include psychology, economics, and nursing. Roughly 30 percent of seniors continue directly to graduate programs.

UConn's 83 percent graduation rate, among the highest for public universities, is 4 percentage points above expectations for institutions serving similar students.

UNIVERSITY OF DELAWARE (DE)

At Delaware, the University 101 program eases all first-year students through an eight-week transition into college life, providing peer mentoring, faculty guidance, and other resources to help everyone adjust. Classes are generally small (62 percent have fewer than thirty students). Business and engineering programs attract nearly one-third of undergraduates. Direct Amtrak access opens up internship opportunities across major East Coast cities, supporting strong career outcomes alongside robust graduate school placement for one-third of seniors. Delaware's location along the Northeast Corridor powers professional connections from Washington, D.C., to New York City. Alumni secure positions at Merck, Capital One, and AstraZeneca.

Delaware graduates earn nearly $72,000 annually, on average, ten years after enrollment, reaping strong returns on their net-price investment of around the same amount.

UNIVERSITY OF ILLINOIS URBANA-CHAMPAIGN (IL)

The Grainger College of Engineering, which produced web browser pioneer Marc Andreessen in the 1990s, helped establish the University of Illinois's reputation for technical innovation and career preparation. Students work alongside more than 100 corporations at Research Park, an on-campus tech hub, while the Siebel Center for Design provides 5,000 square feet of prototyping space, replete with 3D printers and laser cutters. For those more interested in management, finance, or accounting, the Gies College of Business creates direct pathways to top firms and corporations, with recent graduates securing positions at KPMG, Deloitte, PwC, and United Airlines. Regardless of major, every student has access to leadership development through the Illinois Leadership Center's certification programs and retreats.

STANDOUT FACTOR

Ten years after enrollment, graduates earn—annually, on average—1.25 times the school's four-year net price. That ratio places Illinois among the top public institutions for return on investment.

UNIVERSITY OF IOWA (IA)

From its renowned Iowa Writers' Workshop to its innovative bike-building curriculum bridging art and engineering, the University of Iowa exemplifies creativity in education. The school pioneered the Iowa GROW program, where student workers engage in structured conversations with supervisors to develop career skills through campus jobs, inspiring hundreds of institutions to adopt a similar approach. About 30 percent of its 22,000 undergraduates participate in research, and more than 40 percent come from outside Iowa. Alumni find success working for companies such as Epic, Chase, BMO Financial Group, and 3M.

STANDOUT FACTOR

Iowa's 74 percent graduation rate outperforms the average for similar institutions by 4 percentage points—a reflection of strong student support systems.

UNIVERSITY OF KENTUCKY (KY)

Every first-year student at Kentucky receives an iPad through the Smart Campus Initiative, which sets the tone for a tech-enabled learning environment throughout the university. Although around 24,000 undergraduates go to this school, most classes are on the small side, between twenty and thirty students. Its programs run the gamut. The Gatton College of Business and Economics excels in finance and entrepreneurship, while the College of Agriculture leads peer institutions in agricultural research. Graduates often secure positions at Humana, Toyota North America, and Microsoft. Nursing, marketing, and psychology rank among the most popular majors.

STANDOUT FACTOR
Kentucky graduates earn nearly $2,000 more annually than predicted based on student characteristics.

UNIVERSITY OF MARYLAND, COLLEGE PARK (MD)
Minutes from the nation's capital, Maryland's main campus features an honors college with eight specialized living-learning cohorts—such as Gemstone, which offers a four-year interdisciplinary research experience. Strong programs in business, engineering, and journalism attract employers like Northrop Grumman, Deloitte, Amazon, and National Geographic. The university's pre-med preparation stands out as well. Medical school acceptance rates exceed 60 percent, about twenty points above the national average. While 17 percent of classes enroll fifty or more students, nearly half maintain fewer than twenty students.

STANDOUT FACTOR
Maryland's 89 percent graduation rate ranks among the highest for public universities, outperforming peer institutions by 6 percentage points.

UNIVERSITY OF MASSACHUSETTS AMHERST (MA)
Unusually intimate for a research university of its size, UMass has fewer than twenty students in nearly half its courses. And yet, this

public flagship attracts undergraduates from all over, with more than a quarter of those who enroll coming from out of state. Students can expand their academic options through the Five College Consortium, which allows them to take courses at nearby Amherst, Smith, Mount Holyoke, and Hampshire colleges. Major tech employers such as Google, Microsoft, and Amazon actively recruit computer science graduates, while the university's location in Western Massachusetts channels business majors into Boston's financial sector less than two hours away.

STANDOUT FACTOR
The university's six-year graduation rate of 84 percent exceeds expectations for similar institutions by 4 percentage points.

UNIVERSITY OF MINNESOTA TWIN CITIES (MN)
Among major public research universities, Minnesota's flagship campus stands out for balancing broad access with individual student success. It accepts 75 percent of applicants, and its 30,000-plus undergraduates achieve an 84 percent graduation rate. The university's location in Minneapolis–St. Paul connects students to one of the Midwest's largest employment centers, where they can explore an array of internship and job opportunities. Graduates earn approximately $65,000 annually ten years after enrollment.

STANDOUT FACTOR
Target, Medtronic, 3M, and sixteen other Fortune 500 companies headquartered in Minneapolis–St. Paul provide students with an exceptionally rich employment ecosystem within minutes of campus.

UNIVERSITY OF MISSOURI–COLUMBIA (MO)
For a large public flagship, this university provides a wealth of learning-by-doing opportunities. Indeed, it is widely known for its hands-on approach to education—the so-called Missouri Method.

For example, the Mizzou School of Journalism puts theory into practice through real-world training at the university-owned NBC affiliate, KOMU-TV. And the College of Health Sciences, Missouri's only state-supported allied health school, provides clinical exposure and training, creating a direct pipeline into health care careers. The university's location in Columbia, consistently ranked among top college towns, offers strategic access to employers in both St. Louis and Kansas City, including Burns & McDonnell, Bayer, Amazon, and Centene Corporation.

STANDOUT FACTOR

Mizzou graduates earn, on average, $61,073 annually ten years after enrollment against a total net price of $71,596. The practical training they received as students gives them a head start when they compete for entry-level jobs that nonetheless require some experience.

UNIVERSITY OF OKLAHOMA (OK)

Located just outside Oklahoma City, this university combines strong professional programs with unique research opportunities shaped by regional geography. For instance, Oklahoma's meteorology program benefits from its position in Tornado Alley. The college of business is known for its programs in accounting, finance, marketing, and management information systems, with engineering offering its biggest programs in aerospace, biomedical, and petroleum engineering. Both schools connect students with major employers, such as Paycom, Amazon, and Devon Energy. The university's Center for Major & Career Exploration assists students in identifying suitable majors through personalized assessments and advising.

STANDOUT FACTOR

Relative to expectations for peer institutions, the university's graduation rate of 76 percent is 3 percentage points higher, and graduates earn nearly $3,000 more annually.

UNIVERSITY OF PITTSBURGH (PA)

From its home in Pittsburgh's Oakland neighborhood, Pitt offers students a true urban-campus experience. They can easily walk to the Carnegie Museums, for example, and can enjoy watching Division I football at Acrisure Stadium, shared with the NFL's Steelers. The school deserves high marks for academics and career preparation as well. For highly qualified undergraduates, Guaranteed Admissions Programs provide clear pathways to Pitt's medical, law, business, and other professional schools. The Swanson School of Engineering consistently attracts high-achieving students, enrolling applicants with SAT scores in the 97th percentile. More than half of undergraduates participate in research, supported by a low student-faculty ratio of 13:1. Given the university's location, students have ready access to employers in and around the city, such as UPMC, PNC, and BNY Mellon, and they capitalize on a growing tech presence from Amazon, Google, and Microsoft.

STANDOUT FACTOR

With an 84 percent graduation rate and average earnings of $61,744 ten years after enrollment, Pitt achieves outcomes on par with more selective institutions while maintaining its broader acceptance rate of 49 percent.

UNIVERSITY OF UTAH (UT)

Utah's flagship university has emerged as a key source of talent for Salt Lake City's surging tech sector. The School of Business and College of Engineering have built strong pipelines to employers like Goldman Sachs, Adobe, and Microsoft, with 56 percent of students completing at least one internship. Popular majors include psychology, communication and media studies, and computer science. Each year, more than 2,700 students collaborate with faculty mentors and present their work at the annual Undergraduate Research Symposium.

STANDOUT FACTOR

The average annual earnings of Utah graduates, $64,456 ten years after enrollment, significantly exceed the four-year net price of $51,468.

VIRGINIA TECH (VA)

Engineering and computer science are central to Virginia Tech's identity. Roughly 43 percent of graduates emerge from these programs, catching the attention of security and defense contractors like Lockheed Martin and Northrop Grumman. The university's location in the Blue Ridge Mountains doesn't isolate students from opportunity: 53 percent secure paid internships with employers ranging from Amazon to Dominion Energy. Alongside all the tech, the College of Business (accounting for 20 percent of degrees) maintains strong recruiting relationships with major accounting firms, including Deloitte, KPMG, and EY. Each year, more than 1,200 students study abroad in locations ranging from Switzerland to New Zealand.

STANDOUT FACTOR

Virginia Tech's 86 percent graduation rate exceeds predictions for similar institutions by 9 percentage points.

COLLEGE OF WILLIAM & MARY (VA)

As America's second-oldest college, William & Mary infuses its rigorous academics with centuries of tradition, annually hosting long-cherished events like December's Yule Log Celebration and the year-end Royal Ball. The school offers a joint degree with Scotland's St Andrews University, enabling students to split their four years between the two institutions. A global mindset pervades William & Mary, with 55 percent of students studying abroad compared with an average of just 1 percent nationally. The Williamsburg location puts students two hours from Washington, D.C., where graduates build careers at EY, Capital One, and Booz Allen Hamilton after completing majors in business administration, biology, and psychology.

STANDOUT FACTOR

William & Mary achieves a graduation rate 9 percentage points above expectations.

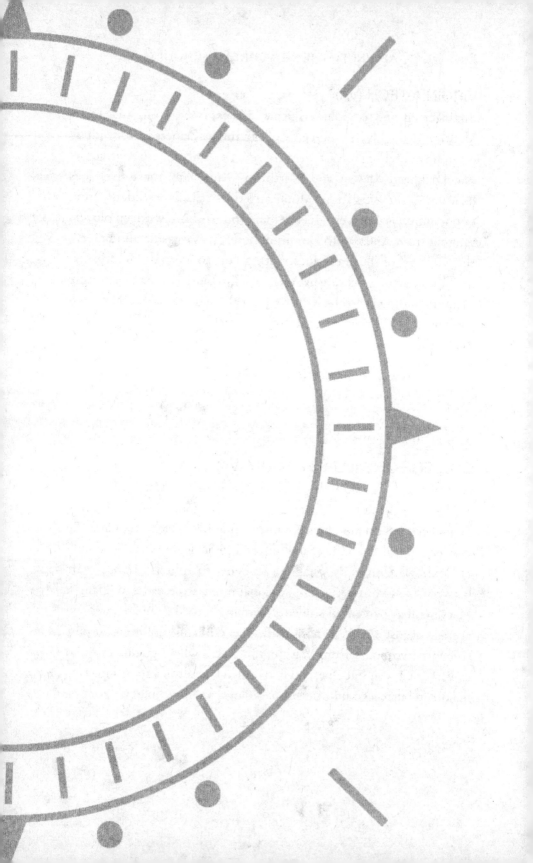

ACKNOWLEDGMENTS

First, I'd like to thank the many cups of coffee at 5 a.m. and deadline-induced panic, without which this book would still be an idea floating somewhere in my head.

The person who first helped draw that idea out was my extraordinary agent, Gail Ross, who, as always, was there with me every step of the way, offering encouragement, answering questions, or just listening. I was fortunate to reunite with my editor, Rick Horgan, whose ability to get to the essence of ideas and anticipate what readers need made all the difference. I'm indebted to his assistant, Sophie Guimaraes, and the exceptional production, marketing, and publicity team at Scribner, whose collective expertise and understanding of an author's journey made this book possible.

The early reporting for this book started with focus groups organized by Debbie Schwartz and her team at Paying for College 101, as well as fellow authors and friends Shereem Herndon-Brown and Tim Fields. Along the way several people helped me hash out my thinking or answered my incessant questions: Diane Campbell, Mike Coyne, James Murphy, and Jon Boeckenstedt. A special thanks to Allison Slater Tate, whose friendship, encouragement, and willingness to answer any question at any time of day were invaluable.

ACKNOWLEDGMENTS

I'm indebted to the partners who fulfilled my requests for how the application landscape has changed by mining their databases: Athena Meyers and the team at Niche, as well as Kevin McCloskey, the cofounder of Scoir. Thanks to Shawn VanDerziel at the National Association of Colleges and Employers, Andy Chan at Wake Forest University, and Handshake for their knowledge about the job market and connecting me with those who recruit new college graduates.

Several people and organizations were helpful in providing their expertise, data, and financial support in compiling the Dream School list, including Michael Itzkowitz, Jillian Kinzie and the NSSE Center for Postsecondary Research at Indiana University, Lendl Meyer and Lightcast, Matt Sigelman and the Burning Glass Institute, and Lumina Foundation. Thanks to Liz Gross and Campus Sonar for helping me understand—through the social listening research they conducted for me—how people were talking about higher education in online forums.

So many chapters in this book were informed by my surveys of parents and students. For the parent survey, thank you to Nicholas Balisciano and John Pryor for not only lending their expertise and insight, but also for their skilled work in designing the surveys and analyzing the crucial data they yielded. Lots of people promoted the survey, including two friends who have been some of my biggest supporters through several books, Lisa Heffernan and Mary Dell Harrington at Grown & Flown. I'm also grateful to Rob Buelow and Vector Solutions for adding my questions to their massive survey that accompanies their online training modules for undergraduates.

I owe an immeasurable debt to the students, parents, and counselors who trusted me with their stories. Their willingness to speak honestly about both struggles and successes has shaped every page of this book. I continue to be moved by their hope for the future.

I'm incredibly lucky to be surrounded by a team who helped get this book to the finish line. Scott Smallwood remains a good friend and one of the most trusted editors I've ever had the honor to work with—his advice, words, thoughtful edits, and data analysis are present on virtually every page. I'm so thankful our paths crossed all those years ago at *The Chronicle of Higher Education*. I'm forever grateful to my *Future U.* podcast cohost and friend, Michael B. Horn, for introducing me to Lisa Burrell, whose editing skills transformed this manuscript. As with my previous books, Sheila McMillen provided invaluable edits that made the book better. Paul Compton's artful eye created the graphics throughout. For research support, thank you to Tiffany MacLennan and Cassy Pressimone Beckowski. Any errors of fact or interpretation are mine alone. My assistant, Kiri Mohan, kept my calendar (and life) in some semblance of order to be sure I got everything done, while Margie Whiteleather ensured the various trains that make up my day-to-day work continued to run on time and also contributed valuable research and ideas that found their way into this work.

This manuscript was also improved by feedback from a collection of early readers: Shana Bass, Amalia Cunningham, Jon Forslund, Ella Leitner, Lance Patterson, Jackie Stancil, Martin VanDerWerf, John Wilkerson, David English, and Hugh McIntosh.

I'm able to write because of people who support my work, and I'm especially thankful to Michael Crow and Jim O'Brien at Arizona State University, who have given me a front-row seat to how higher education should be for the past ten-plus years.

And finally, my family: To my parents, Jim and Carmella, thank you for all you have done for me—and still do—but most of all for giving us the gift of a college education. Beyond your unconditional love and support, it is perhaps the greatest gift a parent can give their children. To Jamie and Dave, I love you both. To my in-laws, Gene and Sandy, thank you for being there, always. To Maria Orozco, I couldn't have finished another book without your help. You'll always be part of our family.

To Hadley and Rory, watching you grow up with each book I have written has been a source of pride, inspiration, but most of all, joy. I'm never happier than when I'm with the two of you and Mom. And to that mom—my wife, Heather, a partner, best friend, companion who is constantly challenging me to be better, but most of all cheering me along (and just listening)—thank you. You and the kids are the dream that matters most—the one that made all of this possible.

NOTES

This book is the result of more than two years of reporting and research during which I interviewed and spoke with hundreds of students, parents, high school counselors, college admissions officers, and other experts on higher education, the post-college workforce, parenting, and teen and young adult psychology. Much of the material in this book is from those interviews and discussions. Where I relied on books, articles, or reports for statistics or information, I listed those sources in the text itself or in the notes below.

Unless otherwise noted, data about colleges and universities in the book come from the federal government's Integrated Postsecondary Education Data System, known as IPEDS (https://nces.ed.gov/ipeds), or a school's report to the Common Data Set. References to *U.S. News & World Report* rankings come from the 2025 edition, which was released in September 2024.

INTRODUCTION

4   *"colleges evaluate students"*: Hector Chade, Gregory Lewis, and Lones Smith, "Student Portfolios and the College Admissions Problem," *Review of Economic Studies* 81, no. 3 (2014): 971–1002, https://doi.org/10.1093/restud/rdu003.

7 *"the skills and values": Purpose of Education Index*, Populace, September 2022, https://populace.org/research.

7 *I conducted two surveys of more than 3,000 parents:* I conducted two surveys of parents for this book. Each survey contained different questions, but the second survey was composed of a follow-up group of parents from the first survey. As a result, collectively throughout the book, they are referred to as a "survey." The first survey was conducted in March 2024, with the assistance of Nicholas Balisciano, a researcher at the Harvard Graduate School of Education. It had 3,079 responses. The second survey, in September 2024, was conducted with the assistance of John Pryor, former director of the Cooperative Institutional Research Program at the University of California, Los Angeles, and the founder of Pryor Education Insights. It had 1,116 respondents.

8 *achievement pressure that rises in middle- and upper middle-class neighborhoods:* S. S. Luthar and C. C. Sexton, "The high price of affluence," *Adv Child Dev Behav* 32 (2004): 125–62, doi: 10.1016/s0065-2407(04)80006-5. PMID: 15641462; PMCID: PMC4358932.

12 *Jay Caspian Kang calls the "panicking class":* From Jay Caspian Kang, "Summer Camps and Parenting Panics," *New Yorker*, May 24, 2024, https://www.newyorker.com/news/fault-lines/summer-camp-and-parenting-panics.

CHAPTER 1: GREAT EXPECTATIONS

19 *Applications skyrocketed 24 percent:* Calculated from data colleges report to the National Center for Education Statistics. Colleges that admitted 20 percent or fewer of their applicants in 2021 were included in this year-to-year comparison.

20 *the combined number of applications filed for both ED and EA:* Application snapshot provided by Mark Freeman, Vice President of Data Analytics and Research, Common App, March 8, 2024.

23 *they suffer from overconfidence bias:* J. R. Magnus and A. A. Peresetsky, "Grade Expectations: Rationality and Overconfidence," *Front Psychol* (2018): 8, 2346, doi: 10.3389/fpsyg.2017.02346. PMID: 29375449; PMCID: PMC5770583.

23 *grades have been rising for at least two decades:* 2019 NAEP High School Transcript Study (HSTS) Results, National Center for Education, https://www.nationsreportcard.gov/hstsreport /#coursetaking_1_0_el; Edgar Sanchez and Raeal Moore, "Grade Inflation Continues to Grow in the Last Decade, ACT, May 2022, https://www.act.org/content/dam/act/secured/documents/pdfs /Grade-Inflation-Continues-to-Grow-in-the-Past-Decade-Final-Acce ssible.pdf.

25 *Clemson and USC offered early action . . . facing another thick pile of files:* The following section is adapted from Jeff Selingo, "The Cynical Reason College Applications Are Surging," *New York Times*, March 16, 2023, https://www.nytimes.com/2023/03/16/opinion/college-admissions -common-app.html.

26 *"we cannot prevent emotional pain in our teenagers":* Lisa Damour, *The Emotional Lives of Teenagers: Raising Connected, Capable, and Compassionate Adolescents* (Ballantine Books, 2023); Lisa Damour, interview with author, February 26, 2024.

28 *about half of families are setting foot on campus:* Jeff Selingo, "A Virtual Spring for Higher Ed," LinkedIn, March 20, 2020, https://www .linkedin.com/pulse/virtual-spring-higher-ed-jeff-selingo/.

33 *In 2024, nearly one in five applicants:* Mark Freeman, "First-year applications per applicant," Common Application, December 12, 2022, https://s3.us-west-2.amazonaws.com/ca.research.publish/Research _Briefs_2022/2022_12_09_Apps_Per_Applicant_ResearchBrief.pdf.

33 *In 2023, 13.1 million applications were filed:* U.S. Department of Education, National Center for Education Statistics, Integrated Postsecondary Education Data System (IPEDS), Admissions component final data (fall 2014–2021) and provisional data (fall 2022).

33 *the number of high school graduates in the U.S.:* Digest of Education Statistics, IES/National Center for Education Statistics, https://nces .ed.gov/programs/digest/d17/tables/dt17_219.10.asp.

36 *Jeff Makris has become keenly aware:* I originally interviewed Jeff Makris for an article in *New York* magazine, which this section is based on: "What Does an SAT Score Mean Anymore?" *New York*

magazine, February 26, 2024, https://nymag.com/intelligencer/article /what-does-an-sat-score-mean-in-a-test-optional-world.html.

40 *"We certainly did not increase our staff . . . require test scores again:* This section on MIT and Stu Schmill is a combination of reporting for the book as well as from my article "What Does an SAT Score Mean Anymore?" for *New York* magazine.

41 *At Case Western, for instance, test-optional:* According to Rick Bischoff, vice president for enrollment management at Case Western Reserve University, interview with author, February 29, 2024.

CHAPTER 2: SWIMMING IN CALMER WATERS

49 *the big fish–little pond effect that Beth alluded to, was introduced:* H. W. Marsh and J. W. Parker, "Determinants of student self-concept: Is it better to be a relatively large fish in a small pond even if you don't learn to swim as well?," *Journal of Personality and Social Psychology* 47, no. 1 (1984): 213–231, https://doi.org/10.1037/0022-3514.47.1.213.

49 *As Marsh later told Malcolm Gladwell:* Malcolm Gladwell, *David and Goliath: Underdogs, Misfits, and the Art of Battling Giants* (Little, Brown, 2013).

50 *"For every 10-point increase in the average SAT score":* Mitchell J. Chang, Oscar Cerna, et al., "The Contradictory Roles of Institutional Status in Retaining Underrepresented Minorities in Biomedical and Behavioral Science Majors," *Review of Higher Education* 31, no. 4 (2008): 433–464, https://dx.doi.org/10.1353/rhe.0.0011.

53 *When we met for breakfast in Cambridge:* This section on Deming is from my interview with him in Cambridge, Massachusetts, June 10, 2024, and from his Substack newsletter, *Forked Lightning.*

54 *the "explore and exploit" trade-off:* For a full discussion of this theory, see Brian Christian and Tom Griffiths, *Algorithms to Live By: The Computer Science of Human Decisions* (Henry Holt, 2016).

56 *Do Ivy-plus graduates have a better shot of landing in the top 1 percent of income?:* J. Wai, S. M. Anderson, et al., "The most successful and influential Americans come from a surprisingly narrow range of 'elite' educational backgrounds," *Humanit Soc Sci Commun* 11 (2024): 1129, https://doi.org/10.1057/s41599-024-03547-8.

57 *Let's consider another study by Deming:* Raj Chetty, Matthew O. Johnson, et al., "Social capital II: determinants of economic connectedness," *Nature* 608 (2022): 122–134, https://doi.org/10.1038 /s41586-022-04997-3; https://www.nature.com/articles/s41586-022-04 997-3.pdf.

CHAPTER 3: THE RISE OF THE OUT-OF-STATE RECRUIT

72 *James Rhodes promised a college within thirty miles of every resident:* Jeffrey Selingo, "Location, Location, Location. Urban Hot Spots Are the Place to Be," *Chronicle of Higher Education,* July 28, 2014, https:// www.chronicle.com/article/location-location-location-urban-hot -spots-are-the-place-to-be.

72 *what's been dubbed the Great Student Swap:* For example, see Aaron Klein, "The Great Student Swap," Brookings Mountain West, September 7, 2022, https://www.brookings.edu/articles/the-great-student -swap/.

74 *one-third of the cost of their education:* Karen Fischer and Jack Stripling, *Chronicle of Higher Education,* March 2, 2014, https://www.chronicle .com/article/an-era-of-neglect/.

74 *raise a lot more money much faster by recruiting out-of-state:* For research on how out-of-state enrollment at flagships increased following declines in state appropriations, see: Ozan Jaquette and B. R. Curs, "Creating the Out-of-State University: Do Public Universities Increase Nonresident Freshman Enrollment in Response to Declining State Appropriations?," *Research in Higher Education* 56 (2015): 535– 565, https://doi.org/10.1007/s11162-015-9362-2.

75 *biggest growth in applications filed through the Common App since 2014:* Rodney Hughes et al., "End-of-season-report, 2023–2024: First-Year application trends," Common App, (2024): 23–24, https://www .commonapp.org/files/FY_application_trends_end_season_report _23-24.pdf.

76 *one-third of the nation's flagships . . . turned away their own state's residents to make room:* Bradley Curs and Ozan Jaquette, "Crowded Out?: The Effect of Nonresident Enrollment on Resident Access to Public

Research Universities," *Educational Evaluation and Policy Analysis* 39, no. 4 (2017): 644–669, 10.3102/0162373717704719.

77 *The average GPA of entering freshmen:* Data from University of Alabama's Common Data Set, Office of Institutional Analysis and Assessment, University of Alabama; and Laura Pappino, "How the University of Alabama Became a National Player," *New York Times*, November 3, 2016, https://www.nytimes.com/2016/11/06/education /edlife/survival-strategies-for-public-universities.html.

77 *Then Alabama went fishing for students:* Crystal Han et al., "Recruiting the Out-of-State University," Joyce Foundation, https://emraresearch .org/sites/default/files/2019-03/joyce_report.pdf.

80 *students who moved to the region for school:* Douglas Belkin and Andrea Fuller, "Sorry Harvard. Everyone Wants to Go to College in the South Now," *Wall Street Journal*, September 27, 2024, https://www .wsj.com/us-news/education/sorry-harvard-everyone-wants-to-go-to -college-in-the-south-now-235d7934.

82 *While many honors programs can be traced:* Richard I. Scott, Patricia J. Smith, and Andrew J. Cognard-Black, "Demography of Honors: The Census of U.S. Honors Programs and Colleges," *Journal of the National Collegiate Honors Council* 18, no. 1 (2017): 548, http://digitalcommons .unl.edu/nchcjournal/548/.

84 *"search for kinship":* Ron Lieber, *The Price You Pay for College: An Entirely New Road Map for the Biggest Financial Decision Your Family Will Ever Make* (Harper, 2002).

88 *Psychologists call this phenomenon social proof:* The concept of social proof was first identified and named by Robert B. Cialdini. The material in this section comes from his book *Influence: The Psychology of Persuasion* (Collins, 2007).

90 *Southeastern Conference . . . sends the largest share of its graduates:* Danny Dougherty, Brian McGill, Dante Chinni, and Aaron Zitner, "Where Graduates Move After College," *Wall Street Journal*, May 15, 2018, https://www.wsj.com/graphics/where-graduates-move-after -college/.

CHAPTER 4: VALUE OVER PRESTIGE

96   *In a survey by* The New York Times: Morning Consult poll included in Frank Bruni, "There's Only One College Rankings List That Matters," *New York Times*, March 27, 2023, https://www.nytimes.com /2023/03/27/opinion/problem-college-rankings.html.

98   *University of Georgia has the third-highest share of students:* The Upshot, "Economic diversity and student outcomes at the University of Georgia," *New York Times*, January 18, 2017, https://www.nytimes.com /interactive/projects/college-mobility/university-of-georgia.

98   *In the decade-plus after the Great Recession of 2008:* Based on 2008 tuition figures from College Board, https://research.collegeboard.org /media/pdf/trends-college-pricing-2008-full-report.pdf; and College Board 2024, https://research.collegeboard.org/media/pdf/Trends%20 Report%202023%20Updated.pdf.

98   *"Unless you have developed some Enron-level accounting":* Nicole LaPorte, "Duke, Baruch, or Bust: Parents Debate If Pricey Private Schools Are Still Worth It," *Town & Country*, August 3, 2023, https://www .townandcountrymag.com/society/money-and-power/a44666515 /2024-college-cost-debate-ivy-league-value/.

99   *the chances of Ivy-plus admission are lowest:* Raj Chetty, David Deming, et al., "Diversifying Society's Leaders?: The Determinants and Causal Effects of Admission to Highly Selective Private Colleges," NBER Working Papers, National Bureau of Economic Research, no. 31492 (July 2023), doi 10.3386/w31492.

105   *In the mid-2010s, around 85 percent . . . to focus on colleges that cost them less:* From author analysis of various years of "How America Pays for College," 2015–2024, https://www.salliemae.com/about/leading-research/how-america-pays-for-college/.

105   *Fewer than half of young adults:* Rachel Minkin, Kim Parker, et al., "Parents, Young Adult Children and the Transition to Adulthood," Pew Research Center (January 2024), https://www.pewresearch.org /social-trends/2024/01/25/parents-young-adult-children-and-the-trans ition-to-adulthood/.

105   *switching jobs in your twenties:* Martin Gervais, Nir Jaimovich, et al., "What Should I Be When I Grow Up?: Occupations and Unemployment over the Life Cycle," NBER Working Papers, National Bureau of Economic Research, no. 20628 (October 2014), doi.10.3386/w20628.

111   *one-third of students above that income level:* From author analysis of various years of "How America Pays for College," 2015–2024, https://www.salliemae.com/about/leading-research/how-america-pays-for-college/.

112   *studied what happened with pricing at a group of liberal arts colleges:* N. Askin and M. S. Bothner, "Status-Aspirational Pricing: The 'Chivas Regal' Strategy in U.S. Higher Education, 2006–2012," *Administrative Science Quarterly* 61, no. 2 (2016): 217–253, https://doi.org/10.1177/0001839216629671.

CHAPTER 5: THE AGE OF AGENCY

117   *the rates of anxiety and depression:* Richard Weissbourd et al., "On Edge: Understanding and Preventing Young Adults' Mental Health Challenges," Harvard School of Education, 2023, https://static1.squarespace.com/static/5b7c56e255b02c683659fe43/t/6537db8894f0802b6480d38e/1698159503140/On+Edge_FINAL.pdf.

118   *enrollment in those degrees rose 16 percent:* Te-Ping Chen, "How Gen Z Is Becoming the Toolbelt Generation," *Wall Street Journal*, April 1, 2024, https://www.wsj.com/lifestyle/careers/gen-z-trades-jobs-plumbing-welding-a76b5e43.

119   *"Agency is churn, the essence of upward mobility":* Scott Galloway, "No Mercy/ No Malice," audio recording, May 31, 2024, https://www.profgalloway.com/agency/.

120   *colleges want teenagers to come in knowing what they will study:* X. Su et al., "Restructuring Degree Roadmaps to Improve Timely Graduation in Higher Education," *International Journal of Educational Management* 34, no. 2 (2020): 432–449, https://eric.ed.gov/?id=EJ1240155.

122   *survey of more than 325,000 undergraduates:* Survey of 329,974 college students as part of digital training, *AlcoholEdu® for College* and *Sexual*

Assault Prevention for Undergraduates, provided by Vector Solutions, a strategic software partner for higher education institutions.

122 *Most of the advice they receive comes from family and friends:* Gallup, Inc., and Strada Education Network, "Major Influence: Where Students Get Valued Advice on What to Study in College," Report, Gallup, Inc., September 2017, https://stradaeducation.org/video/major-influence-where-students-get-valued-advice-on-what-to-study-in-college/.

122 *study examining the extent to which earnings affected choice of major:* Matthew Wiswall and Basit Zafar, "Determinants of College Major Choice: Identification Using an Information Experiment," *Review of Economic Studies* 82, no. 2 (2015): 791–824, http://www.jstor.org/stable/43551547.

123 *marrying someone with a higher-earning degree:* Arpita Patnaik et al., "The role of heterogeneous risk preferences, discount rates, and earnings expectations in college major choice," *Journal of Econometrics* 231, no. 1 (2022): 98–122, ISSN 0304-4076, https://doi.org/10.1016/j.jeconom.2020.04.050.

123 *less swayed by money as they moved through college:* Matthew J. Wiswall and Basit Zafar, "New Approaches to Understanding Choice of Major," *The Reporter*, June 30, 2021, https://www.nber.org/reporter/2021number2/new-approaches-understanding-choice-major.

124 *delaying specialization in college:* David Epstein, *Range: Why Generalists Triumph in a Specialized World* (Riverhead, 2019).

125 *study of English and history:* Nathan Heller, "The End of the English Major," *New Yorker*, February 27, 2024, https://www.newyorker.com/magazine/2023/03/06/the-end-of-the-english-major.

CHAPTER 6: ON THE HUNT FOR A GOOD SCHOOL

129 *Congressional aides gathered . . . Student Right-To-Know and Campus Security Act:* Based on interview with Terry Hartle, August 14, 2024, and The Student Right-To-Know and Campus Security Act, Pub. L. 101-542, 104 Stat. 2381 (1990), https://www.congress.gov/bill/101st-congress/senate-bill/580.

131   *the average acceptance rate:* Calculation based on roughly 1,600 colleges and universities that report admit rates to the U.S. Department of Education and weighted by school based on number of applications.

132   *After the passage of the 1990 bill:* Jeffrey Selingo, "The Rise and Fall of the Graduation Rate," *Chronicle of Higher Education*, March 12, 2012, https://www.chronicle.com/article/the-rise-and-fall-of-the-graduation-rate/.

133   *30 percent response rate:* Robert Morse and Eric Brooks, "How US News Calculated the 2025 Best Colleges Rankings," U.S. News .com, September 23, 2024, https://www.usnews.com/education/best-colleges/articles/how-us-news-calculated-the-rankings.

133   *When a reporter for* Inside Higher Ed: Stephanie Lee, "Reputation Without Rigor," *Inside Higher Ed*, August 18, 2009, https://www .insidehighered.com/news/2009/08/19/reputation-without-rigor#.

134   The New York Times *released its own college-ranking tool:* Quoctrung Bui and Jessia Ma, "Build Your Own College Rankings," *New York Times*, November 9, 2023, https://www.nytimes.com/interactive/2023 /opinion/build-your-own-college-rankings.html.

136   *"To be prepared against surprise":* James P. Carse, *Finite and Infinite Games* (Penguin Books, 1987).

138   *When we are overloaded with information at once:* J. Aislinn Bohren et al., "A Cognitive Foundation for Perceiving Uncertainty," National Bureau for Economic Research Working Paper Series (January 25, 2024), doi10.3386/w32149.

143   *In his speech that day:* Barack Obama, "Remarks by the President on College Affordability—Buffalo, NY," August 22, 2013, National Archives and Records Administration, https://obamawhitehouse .archives.gov/the-press-office/2013/08/22/remarks-president-college-affordability-buffalo-ny.

144   *described a "datapalooza":* Kelly Field, "Obama Plan to Tie Student Aid to College Ratings Draws Mixed Reviews," *Chronicle of Higher Education*, August 22, 2013, https://www.chronicle.com/article /obama-plan-to-tie-student-aid-to-college-ratings-draws-mixed -reviews/.

144 *omits about one-third of college students:* The College Scorecard, U.S. Department of Education, June 2024, https://collegescorecard.ed.gov /assets/InstitutionDataDocumentation.pdf.

146 *compared with $60,000 nationally:* The Federal Reserve Bank of New York, "The Labor Market for Recent College Graduates," February 22, 2024, https://www.newyorkfed.org/research/college-labor-market#-- :explore:wages.

148 *Bain's results weren't surprising:* Will Miller et al., "Beating the Odds: Improving Student Outcomes in Higher Education," Bain & Company, May 21, 2024, https://www.bain.com/insights/beating-the-odds-improving-student-outcomes-in-higher-education/.

149 *Nassim Taleb calls a "haystack" of data:* Nassim N. Taleb, "Beware the Big Errors of 'Big Data,'" *Wired*, February 8, 2013, https://www.wired .com/2013/02/big-data-means-big-errors-people/.

CHAPTER 7: MENTORS MATTER

154 *Decades of research:* Matthew J. Mayhew et al., *How College Affects Students: 21st Century Evidence that Higher Education Works, Volume 3* (Jossey-Bass, 2016).

155 *focus specifically on college professors:* In a Gallup survey, some two-thirds of students who had a mentor in school said that person was a professor. See: https://news.gallup.com/poll/244019/recent-college-grads-say-professors-frequent-mentors.aspx.

155 *"Good teaching . . . which institutions affect students":* How College Affects Students: 21st Century Evidence that Higher Education Works, Volume 3 (Jossey-Bass, 2016).

155 *Sometimes a single exchange:* Daniel F. Chambliss and Christopher G. Takacs, *How College Works* (Harvard University Press, 2014).

157 *"It's not clear how those administrators":* Beth McMurtrie, "Americans Value Good Teaching. Do Colleges?," *Chronicle of Higher Education*, September 20, 2023, https://www.chronicle.com/article/americans-value-good-teaching-do-colleges.

157 *have actually decreased their spending:* Corbin M. Campbell et al., "Prestige or Education: College Teaching and Rigor of Courses in

Prestigious and Non-Prestigious Institutions in the U.S.," *Higher Education* 77, no. 4 (2019): 717–38, https://doi.org/10.1007/s10734-018-0297-3.

159   *described as "middling":* Corbin M. Campbell, *Great College Teaching: Where It Happens and How to Foster It Everywhere* (Harvard Education Press, 2023).

160   *the results were unambiguous:* Corbin M. Campbell, "A Rally Call for Teaching Excellence: Colleges and Universities: Your Role in the Movement," *Change* 56, no. 5 (2024): 13–21, https://doi.org/10.1080/00091383.2024.2385251.

163   *"bait-and-switch" maneuver:* Michele Miller, "Bonus post: Is your IHE truly teaching-focused?," *R3Newsletter*, July 11, 2013, https://michellemillerphd.substack.com/p/bonus-post-is-your-ihe-truly-teaching.

163   *tenure doesn't affect the academic rigor:* Jessica Michel, Diana Chadi, et al., "Ignis Fatuus Effect of Faculty Category: Is the Tenure Versus Non-Tenure Debate Meaningful to Students' Course Experiences?," *Innovative Higher Education* 43 (2018), 10.1007/s10755-017-9420-0.

163   *most are adjunct professors or lecturers:* Glen Colby, "Data Snapshot: Tenure and Contingency in US Higher Education," AAUP, March 2023, https://www.aaup.org/article/data-snapshot-tenure-and-contingency-us-higher-education.

164   *They give lower ratings:* R. J. Kreitzer and J. Sweet-Cushman, "Evaluating Student Evaluations of Teaching: A Review of Measurement and Equity Bias in SETs and Recommendations for Ethical Reform," *J Acad Ethics* 20 (2022): 73–84, https://doi.org/10.1007/s10805-021-09400-w.

166   *someone in college cared about them as a person:* Julie Ray and Stephanie Marken, "Life After College," Gallup, May 6, 2014, https://news.gallup.com/poll/168848/life-college-matters-life-college.aspx.

166   *Yet fewer than a quarter of the alumni:* Stephanie Marken and Zac Auter, "Recent College Grads Say Professors Most Frequent Mentors," Gallup, October 30, 2018, https://news.gallup.com/poll/244019/recent-college-grads-say-professors-frequent-mentors.aspx.

167   *majored in the arts and humanities:* Steve Crabtree, "Student Support From Faculty, Mentors Varies by Major," Gallup, January 24, 2019, https://news.gallup.com/poll/246017/student-support-faculty-mentors-varies-major.aspx.

170   *"mentor mindset":* David Yeager, *10 to 25: The Science of Motivating Young People: A Groundbreaking Approach to Leading the Next Generation—And Making Your Own Life Easier* (Avid Reader Press / Simon & Schuster, 2024).

CHAPTER 8: FINDING YOUR PEOPLE

178   *students at highly selective colleges:* Lisa M. Nunn, *College Belonging: How First-Year and First-Generation Students Navigate Campus Life* (Rutgers University Press, 2021).

179   *almost 40 percent of college students:* Zach Hrynowski and Stephanie Marken, "College Students Experience High Levels of Worry and Stress," Gallup, August 10, 2023, https://www.gallup.com/education/509231/college-students-experience-high-levels-worry-stress.aspx.

179   *about a quarter of college freshmen:* "Persistence and Retention," National Student Clearing House Research Center, June 27, 2024, https://nscresearchcenter.org/persistence-retention/.

179   *seeds are planted:* Tim Renick, executive director of the National Institute for Student Success, interview by author, November 15, 2021.

180   *"belonging uncertainty":* G. M. Walton and G. L. Cohen, "A question of belonging: Race, social fit, and achievement," *Journal of Personality and Social Psychology* 92, no. 1 (2007): 82–96, https://doi.org/10.1037/0022-3514.92.1.82.

181   *A decade later, Cohen and Walton . . . snowball effect over time:* G. M. Walton, M. C. Murphy, et al., "Where and with whom does a brief social-belonging intervention promote progress in college?," *Science* 380, no. 6644 (2023): 499–505, doi: 10.1126/science.ade4420.

181   *Another follow-up study of these students:* David Yeager, *10 to 25: The Science of Motivating Young People: A Groundbreaking Approach to Leading the Next Generation—And Making Your Own Life Easier* (Avid Reader Press / Simon & Schuster, 2024).

183 *three domains of undergraduate:* Several researchers have talked about the different domains of belonging in college, including Lisa M. Nunn et al., "Four Domains of students' sense of belonging to university," *Studies in Higher Education* 45, no. 3 (2018): 622–34, https://doi:10.1080/03075079.2018.1564902; Eliel Cohen and Julianne Viola, "The role of pedagogy and the curriculum in university students' sense of belonging," *Journal of University Teaching & Learning Practice* 19, no. 4 (2022), https://ro.uow.edu.au/jutlp/vol19/iss4/06.

184 *When McMurtrie asked:* Beth McMurtrie, "A Stunning Level of Disconnection," *Chronicle of Higher Education*, April 5, 2022, https://www.chronicle.com/article/a-stunning-level-of-student-disconnection.

184 *One study of belonging among first-year business and economics students:* Suzanne Kane et al., "Notions of belonging: First year, first semester higher education students enrolled on business or economics degree programmes," *International Journal of Management Education* 12, no. 2 (2014): 193–201, https://doi.org/10.1016/j.ijme.2014.04.001.

184 *Getting to know faculty members:* "Beginning College Survey of Student Engagement," National Survey of Student Engagement, Bloomington, IN: Indiana University Center for Postsecondary Research and Planning BCSSE 2020, https://wp.stolaf.edu/iea/beginning-college-survey-of-student-engagement-bcsse/.

185 *finding your academic footing:* "The Sense of Belonging," National Survey of Student Engagement, Bloomington, IN: Indiana University Center for Postsecondary Research and Planning NSSE 2020, https://tableau.bi.iu.edu/#/site/prd/views/NSSESenseofBelonging/.

186 *more than nine in ten colleges provide some sort of first-year experience:* T. L. Skipper, ed., *What makes the first-year seminar high impact? An exploration of effective educational practices*, National Resource Center for The First-Year Experience and Students in Transition (Columbia, SC: University of South Carolina, 2017), http://sc.edu/fye.

186 *"Good advising":* Richard J. Light, "The Power of Good Advice for Students," *Chronicle of Higher Education*, March 2, 2001, https://www.chronicle.com/article/the-power-of-good-advice-for-students/.

187 *"experience instead of just being an audience":* Beth McMurtrie,

"Teaching," *Chronicle of Higher Education*, April 21, 2022, https://www .chronicle.com/newsletter/teaching/2022-04-21.

187   *Frequent and timely feedback:* Susan Ambrose et al., "What kinds of practice and feedback enhance learning?," in *How Learning Works: Seven Research-Based Principles for Smart Teaching* (Jossey-Bass, 2010), 121–152.

188   *among freshmen at Dartmouth College:* Bruce Sacerdote, "Peer Effects with Random Assignment: Results for Dartmouth Roommates," *Quarterly Journal of Economics* 116, no. 2 (2001): 681–704, http://www .jstor.org/stable/2696476.

189   *"the potential to make a misstep":* Laura Hamilton et al., "Providing a 'Leg Up': Parental Involvement and Opportunity Hoarding in College," *Sociology of Education* 91, no. 2 (2018), https://journals.sagepub.com /doi/10.1177/0038040718759557.

189   *"If you can get the cost down":* Jeffrey Selingo, "Why Universities Are Phasing Out Luxury Dorms," *Atlantic*, August 21, 2017, https://www .theatlantic.com/education/archive/2017/08/why-universities-are- phasing-out-luxury-dorms/537492/.

190   *bad roommate relationships:* Madeleine Golding et al., "Negative Room- mate Relationships and the Health and Wellbeing of Undergraduate College Students," *Journal of Public Health Student Capstones*, https:// jphsc.org/index.php/JPHSC/onlinefirst/view/35.

191   *researchers analyzed the networks of 20 million people on LinkedIn:* Karthik Rajkumar et al., "A Casual Test of the strength of weak ties," *Science* 377, no. 6612 (2022): 1304–1310, https://www.science.org/doi/10.1126 /science.abl4476.

192   *"when something doesn't work out . . . super small":* Jeff Selingo and Michael Horn, "How colleges can cultivate relationships to improve the student experience," *Future U.*, podcast, November 7, 2023, https://www.futureupodcast.com/episodes/how-colleges-can -cultivate-relationships-to-improve-the-student-experience/.

192   *linked to academic success and student well-being:* Among studies that have found this: C. A. Kilgo et al., "The estimated effects of college student involvement on psychological well-being," *Journal of College*

Student Development 57, no. 8 (2016): 1043–1049; K. L. Webber et al., "Does involvement really matter? Indicators of college student success and satisfaction," *Journal of College Student Development* 54, no. 6 (2013): 591–611; Center for the Study of Student Life (2020). Involvement, Leadership and Student Outcomes at Graduation. The Ohio State University, Columbus, Ohio.

193   *"If I never had that interaction"*: Erin Gretzinger and Maggie Hicks, "Why Campus Life Fell Apart," *Chronicle of Higher Education*, January 26, 2024, https://www.chronicle.com/article/why-campus-life -fell-apart.

CHAPTER 9: THE DOOM LOOP OF COLLEGE FINANCES

198   *"If dirt isn't flying"*: Audrey Williams, "After Costly Foray Into Big-Time Sports, a College Returns to Its Roots," *Chronicle of Higher Education*, May 18, 2017, https://www.chronicle.com/article/after-costly -foray-into-big-time-sports-a-college-returns-to-its-roots/.

198   *dwindled to around 700 students*: Josh Moody, "Birmingham-Southern Announces Abrupt Closure," *Inside Higher Ed*, March 27, 2024, https://www.insidehighered.com/news/business/financial-health /2024/03/27/birmingham-southern-announces-abrupt-closure.

199   *study by the consulting firm Bain & Company*: Jeff Denneen and Tom Dretler, "The Financially Stable University," Bain & Company, July 6, 2012, https://www.bain.com/insights/financially-sustainable-university/.

199   *A decade later, a follow-up report*: Mark Craft, Jeffrey Deneen, et al., "The Financially Resilient University," Bain & Company, May 22, 2023, https://www.bain.com/insights/financially-resilient -university/.

200   *136 schools have closed*: "Digest of Education Statistics," National Center for Education Statistics, 2021, https://nces.ed.gov/programs/digest /d21/tables/dt21_317.50.asp. Note: Counts include nonprofit colleges only.

200   *private colleges with fewer than 1,000 students*: Robert Kelchen, Dubravka Ritter, and Douglas Webber, "Predicting College Closures and

Financial Distress," WP 24-20. Federal Reserve Bank of Philadelphia, December 2024, https://doi.org/10.21799/frbp.wp.2024.20.

200   *slashed majors*: Josh Moody, "Another Wave of Campus Cuts," *Inside Higher Ed*, February 20, 2024, https://www.insidehighered.com/news /business/cost-cutting/2024/02/20/another-wave-campus-cuts-hits-midwest-especially-hard.

201   *"Serious challenges remain"*: "Moody's-upgrades-Birmingham-Southern-College-AL-bonds-to-B3-outlook," Moody's Investors Services, March 5, 2014, https://www.moodys.com/research/Moodys-upgrades -Birmingham-Southern-College-AL-bonds-to-B3-outlook-PR _294305.

201   *"discount rate continues to move upward"*: "Moody's Revises Birmingham-Southern College-AL-outlook to negative, Affirms B3-rating-action," Moody's Investors Services, March 5, 2014, https://www.moodys.com /research/Moodys-revises-Birmingham-Southern-College-AL-outlook -to-negative-affirms-B3-Rating-Action-PR_338495.

206   *Moody's revised its outlook for Clarkson to negative*: "Moody's revises Clarkson University's (NY) outlook to negative; affirms Baa1 issuer and debt ratings," Moody's Investors Services, March 16, 2023.

208   *"one of the biggest drivers"*: Melissa Korn and Shane Shiflett, "Swimming Pools and Granite Countertops: How College Dorms Got So Expensive," *Wall Street Journal*, December 20, 2023, https://www .wsj.com/us-news/education/college-housing-dorms-cost-tuition-9d9 8c1a4.

214   *Most endowment wealth*: Bruce A. Kimball, *Wealth, Cost, and Price in American Higher Education: A Brief History* (Johns Hopkins University Press, 2023).

216   *roughly half of new majors*: "Bad Bets: The High Cost of Failing Programs in Higher Education," Burning Glass Technologies (now Lightcast), November 2020, https://lightcast.io/bad-bets-failing -programs.

217   *Overall athletic participation is growing*: Aaron Basko, "Can Athletics Save Small Colleges," *Chronicle of Higher Education*, September 5, 2023, https://www.chronicle.com/article/can-sports-save-small-colleges.

217 *Adrian College:* Liam Knox, "Seeking an Enrollment Hail Mary, Small Colleges Look to Athletics," *Inside Higher Ed,* December 4, 2023, https://www.insidehighered.com/news/admissions/traditional-age/2023/12/04/small-colleges-bet-new-sports-boost-enrollment.

217 *Fairleigh Dickinson University:* Dan Murphy, "Could adding athletic programs decrease financial woes for some schools? FDU is banking on it," ESPN, March 11, 2021, https://www.espn.com/college-sports/story/_/id/31038654/could-adding-athletic-programs-decrease-financial-woes-some-schools.

CHAPTER 10: BETTER THAN AVERAGE

224 *individuals who are satisfied:* Alberto Prati, "Hedonic recall bias. Why you should not ask people how much they earn," *Journal of Economic Behavior & Organization* 143 (2017): 78–97, https://doi.org/10.1016/j.jebo.2017.09.002.

229 *Heading into the early 2000s:* Robert G. Valletta, "Recent Flattening in the Higher Education Wage Premium: Polarization, Skill Downgrading, or Both?," National Bureau of Economic Research, December 2016, DOI 10.3386/w22935.

229 *Nearly six out of every ten graduates:* Eric Yan and Sarah Girma, "The Graduating Class of 2024 by the numbers," *Harvard Crimson,* https://features.thecrimson.com/2024/senior-survey/after-harvard./

230 *analyzed job postings data . . . relatively scarce within a field:* The details and some of the language in this section appeared in a report that Sigelman, his team, and I wrote about our research: "Making the Bachelor's Degree More Valuable," https://www.burningglassinstitute.org/research/making-the-bachelors-degree-more-valuable.

232 *70 percent:* Ashley P. Finley, "The Career-Ready Graduate; What Employers Say About The Difference College Makes," American Association of Colleges and Universities, 2023, https://www.aacu.org/research/the-career-ready-graduate-what-employers-say-about-the-difference-college-makes.

232 *"credegree":* Brandon Busteed, "Why Colleges Will Soon Be About Credegrees And Co-Ops," *Forbes,* March 11, 2019, https://www

.forbes.com/sites/brandonbusteed/2019/03/11/why-college-will-soon
-be-about-credegrees-and-co-ops/.

233   *one-third of college graduates*: Nichole Torpey-Saboe et al., "The Power of Work-Based Learning," Strada Education, 2022, https://stradaeducation.org/wp-content/uploads/2022/03/031522-PV-report.pdf.

233   *failed to secure an internship*: Andrew Hanson et al., "Talent Disrupted," Strada Education, 2024, https://stradaeducation.org/wp-content/uploads/2024/02/Talent-Disrupted.pdf.

236   *biggest companies offer full-time roles to two-thirds of their interns*: "2024 Internship and Co-op Report," National Association of Colleges and Employers, April 2024, https://naceweb.org/docs/default-source/default-document-library/2024/publication/executive-summary/2024-nace-internship-and-coop-report-executive-summary.pdf.

236   *"Our internship program ... get an offer"*: As quoted in Kristen Cooper and Eizabeth Diley, "Early Careers Talent Strategy: How Organizations are Fairly and Efficiently Finding the Right Talent" (webinar from National Association of Colleges and Employers, November 6, 2023), https://www.youtube.com/watch?v=kD127955830.

236   *"Work ethic"*: "Interns Take a Star Turn," *Gap Letter*, June 7, 2024, https://gapletter.com/letter_144.php.

237   *ranks near the bottom of factors*: "Job Outlook 2024," National Association of Colleges and Employers," November 2023.

237   *"He who gets them last"*: As quoted in my book *There Is Life After College: What Parents and Students Should Know About Navigating School to Prepare for the Jobs of Tomorrow* (New York: William Morrow, 2016).

CONCLUSION: DREAMS

242   *averages are conclusive*: Todd Rose, *The End of Average: How We Succeed in a World That Values Sameness* (New York: HarperCollins, 2016).

243   *That dream was first articulated*: James Truslow Adams, *The Epic of America* (Boston: Little, Brown, 1931).

INDEX

*Main entries for colleges on the "New" Dream School List appear in **bold type**. States' universities appear in alphabetical order under "University of."*

acceptance rates
  Arizona State's charter and high accessibility, 273
  Butler promising greater access than selective schools, 253
  Case Western's rate as "accessible excellence," 101
  elite and selective schools, 8, 21, 42, 119
  Fairfield's higher overall acceptance rate, 257
  Furman's accessible rate, 258
  George Mason's very accessible rate, 269
  Georgia Southern as an access campus, 269
  Indiana-Bloomington's out-of-state accessible rate, 277
  Lightcast's college comparisons based on acceptance rates, 64
  Minnesota Twin Cities' accessible rate, 288
  MIT's selective rate, 40
  NSSE survey of student engagement based on acceptance rates, 139–43
  Oregon State's accessible rate, 279
  Pitt's outcomes on par with selective schools but broader acceptance rate, 290
  St. Olaf's moderately selective rate, 186
  "scattergrams" data on acceptance probability, 35
  schools accepting fewer than 20 percent of applications, 42
  U.S. average, 131, 306n131
  University of California San Diego, out-of-state rate, 284
  Wisconsin's out-of-state rate as very selective, 33
admissions, 17–45
  adjustments made in the early 2020s, 20

admissions (*cont.*)
AP courses and scores, 43, 48
Carse's theory of a finite game and, 136
criteria for inclusion on "New" Dream Schools list, 249
"deferrals" response, 24, 25
early action (EA) or early decision (ED), 19, 20, 25
ending of affirmative action and, 19
geographic diversity and, 36
GPAs and grades, 23
"The Haves and Have-Nots in Admissions" (*Figure 1.2*), 38
initial reading of applications, 42–43
Landscape tool and, 36–37
looking for more than perfect scores, 39–44
SAT or ACT scores and, 24–25
test-optional policies, 19, 32
U.K. universities vs. U.S., 88
yield management and, 20, 37
Adrian College (MI), 217
Amherst College (MA), 223
application inflation, 30–37
admissions bar raised by, 37
"Application Inflation" (*Figure 1.1*), 34
high schools flooding the system, 36
increased applications to elite colleges, 19
next-tier colleges and, 36
total applications (2023), 33
applications, 17–45
applicants swinging from overconfidence to self-doubt, 22–27
changes in the process post-2020, 17–18
Common App and, 75

example, Mia, deferrals and, 24, 25–26
handling student stress, 26–27
increase in total applications, 42
number sent per student, 33, 34, 35
reach, target, or safety choices, 32
rejections and the new reality, 20–21, 36
resetting expectations, 20–21
"scattergrams" data on chances of acceptance, 35
test-optional schools, 40–41
Apprentice Nation (Craig), 236
Archer School for Girls, Los Angeles, 136
approach to college counseling, 137–38
Arizona State University (AZ), **273**
Barrett Honors College, 86, 273
Selingo's connections with, 251
work experience built into courses, 235, 273
Aspen Institute, 154
Augustana College (IL), **251–52**

Babson College (MA), 252
Bain & Company, 147–48, 211
"Beating the Odds" report, 148–49
Ball State University (IN), 57, 187
Bama Rush (HBO documentary), 82
Baruch College (NY), **265**
Bates College (ME), 112
Becca Schmill Foundation, 44n
belonging, 175–96
academic connection and, 184–87
accessible faculty and, 184–85
"attachment theory" and, 180
"belonging uncertainty," 180
chance for friendships and, 84–85, 178

INDEX

Cohen and Walton's study on, 180–83

declaring a major and, 185

Delaware's transition into college life program, 285

example, student's transfer to University of Minnesota, 1–3, 5, 178

extracurricular activities and, 190–93

first semester freshman year and, 184–86

fit outweighing prestige, 179

freshmen dropouts and lack of, 179

Gallup survey on student loneliness, 179

"helicopter parents" and, 189

Homayoun's "multiple nonoverlapping circles of connection" and, 192

Montclair State's Office of Student Belonging, 270

Plan B and a better fit, 178–79, 193–96

requesting "campus climate" surveys, 190

residential life and, 187–90

St. Olaf's "first year experience," 185–86

selective schools and, 195–96

Selingo at Ithaca, 175–77, 180, 191–92

social-belonging interventions, 180–83

three domains of undergraduate life and, 183–93

what parents expect college to do, 190–91

Bentley University (MA), 221, **252**

Berry College (GA), **252–53**

Binghamton University (NY), 36, 225, **265–66**

Birmingham-Southern College (AL), 197–99, 200, 201, 216

Bloomberg News, 212

Bloomberg ROI college rankings, 145, 146

Boston College (MA), 87

Boston University (MA), 36, 59

Bowdoin College (ME), 91, 95

Bowlby, John, 179–80

Bradley, Bill, 129, 130

Brady, Shannon, 182–83

Brigham Young University (UT), 61

Brown University (RI), 53, 57

Bryn Mawr College (PA), 95, 231

Burning Glass Institute, 228, 251

Butler University (IN), **253**

California Polytechnic State University (CA)
  Pomona, **266**
  San Luis Obispo, 111

California State University (CA)
  earnings vs. cost of a degree, 145
  Fresno, **266–67**

Camden County College (NJ), 231

Cameron, William Bruce, 150

Campbell, Corbin M., 158–61
  Great College Teaching (Campbell), 159–60

Campus Sonar, 79

campus visits, tours, 28, 138
  Alabama and, 80–82
  course correction and, 27–28, 30
  dorm tours, questions to ask, 189–90

campus visits, tours (*cont.*)
  "informational drive-by" (exercise
    recommended), 30
  insight on teaching quality, 163–64,
    187
  NSSE as source of questions to ask,
    139
  "welcome center" and, 39
career goals
  anxiety about career path, 117
  college as a means to a job, 54, 120–21
  delaying or switching majors, 123–26
  Deming and, 53–54
  "explore and exploit," 54, 124–25
  making college transformational, 121
  NSSE and measuring career success,
    139
  personal agency and college choice,
    115–26
  questions to ask about career choice,
    126
  role of money in picking a major,
    121–23
  STEM degrees and, 125
  See also employment after
    graduation; making sure the
    degree pays off
Carleton College (MN), 261
Carlson-Reddig, Thomas, 189
Carnegie Mellon University (PA), 18,
    24, 60–61, 274
Carse, James P., 136
Case Western Reserve University
    (OH), 32, 36, 41, 249, **273–74**
Caulfield, Marybeth, 60
Chambliss, Dan
  How College Works (Takacs and
    Chambliss), 155–56, 170

Chan, Andy, 61
Chetty, Raj, 53
Cialdini, Robert, 89
Ciesil, Blair, 65–66
City University of New York (CUNY)
  credegree at, 232
  earnings vs. cost of a degree, 145
Clarkson University (NE), 206, 207
Clemson University (SC), 24, 25, 27,
    38–39, 219, **274**
CliftonStrengths personality test, 168
Cohen, Geoffrey, 180–81
Colby College (ME), 106, 203, 204
college finances/fiscal health, 197–218
  Birmingham-Southern's closing,
    197–99, 200, 201, 216
  bond-rating reports and, 207–11
  college closings since 2000, 200
  colleges on an "unsustainable
    financial path," 199, 206
  Common Data Set (CDS) and, 210
  criteria for inclusion on "New"
    Dream Schools list, 249–50
  endowments and, 201, 210, 213–14
  enrollment and endowment data,
    212–14
  Federal Audit Clearinghouse data
    and, 210
  federal student loans and, 202
  "Firm Financial Footing" (*Figure 9.1*),
    211
  government assistance and, 202
  Moody's ratings and, 208–9, 213
  net-price-calculator and, 205
  projected closings and mergers, 200,
    206
  public universities and, 209–10
  red flags, 200–207, 209, 212, 217–18

ways to measure financial health, 207–16

Wells College's closing, 216–17

College of New Jersey (TCNJ) (NJ), 248, **267**

College Scorecard, 143–47, 223, 224, 242

college search

"Alt-Ivies" list, 134

analogy of choosing to stand in line, or not, 116–17

"averages" unhelpful, 242

big fish–little pond advantages, 48–49, 51–52, 66

campus visits, tours, importance of, 27–28

changing your mindset, 115–26

charting job prospects and, 60–62, 164

choices close to home, 71, 72

College Scorecard and, 143–47

consumer information available about colleges, 129–51

course correction for, 26–30

decisions to make, 118

defining what you value, 6, 29, 110, 134

determining teaching quality, 161–63

elite schools vs. everyone else, 4, 66, 139–43

example, Abby and April, applying to elite schools and less-selective publics, 109

example, Mia, pivoting after deferrals, 22–24, 27–30, 38–39

factor to consider: college location may determine future residence, 89–90

five ways to maximize value, 108–12

GPAs, grades, and, 23–24

identifying best choices, 6–7

information overload and focus on "outliers," 138

July before senior year, what happens, 23

"list creep," 32

the "money talk," 28, 111–12

Naviance tool, 26

New York Times build-your-own college ranking tool, 134

Niche.com, 22

others defining your dream school, 4–5, 115–16, 219–20

overconfidence bias, 23–24, 32

Plan B and, 5, 6, 17–45, 124, 172–73, 178–89, 193–96, 244 (*see also* "New" Dream Schools list)

rankings and, 156–64

reach, target, or safety choices, 32

#RushTok's influence, 4

seeking the Easy Button, 171

setting a price limit, 205–6, 220

slowing down the search, 110, 138

"social proof" and, 88–89

three questions to ask before starting, 29

top schools vs. good schools, 39

typical duration of the search, 118

"undermatching" to "chase merit," 93, 109

the *why*, not just the *where*, 138

widening your lens, 33, 39, 96, 110, 194, 219–20

See also belonging; cost; employment after graduation; residence halls/dorm life

Colleges That Change Lives (Pope), 6, 197, 198

Colorado School of Mines (CO), 221
Colorado State University (CO), 32, **275**
Columbia University (NY), 1–5, 159, 178, 193
Common Application (Common App), 20, 27, 40, 75, 79
Common Data Set (CDS) on a college's website, 204, 210
 "Firm Financial Footing" (*Figure 9.1*), 211
community college, 110–11, 118
 example, Amy, and advantages of Sierra College, 111
Cornell University (NY), 106, 242, 258
cost, 8, 9, 11, 241
 assessing financial fit, 92
 "Chivas Regal effect," 112–14
 college pricing hidden until after acceptance, 28, 92
 decline of full payers, 103–5, 113
 earnings-to-net-price ratio/return on investment, 143–47, 250, 256, 265, 266, 267, 268, 275, 278, 280, 286, 290 (*see also specific schools*)
 example, Abby's choice of William & Mary over elite schools, 91–93
 example, April's choice of SMU over elite schools, 106–8
 Facebook groups on, 93
 family's budget for, 29, 205–6, 220
 increased price for college, 93, 94, 97, 143
 international universities, 88
 Levine's research on, 94
 loan debt and, 54
 net-price calculator, 28, 204–5, 222–23
 parents talking to teens about, 111–12
 price of prestige, 9, 112–14
 pricing and "consumer surplus," 97
 public universities and affordability, 75, 88, 94, 145, 263, 267, 268, 271, 275, 277, 278, 289, 290
 relationship between discounts and rankings, 113
 starting at a community college, 111
 tuition compared to airline pricing, 92
 "undermatching" to "chase merit," 93, 109
 value over prestige, 91–114
 weighing value and, 75, 220–21
 See also financial aid and discounts
course correction (for college search), 26, 27–30
 allow time to process a change, 28–29
 consider affordability, 28, 91–114
 example, Abby widening her lens, 96
 take your own "College 101" course, 30
 understand what you value, 29
 value of small classes, 96
 value over prestige: getting a deal, 91–114
 visit a campus, or revisit a campus, 27–28
Craig, Ryan, *Apprentice Nation*, 236–37
Creighton University (NE), **253–54**

Damour, Lisa, *The Emotional Lives of Teenagers*, 26
Dartmouth College (NH), 41, 181, 188
David and Goliath (Gladwell), 49–50, 51
Davidson College (NC), 95
Davis, Elizabeth, 167, 170
"deferrals," 24
 by "backup schools," 38

colleges' ignoring deferred students, 26

colleges' increasing use of, 25–26

example, highly qualified student, 25–26

reach schools and, 33

Deming, David, 52–55, 227, 244

"extra lottery ticket" analogy, 55–57

signaling effect of job held at age twenty-five, 58, 64

study on social connectedness, 57–58

study on elite college alumni, 55–57

Denison University (OH), 170–71, 248, **254**

Department of Education's College Navigator, 132

DePaul University (IL), **254–55**

DePauw University (IN), 181, **255**

D'Evelyn Junior/Senior High School, Denver, applications and acceptances to select colleges, 30–32

Dickinson College (PA), 146, **255–56**

Dougherty Valley High School (CA), applications and acceptances to USC, 35

dream school. *See* "New" Dream Schools; "New" Dream Schools list

Drew University (NJ), 210

Drexel University (PA), 22, 179, 235, **275**

Duke University (NC), 18, 42–43, 57, 223, 278

admissions dean, Christoph Guttentag, 42

what gets students into Duke, 43

Dvortsyn, Matt, 231–32, 238

early action (EA) and early decision (ED) admissions, 19, 25, 109–10

elite and selective colleges

acceptance as a "winning lottery ticket," 1, 43

alternatives and a better fit, 4–6, 85, 96–97, 115–26

backup plan needed, 6, 17–45

career ambitions and degree from, 47–57

competitive culture of, 51, 84–85

cost, 9, 112–14

decline in sense of belonging at, 196

feeder schools for, 37

Fortune 50 recruitment at, 66

graduation rates, 146–47

increased applications to, 19

Landscape tool used by admissions, 36–37

limited number of seats at, 74

little fish–big pond disadvantages, 49–50

outcomes for students, 49, 55–57, 63, 147

overestimating importance, 7

"panicking class" and, 12, 131, 188, 244

percentage of acceptances, 8, 21, 42, 119

prestige and desirability, 1, 5, 6, 7, 8, 52, 97, 196

randomness of acceptance, 43

role of faculty, 157, 160–61

"rubbing elbows" aspect, 57–58

social hierarchy at, 106, 188

social pressures to apply, 116

"Student Engagement: Elite Schools vs. Everyone Else" (*Figure 6.1*), 141

students from ultra-competitive high schools and, 37

"super" or "ultra" selective colleges, 21

elite and selective colleges (*cont.*)
test score requirements, 24, 41
U.S. presidents with Ivy
backgrounds, 66
Elmira College (NY), 210
Elon University (NC), 190, **256–57**
president, Leo Lambert, 256
Emory University (GA), 53
Emotional Lives of Teenagers, The
(Damour), 26
employment after graduation, 58
acquiring skills employers want,
230–33
alumni networks and, 60, 61
alumni running Fortune 500
companies, 57
college choice and, 60–62, 115, 116,
164
College Scorecard and, 143–47, 224
criteria for inclusion on "New"
Dream Schools list, 251
earnings calculators and rankings,
145, 226–27
earnings data and geography, 145, 222
elite and selective schools, 57–58, 63,
66, 145–46, 222, 227, 229
employment of alumni, Southeastern
Conference schools, 90
example, April after SMU, 108
example, Katelynn's college search
and choosing Loyola, 222–25
First Destination Survey, 63
first employer as important, 59, 237
Granovetter's "strength of weak
ties," 191
Lightcast data on, 63–64
LinkedIn's "People You May Know"
and, 191

majors as factor in hiring and future
earnings, 125, 146, 221, 223, 227,
229, 230–31
microcredentials and, 232–33
Payscale website, 223, 224
placement rates, 7, 8, 204, 221, 258,
260, 276
recruiters' hiring strategies, 59
region-based hiring, 59–61, 66, 89, 222
scoring colleges on the return on
investment, 143–47
tips to start a job search, 62–63
what parents expect college to do,
190–91
when prestige can hurt you, 61
where employers hire and why, 59,
65, 146, 222
who Fortune 50 companies hire,
64–66
employment after graduation: "New"
Dream Schools' alumni employers
and earnings
Alabama, 283
Augustana, 252
Baruch, 265
Butler, 253
Cal Poly Pomona, 266
Cal State Fresno, 266, 267
Case Western, 274
Clemson, 274
Colorado State, 275
Creighton, 254
Dayton, 263
Delaware, 285
Denison, 254
DePaul, 255
Dickinson, 146, 256
Drexel, 275

INDEX

Elon, 256

Fairfield, 257

Florida International, 268

Furman, 258

George Mason, 268

Georgia Southern, 269

Gettysburg, 258

Howard, 276

Indiana, 277

Iowa, 286

Ithaca, 259

Kentucky, 287

Loyola, 223–24, 260

Marquette, 270

Miami Ohio, 278

Michigan State, 278

Minnesota Twin Cities, 288

Missouri-Columbia, 289

Montclair State, 270

Oklahoma, 289

Oregon State, 279

Pacific, 264

Pitt, 290

Puget Sound, 272

RIT, 280

Rutgers, 280

Saint Mary, 261

St. Olaf, 262

Santa Clara, 261

SMU, 281

Spelman, 281

Stevens Institute, 262

Syracuse, 281

UConn, 284–85

UC San Diego, 284

UMass-Amherst, 287

UNC Asheville, 271

Urbana-Champaign, 286

Utah, 290

Virginia Tech, 291

Washington State, 272

William & Mary, 291

End of Average, The (Rose), 242

Energy Institute High School, Houston, and dropping out of a STEM program, 50

Epstein, David, *Range*, 124–25

extracurricular activities, 190–93

belonging and, 191–92

developing multiple identities and, 192

employment after graduation and, 191

Homayoun's "multiple nonoverlapping circles of connection" and, 192

identifying existing clubs, 193

starting a new club, 193

Facebook

College Talk group, 93

Paying for College 101 group, 93, 204

FAFSA (Free Application for Federal Student Aid), 204

Fairfield University (CT), **257**

Fairleigh Dickinson University (NJ), 217

financial aid and discounts

college choice and, 28

Common Data Set (CDS) on a college's website, 28

"donut hole" of financial aid, 93–94

example, Abby's offers as seemingly arbitrary, 95

formula for FAFSA, 204

"hard look," 91

merit aid, 8, 10, 28, 77, 92, 100, 102, 112–13, 204, 250, 263, 280, 283

financial aid and discounts (*cont.*)
need-based aid, 10, 77
net-price calculator, 205
"pre-read" or "early read" for, 91, 95
public universities and full-rides for
academic superstars, 76
financial aid and discounts: "New"
Dream Schools
Alabama's aggressive merit-aid
packages, 77, 80, 283
Augustana's 100 percent of
demonstrated need as well as aid
without need, 252
Bentley discounts, 252
Birmingham-Southern as a warning,
197–99
Butler's awards, 253
Case Western's merit discounts, 274
Dayton's transparent model, 263
Denver's aid without financial need,
264
DePaul's average merit discount, 255
DePauw's budget and, 255
Dickinson's discounts and net price,
256
Elon's discounts/average award,
256–57
Loyola discounts, 225
Pacific's merit-based aid, 264
Puget Sound's discounts/average
merit award, 272
Rutgers's merit aid, 280
Trinity's endowment per student
and, 263
First Destination Survey, 63
Fischman, Wendy, *The Real World of
College*, 120–21, 195–96
Fitzgerald, Susan, 208, 213

Florida A&M University (FL), **267–68**
Florida International University (FL),
156, **268**
Forbes
"American Leaders List," 149
"financial grades" for colleges, 211
"38 Great Colleges With Less
Admissions Stress," 149
Fordham University (NY), 22, 27, **276**
Franek, Rob, 30–31
Franklin & Marshall College (PA) 27,
44, 154, 220
Friedman, John, 53
friendships and community, 2, 85, 109,
150, 153, 166, 167
college environments that foster
them, 155
Denison University and, 254
importance, before and after
graduation, 154–55
See also belonging
Furman University (SC), 114, **257–58**
president, Elizabeth Davis, 150, 167
"scaffolding" at, 165–70

Galloway, Scott, 118
Gallup Alumni Survey (2013), 166–67
Gallup survey on student loneliness,
179
Gardner, Howard, *The Real World of
College*, 120–21, 195–96
George Mason University (VA),
268–69
Georgetown University (DC), 154, 223,
235
George Washington University (DC), 114
Georgia Southern University (GA), **269**
Gettysburg College (PA), **258**

INDEX

Gladwell, Malcolm, *David and Goliath*, 49–50, 51

Golden Gate University (CA), 210

Granovetter, Mark, 191

Great College Teaching (Campbell), 159–60

Greek life (sororities and fraternities), 4, 30, 75, 78, 79, 82, 171
  Alabama and, 77, 283
  SMU and, 107
  Syracuse and, 282

Grinnell College (IA), 213

Gutierrez, Norma, 34–35

Guttentag, Christoph, 42–43

Hamilton, Laura, 187–89

Hamilton College (NY), 82

Handshake (job-search platform), 61

Harrington, Molly, 31–32

Hartle, Terry, 130, 132

Harvard Graduate School of Education
  Making Caring Common initiative, 117
  Weissbourd's study about anxiety and depression in young adults, 117, 126

Harvard Law School
  shark mentality of some students, 52
  student, Beth and undergraduate experience, 47, 48–49, 51–52, 85

Harvard University, 54
  budget percent from endowment, 201
  career ambitions of students, 56–57
  career fields for one-third of students, 54
  Deming as a faculty dean at, 54
  employment after graduation, 229
  endowment size, 213
  financial health of, 213
  graduate success and, 55–57, 58
  Kennedy School of Government, 52
  Opportunity Insights, 52–53, 55
  test score requirements reinstatement, 41

Harvey Mudd College (CA), 156

Hauck, Ivan, 136–38

Hechinger Report, The, 212

Highland High School, Medina, OH, 9–10

Hobart and William Smith Colleges (NY), **258–59**

Holy Cross (MA), 75, 77, 220, 222–23

Homayoun, Ana, 191

honors colleges, 76, 77, 82–87
  advantages of, 82
  at Alabama, 77, 85, 283
  at Arizona State, 86
  at Clemson, 274
  example, Emily's choice of Ole Miss, 82–83
  growth of, number of today, 82
  housing provided by, 87
  at Michigan State, 278
  quality of advisors, 86–87
  tips for evaluating, 85–87
  university's ranking and, 82
  value of the benefits, 86
  at Wisconsin, 85

Howard University (DC), **276**

How College Works (Chambliss and Takacs), 155–56

Human Capital Research Corporation, 112–13

Indiana University (IN), 73, 139–43, 187–88
  Bloomington campus, **277**

International Baccalaureate curriculum, 43
international universities, 88
internships, 63, 233–38
  college search and, 235
  companies hiring directly from intern pools, 236, 237
  Denver and, 263
  DePauw and, 255
  Drexel's paid co-op experiences, 235, 275
  elite colleges and, 234–35
  Furman and, 257
  Georgia Southern and, 269
  Indiana and, 277
  Ithaca and, 242–43, 259
  Macalester and, 260
  pacing yourself for, 237
  searching for and finding the right opportunities, 237–38
  "Underemployment and Internships" (*Figure 10.1*), 234
  Virginia Tech's paid internships, 291
  Washington State and, 272
Iowa State University (IA), 72, 190
Ishop, Kedra, 25–26
Ithaca College (NY), 150, 242, **259**
  internships and student McAllister's experience, 242–43
  Park School of Communications: Los Angeles program, 61, 242
  Selingo and, 12, 175–77, 180, 191–92, 251
Itzkowitz, Michael, 143–45, 149

James Madison University (VA), 58
job placement, 7, 9
  alumni networks and, 60, 61, 62
  Handshake (job-search platform), 61

Oklahoma's Center for Major & Career Exploration, 289
  rates, 7, 8, 204, 221, 258, 260, 276
  region-based hiring and, 59–61
  Wake Forest University's career center, 61
John Carroll University (OH), 209
Johns Hopkins University (MD), 223, 274
Jones, Alexander, 193

Kang, Jay Caspian, 12
Kennedy, Edward M. "Ted," 129–30
Kenyon College (OH), 114
Kettering University (MI), 57, 221
Kho, Simon, 59, 60–61, 63, 236
Kinzie, Jillian, 139–40

Lambert, Leo, 256
Landscape tool (from College Board), 36–37
LeBlanc, Diane, 185–86
Lehigh University (PA), 32, 232
Levine, Phillip, 94
Lewis & Clark College (OR), 182
Lieber, Ron, 84
  The Price You Pay for College (Lieber), 8
Lightcast, 63–64, 90, 216
LinkedIn, 62, 191
Louisiana State University (LA), 57
Loyola University (MD), 222–25, **260**
Lumina Foundation, 251

Macalester College (MN), **260**
making sure the degree pays off, 219–39, **275**
  College Scorecard and, 223, 224
  criteria for inclusion on "New" Dream Schools list, 250

engaging in college with an eye
toward job interviews, 238–39
how students can build marketable
skills, 7, 48–49, 230–38, 251, 279
how students can influence
outcomes, 227–30
"microcredentials," 232–33
Payscale website and, 223, 224
scoring colleges on the return on
investment, 143–47, 256
"Underemployment and Internships"
(*Figure 10.1*), 234
See also internships
making sure the degree pays off: "New"
Dream Schools
Arizona State, innovation zones,
235, 273
Augustana, research projects, 251–52
Berry, LifeWorks program, 253
Binghamton, research projects, 265
Case Western, experiential learning,
273–74
Clemson, Leadership Certificate, 274
Colorado State, research
opportunities, 275
Creighton, experiential learning, 253–54
Denison, workforce prep programs,
254
Denver, research and service
projects, 264
Drexel, paid co-op experiences, 235, 275
Elon, cooperative-education
program, 256
Furman, research projects, 257
Georgia Southern, experiential
learning and industry alignment,
269
Gettysburg, research projects, 258

Hobart and William Smith,
"hands-on" approach, 259
Iowa, GROW program, 286
Kentucky, tech-enabled learning,
286–87
Macalaster, Action Fund, 260
Marquette, research, pre-med prep,
and clinical coursework, 269–70
Maryland, living-learning cohorts, 287
Michigan State, research projects, 278
Missouri-Columbia, learning-by-
doing opportunities, 288–89
NC State, research opportunities,
279
Oregon State, research
opportunities, 279
Pacific, accelerated professional and
experiential programs, 264
RIT, cooperative education program
and paid internships, 279–80
Rutgers, research opportunities, 280
SMU, Engaged Learning Fellowship,
280–81
Spelman, dual-degree partnerships,
281
TCNJ, research opportunities, 267
Trinity, hands-on learning, 263
UC Davis, research opportunities,
283
UC San Diego, research
opportunities, 284
UMass-Amherst, Five College
Consortium, 288
UNC, research programs, 271
Urbana-Champaign, technical
innovation and career
preparation, 285–86
Makris, Jeff, 36

Malamud, Ofer, 124–25

Marken, Stephanie, 166

Marquette University (WI), **269–70**

Marsh, Herbert, 49, 51

Massachusetts Institute of Technology
(MIT), 39, 40, 41
Schmill as admissions dean, 24–25,
39, 40, 44–45

McAllister, Colleen, 242–43, 245

McLendon, Matt, 80–81

McMillen, Tom, 129

McMurtrie, Beth, 184

medical school acceptance rates
Hobart and William Smith Colleges,
259
Maryland, College Park, 287
SMU, 281
TCNJ, 267

mentors/putting teaching first, 153–73
Campbell's study on best teachers,
159–60
college environments that foster
them, 155
college professors as mentors, 155
college search, what to look at, 161–63
early signals from a college and, 172–73
finding a college prioritizing, 158–64
finding a college with "scaffolding,"
164–71
Gallup Alumni Survey results and,
166–67
liberal arts colleges and, 160
Porterfield on active learning, 154
rankings' failure to gauge, 156–57
schools deeper in the rankings, 157–58
what types of college did best, 159–60
Yeager's "mentor mindset" and, 170
mentors/putting teaching first: "New"

Dream Schools
Alabama, 283
Augustana, 252
Denison, 170–71, 254
Florida A&M, 267
Florida International, 268
Fordham, 276
Furman, 167–70, 257
Gettysburg, 258
Hobart and William Smith, 259
Indiana, 277
North Carolina, 271
Pitt, 290
Puget Sound, 272
TCNJ, 267
William & Mary, 96

merit aid: *see* financial aid and
discounts

Miami University (OH), 87, **277–78**

Michigan State University (MI), 22, 73,
125, 190, 249, **278**

Middlebury College (VT), 82

Miles, Charles, 165–71

Miller, Michelle, 163

*Mindset Matters: The Power of College
to Activate Lifelong Growth*
(Porterfield), 154

Minnetonka High School,
Minneapolis, application
inflation, 34–35

Miranda, Marie Lynn, 177

Missouri University of Science and
Technology (MO), 221

Montclair State University (NJ), 148, **270**

Moody's, 208–9

Moore, Doug, 216–18

Mount Holyoke (MA), 95

Muhlenberg College (PA), 209

Muir, David, 176
Murthy, Vivek, 179

National Survey of Student
    Engagement (NSSE), 139, 185
  Berry and, 253
  criteria for inclusion on "New"
    Dream Schools list, 250–51
  electronic "pocket guide," 139
  elite colleges and internships, 235
  Gettysburg and, 258
  obtaining results from, 140
  red flag on schools that won't release
    numbers, 186
  St. Olaf's scores, 186, 262
  as source for campus tour questions, 139
  "Student Engagement: Elite Schools
    vs. Everyone Else" (*Figure 6.1*), 141
Naviance, 26
  "scattergrams" feature, 35
"New" Dream Schools, 3, 6–7
  best choices, 4–6
  choosing data for, 149–50
  colleges that outperformed on
    student outcomes, 148
  earnings outcomes vs. cost of degree,
    145
  factors to consider, 4
  "no perfect schools" truism, 148
  redefining what it means, 12–13
  survey of parents, results, 153–54
  three critical components for, 150–51
  what it is, 4
  what it should deliver, 7
  See also belonging; cost; financial aid
    and discounts; mentors/putting
    teaching first
"New" Dream Schools list, 247–91

  backstory, 134–51
  Breakout Regionals, 248–49, 265–72
  criteria for colleges included, 147,
    249–51
  geography and choice, 248
  Hidden Values, 248, 251–64
  Large Leaders, 273–91
  See also specific colleges
New York Times
  build-your-own college ranking
    tool, 134
  Wirecutter, 133
New York University (NY), 136, 214, 244
Niche.com, 22, 204
North Carolina State University (NC),
  278–79
Northeastern Illinois University (IL),
  209
Northeastern University (MA), 36, 95,
  244
Northern Arizona University (AZ), 163

Obama, Barack, 143
Ohio State (OH), 53, 56, 58, 114, 209
Opportunity Insights, 52–53
  study on social connectedness, 57–58
  study on the outcomes of
    matriculants at 34 elite colleges,
    55–58
  study of top 1 percent
    overrepresented at elite colleges, 55
Oregon State University (OR), **279**
out-of-state recruitment and school
    choice, 32, 62, 71–90
  considering location and post-
    graduate employment, 89–90
  costs driving market behavior and,
    74–77

out-of-state recruitment and school
choice (*cont.*)
creating community/honors
programs, 82–87
in-state choices vs., 87–88
international universities
alternative, 88
social proof problem, 88–89
Southern schools and, 78–82

Parker, John W., 49, 51
Pascarella, Ernest T., 192
Payscale website, 223, 224
Maryland schools, 223
math-computer science majors, 223–24
what it is, what it shows, what it
doesn't, 224
Pennsylvania State College (PA), 61, 215
personal agency and college choice,
115–26
be open to switching your major,
123–26
careerism vs. individual agency, 120–21
college search decisions and, 118
making college transformational, 121
questions to ask about career goals,
126
refusing to play the elites'
admissions game, 119
role of money in picking a major,
121–23
stepping away from expectations,
117–18
Plan B
course correction for, 26, 27–30
example, Ethan's rejections and, 194
example, Mia's deferral and, 18–19,
22–25

Oklahoma, as student's Plan B,
successful outcome, 172
pivoting to, outcomes, 172–73, 178–79
problem with not having, 5
rejection by Plan A college, positive
effects, 124, 195
when it is a better fit, 193–96
why applicants need a backup plan,
17–45
widening your lens and, 39, 96, 110, 194
See also "New" Dream Schools list
Pollick, G. David, 198
Pontari, Beth, 168
Pope, Loren, *Colleges That Change Lives*,
6, 197, 198
Porterfield, Dan
the merits of active learning, 154
Mindset Matters (Porterfield), 154
Price You Pay for College, The (Lieber), 8
Princeton Review, 30–31
Princeton University (NJ), 156, 201
Providence College (RI), 18, 206
Purdue University (IN), 32, 61

Range (Epstein), 124–25
Real World of College, The (Fischman
and Gardner), 120–21, 195–96
Reddit r/chanceme, 241
rejections, 33
elite schools encouraging more
applications with ultra-low
acceptance rates, 119
example, outstanding student, Mia,
27
"life is ruined" response, 44–45
new reality of admissions and, 20–21
pivoting to Plan B, outcomes, 5,
172–73, 178–79

trouble fully embracing next school on the list, 171–72

Reservoir High School (MD), applications and acceptance rate to North Carolina at Chapel Hill, 35

residence halls/dorm life, 187–90
asking how roommates are assigned, 190
campus tours and, 189–90
colleges that create communities, 189
cost, 189
Dartmouth study on roommates, 188
Georgia State's lesson about housing, 189
Hamilton study of social class and, 187–88
living-learning communities, 190
Miami Ohio's living and learning, 278
Michigan State's connecting academics with residential living, 190, 278
public-private partnerships for, 208

retention/graduation rates
average SAT scores and retention, 50–51
belonging-intervention and retention, 181
dropping out, Matt Dvortsyn's story, 231–32, 238
economic/social class and likelihood of dropping out, 187–88
elite schools, low drop-out rate, 49–50
factors in dropping out of a STEM program, 50
freshmen dropouts, lack of belonging, 179
student that dropped out of Stanford, 50

retention/graduate rates: "New" Dream Schools that excel
Bentley, 252
Butler, 253
Clemson, 274
Denver, 264
DePauw, 255
Drexel, 275
Furman, 258
George Mason, 269
Georgia Southern, 269
Indiana, 277
Macalester, 260
Marquette, 270
Maryland, College Park, 287
Michigan State, 278
Minnesota Twin Cities, 288
Montclair State, 148, 270
North Carolina State, 279
Oklahoma, 289
Oregon State, 278
Pitt, 290
Rutgers, 280
San Diego State, 271
TCNJ, 267
Texas A&M, 282
UConn, 285
Virginia Tech, 291
William & Mary, 291

Rice University (TX), 84, 106
example, Emily chooses "Ole Miss" over Rice, 84

Rochester Institute of Technology (RIT) (NY), **279–80**

Rose, Todd, *The End of Average*, 242

"Rise and Fall of the Full Payers, The" (*Figure 4.2*), 104

Rutgers University (NJ), 225, 232, **280**

St Andrews University, Scotland, 291
Saint Mary's College of California
    (CA), **261**
St. Olaf College (MN), 248, **261–62**
    "first year experience" at, 185–86
    NSSE scores on engagement and
        satisfaction, 186
San Diego State University (CA), **271**
Santa Clara University (CA), 248, **261**
SAT and ACT testing
    ACT scores at University of
        Alabama, 77
    all-digital SAT, 41–42
    college search and, 24
    double 750s not as meaningful, 42
    should applicants submit scores,
        24–25, 42
    test-optional policies, 19, 32, 39, 41
"scaffolding," 164–71
    example, Furman, 165–70
Schalk, Sami, 184
Schmill, Stu, 24–25, 39, 40, 44–45, 44n
Scoir "scattergrams" feature, 35
Scripps College (CA), 156
Sierra College (CA), 111
Sigelman, Matt, 228–29, 230
"social proof," 88–89
Southern Methodist University (SMU)
    (TX), 86, **280–81**
    example, student chooses over elite
        schools, 106–8, 110
Southern Oregon University (OR), 181
Spelman College (GA), **281**
sports, 4, 30, 75, 83, 191
    Adrian College and doubling
        enrollment with thirty sports
        teams, 217
    Alabama football, 77, 80, 81, 90, 283

Birmingham-Southern's demise and,
    197–98
Binghamton's varsity sports in
    NCAA Division I, 265
Creighton's students in Division I
    athletics, 253
Division III schools and, 217
Fairleigh Dickinson adding two
    sports to drive tuition revenue,
    217
Furman's eighteen sports in NCAA
    Division I, 167
high percentage of students playing
    sports, as financial problem red
    flag, 217–18
North Carolina State, NCAA
    basketball, 278–79
Pitt Division I football at Acrisure
    Stadium, 290
St. Mary's NCAA Division I
    athletics and outsize athletic
    culture, 261
Southern schools and football, 78,
    80, 90, 107, 144
UConn's Division I athletics
    program, 284
UT at Austin and football, 195
Staisloff, Rick, 214–15
Stanford University (CA), 32, 50, 67,
    181
state (public) universities
    choosing a home state university, 75,
        88, 89
    costs for out-of-state students, 75
    disadvantages of, 111
    employment earnings vs. cost of a
        degree, 145 (*see also specific schools*)
    flagship universities, 72–73, 89

full-rides for academic superstars, 76

Great Student Swap, 72–73, 74

honors colleges, 76, 77, 82–87, 278, 283

most value for cost: Cal State and
    CUNY systems, 145

out-of-state students, 32, 62, 71–82,
    271, 272, 284, 286

percentage of in-state students, 72,
    76

in the South, 72

Southern flagships, 76–82

strong value for cost, "New" Dream
    Schools, 275, 277, 278, 280, 285, 286

students opting for "Other State U,"
    75–76

in the West, 72

State University of New York (SUNY)
    (NY), 87–88

Stony Brook campus, 87

Stevens Institute of Technology (NJ),
    236, **262**

"Student Engagement: Elite Schools vs.
    Everyone Else" (*Figure 6.1*), 141

Student Right-To-Know and Campus
    Security Act, 130–31

study abroad/programs, 5, 142, 255–56

Augustana and, 251–52

Delaware and, 28

DePauw and, 255

Dickinson known for, 255–56

Fordham and, 276

Furman and, 167, 257

Hobart and William Smith and, 259

honors colleges and, 86

Macalester and, 260

Mississippi's stipend for, 83

Puget Sound's Pacific Rim Program,
    272

SMU's opportunities, 86, 107, 110

Virginia Tech and, 291

Stuyvesant High School, New York
    City, 36

acceptance rate at top tier schools,
    2016 vs. 2022, 36

Syracuse University (NY), **281–82**

Takacs, Christopher, *How College
    Works*, 155–56

Taleb, Nassim, 149

Temple University (PA), 22

Texas A&M University (TX), 50, 51,
    109, **282**

"38 Great Colleges With Less
    Admissions Stress" (*Forbes*), 149

Town & Country, "Alt-Ivies" list, 134

transfers

Dayton's transfer partnership, 263

Dvortsyn's transfer to Rutgers, 232

example, from Sierra College to Cal
    Poly Tech, 111

percentage of college freshmen, 3,
    179

starting at a community college,
    110–11

Trinity University (TX), **263**

University of Alabama (AL), 39, 76–77,
    80–82, 85, **283**

enrollment and Matt McLendon,
    80–81

honors college, 77, 85, 283

Randall Welcome Center, 81

ranking of, 80

University of Arizona (AZ), 78

University of Arkansas (AR), 78

University of Buffalo (NY), 143

University of California (CA)
Berkeley, 54–55, 76
Davis, 32, **283**
Los Angeles (UCLA), 56, 224
Merced, 188
San Diego, 33, **284**
University of Central Florida (FL),
230–31
University of Chicago (IL), 22, 27, 54, 83
University of Cincinnati (OH), 235
University of Colorado (CO), 32, 109,
215
University of Connecticut (UConn)
(CT), **284–85**
University of Dayton (OH), **263**
University of Delaware (DE), 27, 28,
73, **285**
University of Denver (CO), **264**
University of Edinburgh, Scotland, 88
University of Florida (FL), 56
University of Georgia (GA), 56
University of Hartford (CT), 210
University of Illinois (IL)
Chicago, 177
Urbana-Champaign, **285–86**
University of Iowa (IA), **286**
University of Kentucky (KY), **286–87**
University of Maryland (MD), 249
College Park (main campus), **287**
University of Massachusetts Amherst
(MA), 231, 238, **287–88**
University of Michigan (MI), 32, 73, 76,
223, 267
University of Minnesota (MN), 2–3, 5,
75, 178
Twin Cities, **288**
University of Mississippi (MS)
example, student's choice, with full

ride and perks, 82–84
honors college at, 83–84
University of Missouri-Columbia
(MO), **288–89**
University of Montana (MT), 200
University of Nebraska (NE), 215
University of North Carolina (NC), 76
Asheville, **271**
Chapel Hill, 35, 96, 246, 267, 278
Greensboro, 200
University of Oklahoma (OK), 73, 144,
289
as student's Plan B, successful
outcome, 172
University of Oregon (OR), 73, 160
University of Pennsylvania (PA), 22, 27
University of Pittsburgh (Pitt) (PA),
27, **290**
University of Puget Sound (WA), **271–72**
University of Richmond (VA), 27, 44
University of South Carolina (SC), 58,
73, 78, 82
University of Southern California
(USC) (CA), 25–26, 32, 35, 157–58,
244
University of Tennessee (TN), 78
University of Texas (TX), 232
"credegree" and, 232
University of Texas at Austin (TX), 41
as student's Plan B, 194–95
University of the Pacific (CA), **264**
University of Utah (UT), **290**
University of Vermont (VT), 73
University of Virginia (VA), 82, 267
College at Wise, 193
University of Wisconsin (WI), 32, 33,
73, 85
U.S. colleges and universities, 58

colleges not on elite list with alumni running Fortune 500 companies, 57

colleges on an "unsustainable financial path," 199

coming demographic cliff, 43–44, 217

economic struggles of, 43–44

feeder schools for, 37

fiscal distress and, 197–218

four-year colleges with at least 1,000 undergraduates, 249

land-grant universities, 72, 73

large universities vs. small colleges, number of, 3

major agencies for bond ratings of, 208

Midwest universities, 72

myth about admissions, 131

Northeast, small colleges of, 71

Selingo's five tiers of selectivity, 131

South, big public universities and small church-affiliated colleges, 72

state (public) universities recruiting out-of-state students, 32, 62, 71–82

Student Right-To-Know and Campus Security Act, 130–31

teenagers "ignorant of the types of colleges" that would be a good fit, 4

test-optional policies, 41

total number of, 3, 249

transformation from regional to national/international business, 131

West, few private colleges and large public institutions, 72

U.S. Department of Education's College Navigator website, 215

U.S. News & World Report

"Best Undergraduate Teaching,"

reliant on peer assessment, 157

cherry-picking data and, 149

college ranking guides, 3, 11, 133

failure to gauge teaching and mentorship, 156–57, 159

issues with the rankings, 133–34

most-cited category, 158–59

"peer assessment" score, 133

ranking equated with prestige, 80

ranking for Colby, 203

ranking for Williams, 96

Selingo as intern on college rankings (1994), 132

small liberal arts colleges ranking between 51 and 100, dropping number of full payers, 113

value over prestige: getting a deal

balancing money and brand, 106–8

caution about ED admissions, 109–10

example, Abby's choice of William & Mary, 91–97

example, April chooses SMU over elite schools, 106–8

overall decline of full payers, 103–5

the price of prestige, 112–14

"The Rise and Fall of the Full Payers" (*Figure 4.2*), 104

"Skip-Over Schools: Value Over Prestige" (*Figure 4.1*), 100

trading in an emotional attachment to status for financial practicality, 97–103

ways to maximize value, 108–12

weighing options at different price points, 108

Vanderbilt University (TN), 53, 84, 90, 173, 194

Virginia Commonwealth University (VA), 235

Virginia Tech (VA), 32, **291**

Wake Forest University (NC), 61, 182
    career development, Andy Chan and, 61

Wall Street Journal
    "Half of College Grads Are Working Jobs That Don't Use Their Degrees," 228

Wall Street Journal: Best Colleges list, 156
    Florida International, 268
    Hobart and William Smith, 259
    Loyola, 224, 260
    "student experience" top three schools, 156
    top college, overall rankings, 156

Walton, Gregory, 180–81

Ward, Adam, 237

Washington State University (WA), **272**

Weinberg, Adam, 170

Weissbourd, Richard, 117, 119, 126

Wells College (NY), 216–17

Western Oregon University (OR), 160

West Virginia University (WV), 200, 220

"Who Gets Hired Where" (*Figure 2.1*), 65, 222

Who Gets In and Why (Selingo), 3, 19, 131
    "Buyers and Sellers" list, 10, 92

Willamette University (OR), 210

William & Mary (VA), 95–97, **291**

Williams, Tara, 86, 87

Williams College (MA), 95, 96, 193

Wittenberg University (OH), 210

Workforce, 223

Yale University (CT), 41

Yeager, David, 170

Your College-Bound Kid (podcast), 92

Zucker, Brian, 112–13

Zygmunt, Eva, 187